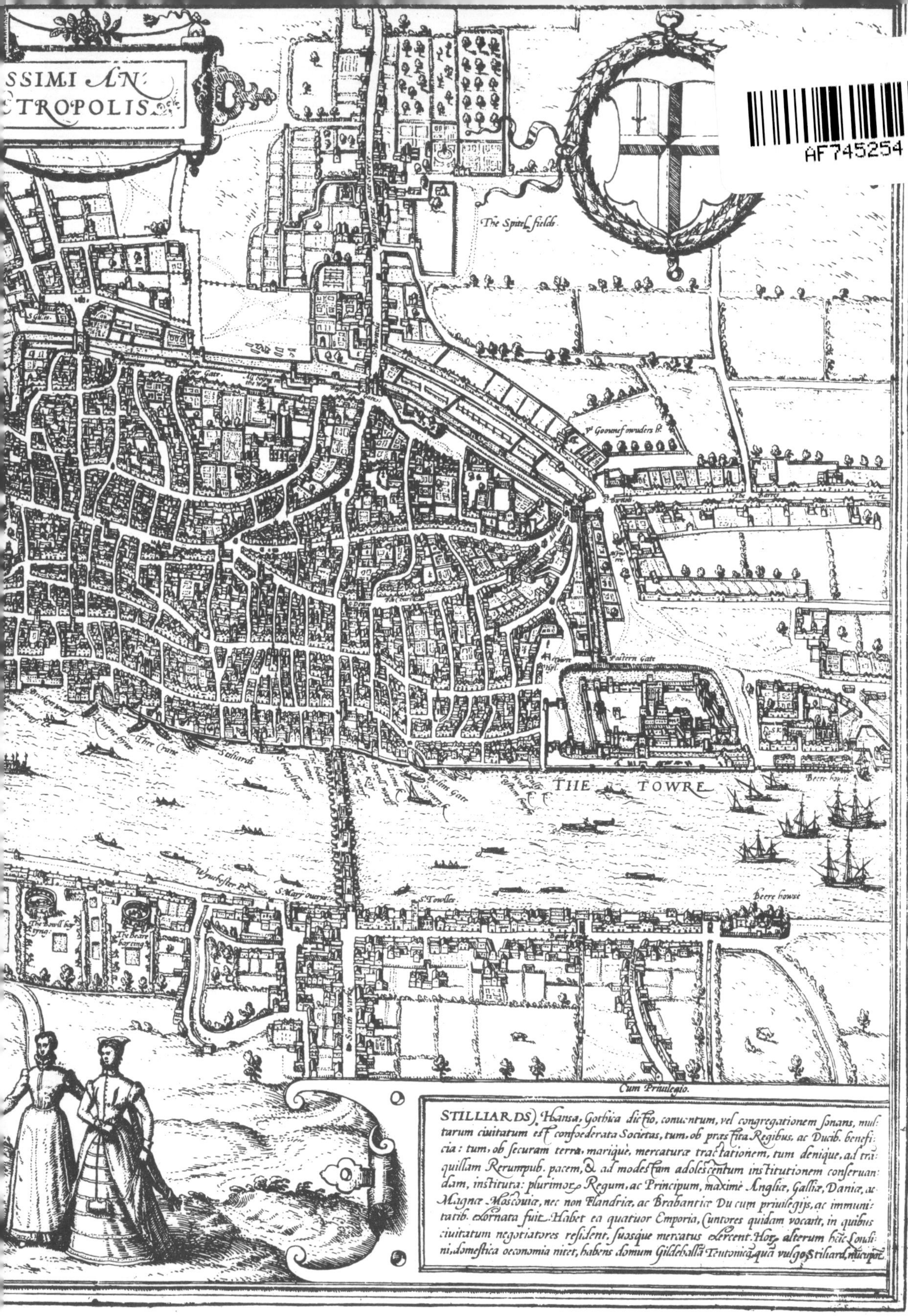

complete with the spire burnt down in 1561. The green south bank has its bullring and bear pit. Among the river craft is a canopied boat being towed up-stream with its halberdiers; this may represent the royal barge, a graceful show of loyalty to the young queen. At the foot are some typical Londoners—a well-to-do tradesman in furred gown and his wife in farthingale, each with an attendant. Top left and right are the royal arms and the arms of the city of London.

THE WAX CHANDLERS OF LONDON

Wax Chandlers' Hall: the 'greate roome' today.

Truth is the Light

THE WAX CHANDLERS OF LONDON

A short history of the Worshipful Company
of Wax Chandlers,
London

by

John Dummelow

MA (Cantab), C Eng
Master 1960-2

PHILLIMORE

1973
Published by
PHILLIMORE & CO. LTD
London and Chichester

Head Office: Shopwyke Hall,
Chichester, Sussex, England

ISBN 0 85033 100 5

Set in 'Monotype' Bembo Series 270
and printed in Great Britain on English antique laid paper
by Eyre and Spottiswoode Ltd, Her Majesty's Printers,
at Thanet Press, Margate, Kent

Contents

List of Illustrations

Unless otherwise indicated, the originals of the illustrations are in the Company's possession.

Foreword

IN PRESENTING this history of the Worshipful Company of Wax Chandlers I would first of all like to pay a personal tribute to our senior Past Master and former Clerk, C. G. Todd, whose devotion and generosity over many years have won him the title of Father of the Company. He was the first Clerk ever to put together a mass of detailed information on the Company's long life, and to mark his retirement from the Clerkship he presented each member with a copy of his work.

This pioneer production evoked keen interest, and Past Master John Dummelow undertook the authorship of the present full and illustrated history. The work that has gone into its making has been immense, but I know it has been a labour of love. It is superfluous to commend the author to his readers – his work speaks for itself – and he is assured of their grateful appreciation.

The Company is also indebted to two members of the Livery, Past Master C. J. W. McCallum and the Rev. W. M. Atkins, for generous donations towards the cost of production.

While it is hoped that this book will be of interest to many outside the Company, its main purpose is for the information of present-day Wax Chandlers and their families. The detailed knowledge of the Company's past now made available in such a readable form may give them further cause for pride in their inheritance.

H. T. PIKE
Deputy
(Master 1970–2)

Acknowledgements

Permission to reproduce illustrations has been given by –

the Trustees of the British Museum – fig. 1.
the Director of the Guildhall Art Gallery – plates 13 and 17.
the Librarian, the Guildhall Library – plates 4 and 12, fig. 3, and back end-paper.
the Trustees of the London Museum – front end-paper.
the Rector of St. Andrew Undershaft, the Ven. H. A. S. Pink – fig. 2.
The Sunday Times Ltd. – fig. 5.
Frederick Warne & Co. Ltd., publishers, *The Armorial Bearings of the Guilds of London*, 1961 – plate 4.

Permission has been received from The Clarendon Press to reproduce the passage on pages 47–8 by John Stow, *A Survey of London*, edited by Kingsford, 1908, and from the Librarian, Guildhall Library, to reproduce the calendar of documents in appendix 17.

Other passages quoted in the text, if not from the Company's own documents or otherwise acknowledged, are from sources mentioned in the bibliography (pages 191–2).

The tail-pieces are from E. St. V. Millay (*A Few Figs from Thistles*), Swift (*The Battle of the Books*), Shakespeare (*Romeo and Juliet*, I.v), Goldsmith (*The Captivity, An Oratorio*), and Shakespeare (*The Merchant of Venice*, V.i).

Transcriptions on pages 18, 131–2, and 135–40 are the work of C. R. H. Cooper, M.A., of the Guildhall Library.

Assistance has been given by many organisations such as –

the Bee Research Association.
the British Museum.
the Cabinet Office (Central Statistical Office).
the Catholic Information Office.
the Central Association of Bee-keepers.
the Church Information Office.
the College of Arms.
Charles Farris Ltd.[1]
the Guildhall Library.
the London Museum.
Price's Patent Candle Co. Ltd.[2]
the Public Record Office.
the Records Office of the Corporation of London.
the Rugby Borough Library.

– and by the Clerks of many City Livery Companies.

[1]Founded in 1845 as Whitmore & Craddock, their works in Bishopsgate was the last candle factory in the City; it was moved to Hounslow in 1931. Charles Farris was admitted to the Freedom of the City in 1886.

[2]They incorporate the business of Francis Tucker & Co. Ltd., which was founded as Wheble, Kendal & Doe in 1730. The manufacture of beeswax candles, originally at Kensington, has been carried on at Battersea since 1953. A former director, C. E. Mold, is a Freeman of the Wax Chandlers.

Preface

'HISTORY', said Kenneth Clark during his marathon run through *Civilisation*, 'is our life-line to the past', and there can be no better justification for yet another history of a livery company. For without their origins and traditions these companies would be just another source of benevolence with little to distinguish them from the general run of philanthropic institutions, but given the historical background they become something greater – a continuing assertion of basic virtues and values. In London the traditions of ceremony, hospitality, and charity have been maintained for six centuries or more, a remarkable achievement for which the status of perpetual corporations and the ownership of landed property cannot claim all the credit. Not for nothing have the companies been called the soul of the city, and it is tempting to believe that a livery spirit, transcending the requirements of trade, has persisted through the years and has inspired each generation in turn with the ideals of its predecessor. But just as fascinating as such metaphysical speculation – and far more fruitful – is the factual side of the story: how the first small bands of craftsmen became the accredited representatives of their industries and a power in the city and how they survived the eventual loss or extinction of their trades, coming to terms with events and combining the preservation of old customs with the wise use of current resources. Of such, in their small but exclusive sphere, is the story of the Wax Chandlers of London, which forms the subject of this book.

The aim was to produce not a definitive history for the scholar's delight, but rather a straightforward narrative designed especially for members of the Company and also having some appeal for the general reader. The historian, like the artist in mosaic, had to choose his pieces from the material available and arrange them to form a recognisable picture. For the foreground there were the Company's own documents dating back to the Plantagenets; the City records, voluminous but with frequent references to individual companies; and the national archives in whose bulk is buried the occasional mention of the Wax Chandlers. To sift the whole mass would have been impracticable, but a surface inspection proved sufficient for the purpose, and in any case much of the evidence has survived by chance and not because of any real significance. Moreover the written sources as they stood were not enough: too often, for example, the Court minutes recorded the decisions taken but not the reasons behind them. So the raw material had to be worked, adding interpretations to events and actions and generalisations to facts and statements. And the picture still required a background, necessitating much reflection on the political, social, and economic history of the period before the Wax Chandlers' activities could be placed in their proper context. Finally the finished material had to be arranged so as to combine two desiderata – chronological order and continuity of subject. The book was therefore divided into five chapters, each covering a stage in the Company's development, and within each chapter the main aspects of Company life were treated in turn; for readers who wished to trace one subject from start to finish, the index would provide an easy route.

So much for the history, its content and construction, but 'what's past is prologue'. Today the Company exists as a trustee, not only of ancient properties but also of ancient traditions – fair dealing, good fellowship, hospitality, and charity – and by continuing to cultivate these virtues the Wax Chandlers pay due homage to their forefathers. But to build up and sustain a viable future it is not enough to look back on the past. One can easily envisage an election-day service being held on the site of our former parish church, St. John Zachary, which is still consecrated ground, or a shop being shared with a candle-maker in the Elizabethan reconstruction projected for the Globe Theatre site on the South Bank. More practically, one can hope for the completion of the long overdue alliance with the professional side of the lighting industry, the successors to our medieval craftsmen, and look forward to the time when lease reversion will enable our major charity to multiply its gifts to the poor and needy. Whatever may be the destiny in store, I for one have no doubt that when it falls to future generations to write a sequel to this history, they will tell of a Company that not only conserved its heritage from the past but also made a not insignificant contribution to the future.

★ ★ ★ ★

Many organisations and individuals have assisted in the making of this book, and to the Company's official acknowledgements on page xi I would add my own personal thanks. Like all writers of social history I am indebted also to those who have gone before, particularly the chroniclers of London. I am further grateful to the various authorities who have given me advice in their own fields and thus helped to ensure that any errors are my own. Among City officers and their staffs I must single out Dr. A. E. J. Hollaender, Keeper of Manuscripts, Mr. J. L. Howgego, Keeper of Prints and Pictures, and Miss Betty R. Masters, Deputy Keeper of Records, who have given ready help. Nearer home, Mr. J. L. Haiste, my Borough Librarian, has made available the excellent facilities of the Rugby Library.

My thanks are also due to many colleagues on the Court and Livery, particularly Deputy H. T. Pike, our immediate Past Master, who has been unfailing in his interest and support; Past Master C. G. Todd, our former Clerk, whose notes on *The Worshipful Company of Wax Chandlers* (privately printed) inspired me to undertake the present work; and T. J. Wood, an Assistant and our present Clerk, who has been always ready to give practical help. Finally, both I and the Company owe a special debt of gratitude to H. R. Aldridge, a Liveryman and formerly a Deputy Keeper in the Department of Manuscripts in the British Museum. He has given freely of his time and energy in transcribing salient passages from the early documents and his wide experience as an historian with a special interest in law has been brought to bear on many intractable problems. Without his expert advice and criticism the book would have been much the poorer.

Bilton, near Rugby. JOHN DUMMELOW

December 1972

Notes to Reader

Supplementary information on many points is given in the footnotes, which for technical reasons are grouped together at the end of each chapter, and reference to these will answer some likely queries.

Dates

The historical year starting on 1 January is used throughout, except in direct quotations from early documents. In England a legal and ecclesiastical year starting on 25 March (Lady Day) was used from the thirteenth century until the New Style calendar of 1752; alternatively legal or official documents were dated by the year of the sovereign's reign. For instance, the year of the first Wax Chandlers' charter, which was sealed on 13 February, was given by contemporaries as 1483 or I Richard III; after 1752, it would be given as 1483/4 or 148$\frac{3}{4}$. But 1 January was always called New Year's Day.

Definitions and derivations

Obsolete or technical terms are explained in the main text or in footnotes on their first occurrence.

In derivations, the following abbreviations are used:

F	French	Med L	Medieval Latin (600–1500)
Gk	Greek	OE	Old English (up to 1100)
L	Latin	OF	Old French (800–1300)
ME	Middle English (AD 1100–1500)	Sp	Spanish

Early documents

Transcriptions are generally verbatim. Phraseology, spelling and punctuation have been altered as little as possible so as to preserve the flavour of the original. Spelling, which up to 1500 was in a fluid state, did not settle down for another hundred years, and, though a wider literacy had followed the growth of printing, clerks could still be hasty or poorly educated. There were often alternative spellings, and many letters were interchangeable, e.g. *i* and *j*, *u* and *v*, *y* and *i*, *ff* and *F*. Interpolations necessitated by gaps or illegibility in the MS are placed in square brackets [ ]. Explanations are in parentheses ( ).

Roman numerals are used in all the early accounts and did not disappear until the 1700's. It was common practice to put *j* for *i*, particularly for the last digit in numbers such as *ij*, *viij*, and *xiiij*.

MS numbers refer to Wax Chandlers documents in the Guildhall Library (appendix 17).

Sources

Primary sources of information consist mainly of the records kept by the company and the city; these go back to the thirteenth century.

The Wax Chandlers' archive is deposited in the Guildhall Library, and the official calendar or précis of its contents is given in appendix 17. It includes original exemplifications of charters, grants-of-arms, and ordinances; minute books, account books, treasury books, registers and other regular records; title-deeds of properties; inventories and wills.

In the city archive, the most rewarding sections are the Letter Books, which contain minutes of the administrative assemblies from 1275 to 1689 and are calendared[1] up to 1495, the Journals of the Court of Common Council from 1416, and the Repertories of the Court of Aldermen from 1495. From 1416, the Letter Books contain transcriptions of the most important passages in the Journals and Repertories.

Occasional use has been made of documents in the national collections, some of which have been calendared.[1]

Value of money

Owing to the changing value of money, the sums quoted for early transactions must be multiplied many times to obtain their equivalent in internal purchasing power today. The comparative value of the £1 depends on so many factors that only very approximate figures can be given, but the multiples to apply at various significant dates in the company's history are as follows:[2]

Year	*Multiple*	
1330	70	Gift of money to Edward III
1484	65	First royal charter
1500	90	Hall site purchased
1540	50	First hall in use
1609	15	Plantation of Ulster
1642	10	Money for the Civil War
1663	10	Current charter
1793	8	Post-fire hall rebuilt
1854	7	Hall rebuilt
1914	7½	
1938	4¾	
1958	2	Present hall built
1972	1	

[1]See *inter alia* R. R. Sharpe (ed.), *Calendar of letter-books of the city of London*, 1899; H. T. Riley (ed.), *Memorials of London and London life (1276–1419)*, 1868; the calendars of close rolls, letters and papers of Henry VIII, patent rolls, and state papers (domestic) in the Public Record Office. Also *English Historical Documents* (vols. 2, 4, 5 & 8, various editors), 1953/69, and R. R. Sharpe (ed.), *Calendar of wills proved and enrolled in the Court of Husting, London . . .*, 1889/90.

[2]E. H. Phelps Brown and Sheila V. Hopkins, *Seven centuries of the prices of consumables . . .*, from *Economica*, November 1965 (for years up to 1793); G. H. Wood, *An introduction to the study of prices*, 1938 (for 1854); and the Central Statistical Office (from 1914).

TO MY WIFE

for her love and forbearance

Introduction

'THE ART or Mistery of Wax Chandlers of the City of London'–to use the proper style – has a history that is documented from the fourteenth century. As an informal association it may go back even further, to the time when wax candles first became articles of commerce and the London craftsmen got together for their mutual benefit, but it was not until 1358 that their standards of quality were underwritten by the city authorities, and in 1484 their organisation was incorporated by royal charter. A flourishing trade in beeswax and its products continued, with the church and the nobility as the principal customers, up to the Reformation. Thereafter the demand fell off considerably: candles were banned from religious ceremonies, and in the nineteenth century new types of wax were developed. Today, candles containing beeswax are seldom used, save by the Roman Catholic church.

As business declined, the membership of the company became less representative, and it had virtually lost its control of the trade before the industrial revolution. Nevertheless a new charter obtained in 1663 has never been cancelled, and the Wax Chandlers', as a perpetual corporation, continues to function. From the site on which its hall has stood since the 1500's, the company administers its corporate property and charitable trusts and fulfils the traditional formalities, including its part in electing the lord mayor and other city officials.

Procedure within the company has changed very little over the years. The first stage of membership is still the freedom, which is obtainable by apprenticeship or 'servitude', inheritance ('patrimony')[1] or purchase ('redemption'). Every freeman of the company can take up the freedom of the City of London, becoming both Citizen and Wax Chandler and, as such, qualified for admission to the main body of members or 'livery', so-called from the costume they are entitled to wear. From the livery are chosen a 'court of assistants', who form the governing body, and from these are elected, every other year, two wardens and a master to preside. A permanent official, the clerk, is the chief executive officer.

The Wax Chandlers' is one of eighty-four London livery companies,[2] and it ranks twentieth in order of precedence. Though the first twelve, known as the 'great' companies,[3] are among the oldest, many others have existed for four or five hundred years, and as organisers of the trades, both manufacturing and merchandising, they can claim to have built up London's commerce, and made it the greatest city in the world. In their heyday they supplied money and men-at-arms for the country's wars, underpinned the civic administration by laying up stocks of corn and coal, and founded schools and almshouses in London and many parts of the country; all this was in addition to their primary function of supervising the trades in which their members were engaged, regulating conditions of employment and apprenticeship, and protecting customers against faulty goods or services. They also promoted good fellowship among their members and gave them and their families practical aid in adversity.

Though many of the original crafts have disappeared or been replaced by industries over which the companies have no control, most of them keep up a trade connection, for instance by fostering technical training or research, and there is often a high degree of common membership between company and trade or profession.[4] In only a very few cases are their responsibilities exercised under the original charters, for example the Fishmongers, who inspect and seize bad fish at Billingsgate market, and the Saddlers who inspect stocks and finished products at saddlery establishments.[5]

In their later years a considerable increase in wealth, resulting principally from the changing value of property in and around the city, has enabled many companies to become large-scale philanthropists. The arts, sciences, literature, medicine and education[6] are among the spheres that benefit to the tune, it can be safely said, of something like £1m. a year. As well as disbursing their own money, most of which originated in the personal contributions of members, the companies are responsible for distributing the income from their charitable trusts; the very large sums often available are used to provide pensions, almshouses and grants of money for the old and needy and to support schools and colleges, assist apprenticeship schemes, and promote many other worthy undertakings.[7]

The Wax Chandlers' has always been one of the smaller companies, the livery having seldom been more than a hundred, and it has never been a really wealthy one.[8] Nevertheless it has taken its full share in public duties such as sending men to fight for the king or to defend London, providing money for crown or protector, storing munitions or grain in the hall, and contributing to royal and civic pageantry. And from its ranks have come a number of city dignitaries including the occasional lord mayor.

Today the company gives its support – as far as its means allow – to general, technical and university education, and it contributes regularly to a variety of organisations concerned with the relief of poverty and suffering or with medical research. In addition, its ancient trusts are kept in a flourishing condition with a view to making the maximum grants of money, not only to charitable institutions but also to individuals, when personal needs can be taken into account; the income available is supplemented from corporate funds.

Like the bee with whose product it originated, the Wax Chandlers' Company is still in business. Its function has changed with the times, but it has preserved its identity for over six hundred years, a thread in the fabric of English history that can be traced back to the Plantagenets. It is there, in the formative period of craft and company, that our story must begin.

My candle burns at both ends;
It will not last the night;
But ah, my foes, and oh, my friends –
It gives a lovely light.

E. St. V. Millay

Notes on Introduction

[1]Among the families represented in the company today, the Field connection dates from before 1581, Gregory from 1765, Allt from 1791, Dummelow from 1800, Todd from 1835 and Harvey from 1840.

[2]For a full list see appendix 18.

[3]In the second half of the fourteenth century, the wealthier crafts began to be recognised as the leaders, and almost every mayor down to 1742 came from one or other of the 'great twelve'. For the next two centuries or so the minor companies supplied the civic head.

[4]For instance, the Apothecaries' licence by examination is a complete qualification for a general medical practitioner.

[5]The Goldsmiths' right to assay gold and silver and the Gunmakers' to prove small arms are maintained by statute and not by charter.

[6]Oundle, Tonbridge and St. Paul's schools, for instance, owe much to the generosity of the Grocers, Skinners and Mercers respectively. The city and the companies founded and still support the City and Guilds of London Institute for the advancement of technical training.

[7]All trusts must be registered under the Charities Act of 1960, and the accounts submitted yearly to the Charity Commissioners or the Department of Education and Science.

[8]The last published figures (in 1954) gave its trust income as £1,250 and its corporate income as £1,900 a year (*Whitaker's Almanack*).

CHAPTER I

The Art and the Mistery: up to 1485

TOWARDS the end of the Middle Ages every class of English society was permeated by voluntary associations known as gilds[1] or fraternities. Those whose intention was not primarily religious[2] took care to add some works of piety to their social objectives of good fellowship, hospitality, and mutual aid, and this had many advantages. Religion was an important part of everyday life. Everyone belonged to the church and recognised its right to control his life in this world and the next. The working day – from dawn to dusk – was interrupted many times for church services, and the only holidays were on Sundays and major festivals; there were nearly a hundred such holy days on which no work was done. For a gild to be attached to a religious establishment, whether church, monastery or hospital, was highly desirable: not only did it provide a meeting place, a patron saint, and prayers for the dead, whose future welfare might thus be assured, but it also afforded protection against the temporal power to whom any sort of combination was suspect.

In London and a few other towns,[3] handicraftsmen and merchants working in the same occupation, often in the same neighbourhood, would form themselves into a craft gild or 'mistery'.[4] They could then lay down conditions under which the members or 'freemen' should trade, and quality, methods, wages, hours and prices could be brought under control. There would be by-laws or ordinances by which all agreed to be bound, and regular contributions would be levied to cover expenses such as sick pay, pensions and funeral benefit. Selected members called keepers, overseers, or wardens would be appointed to see that others kept the rules. A distinctive costume or 'livery'[5] encouraged a gild spirit. Admission to the freedom of the mistery could be gained by apprenticeship (servitude), inheritance (patrimony), or purchase (redemption).

The late thirteenth and early fourteenth centuries have been reckoned the golden age of the misteries, when every craftsman was his own master, creating works of art as well as of utility and selling them direct to the user. Identity of interest brought social equality. But the idyllic picture of a society as classless as the religious fraternities faded with increasing prosperity. The best craftsmen became rich masters, and between them and the apprentices arose a class of journeymen[6] or hired servants earning low wages and having little representation. Traders began to acquire control.

By the mid-fifteenth century the wearing of livery began to be restricted to the more experienced and prosperous, the well-to-do employers and merchants: those on the livery or 'on the cloth' constituted a capitalist class, which controlled the craft and paid for luxuries like charters and halls. There might even be a distinction within the liverymen – between those who wore both gown and hood and those who wore the hood only. And below the livery there was sometimes an intermediate grade: the poorer manufacturing masters who were left 'out of the livery' together with the journeymen formed themselves into a 'yeomanry',[7] which was often semi-independent and capable of dealing with the employers like a trade union.

Side by side with class distinction there grew up an administrative structure. The wardens were provided with assistants, forming a governing body or 'court' with deliberative, administrative and judicial functions. Heading the court was the 'prime warden'[8] or, as he was usually called, the 'master'. A clerk and a beadle, both paid, were the permanent officials.

Behind this formal hierarchy lay the solid core of elders, those who were privileged to wear the craft livery. In the Middle Ages the wearing of liveries was closely guarded by the crown, and from the time of Richard II onwards many acts were passed for their regulation.[9] The entitlement of the authorised crafts had become well established by the fourteenth century or earlier, and in 1406 it was confirmed, in a back-handed way, by a statute,[10] which exempted gilds, fraternities and 'also the men of the misteries' (*les gentz del mistère*) from the necessity to prove their right; similarly, in 1411, when any knight was prohibited from giving a livery to his retainers, the 'gilds, fraternities and people of the crafts' were again declared exempt.[11]

Craft liveries, which derived from the religious associations of the misteries and the gowns and hoods worn by the monks, were originally in two colours. These might be varied from time to time, and, for royal and civic occasions, they were enlivened by trade 'cognisances' embroidered in a conspicuous position. Fresh liveries were ordered at regular intervals and were often charged to the members themselves.

The craft gilds and the city

In London, always the largest city in England, the misteries are first heard of in the twelfth and thirteenth centuries, after which they multiplied rapidly: the 25 crafts listed in 1328 had grown to 111 a hundred years later. During the same period the citizens obtained recognition as a corporate body and developed their own system of government.

London had been divided into wards under aldermen from before the Norman conquest, and in 1191 the future King John (Richard Coeur de Lion being away on the Third Crusade) granted the city a 'commune' or body of free citizens who could choose a mayor.[12] In 1215, a few weeks before being forced to seal Magna Carta,[13] John allowed them the further right of electing a mayor each year, with the proviso that after election he should present himself to the king or his justices for approval. Sheriffs, originally king's officers for collecting revenue and dispensing justice, had been elected annually from 1199, for London and Middlesex. In 1200, 'five and twenty of the more discreet men of the city' were sworn to take counsel with the mayor – this was the first 'court of aldermen' – and in 1285 forty 'good men' (*probi homines*) of all the wards were sworn to consult with the aldermen; here were the seeds of the 'court of common council', which provided the main administrative body.

By the end of the fourteenth century the city government had become democratic, in form at least: the aldermen and common councilmen were elected by the freemen of the wards, the former for life and the latter year by year. The mayor and other high officers were elected annually by a 'congregation', later called 'common hall', which consisted at first of all the freemen and later of the court of common council with other selected citizens. In 1467 the masters and wardens of the misteries were added, and from 1475 election was transferred to the whole of the livery,[14] a very much larger body though one to which the former electors would normally belong. In addition to electing city officials, the livery formed the parliamentary electorate for the city, having replaced the ward representatives in this role in 1375.

'London' originally meant the 325 acres within the Roman wall with its six gates. Under the Saxons 'the liberties of the city' were added, forming a suburban area outside the walls and extending from Temple Bar in the west to Aldgate Bars in the east; the liberties were administered as wards, e.g. Cripplegate Without (the wall). By 1222 the city had spread to its present area of 677 acres, the famous 'square mile' that is still the heart of the metropolis, and in the thirteenth and fourteenth centuries the population may have been 40,000–50,000. It was surrounded by fields and forests, fish and swans swam in the wide clear Thames, and the upper storeys of painted wooden houses overhung the narrow cobbled streets. The Guildhall, the city's town hall, was originally the meeting-place of the gilds, who subscribed towards the cost of a new building in 1411–26; its walls and crypt are incorporated in the present structure.

Between city and gilds there was the natural link provided by common membership and common interests. As will be seen, the crafts formed the main avenue to citizenship and its privileges. No-one could ply his trade unless he was free of the city, and no-one was admitted to the city freedom unless he was vouched for by a craft; only the craft liverymen could vote in the city elections. Moreover, from 1347 not only the ordinances of a craft but also all their proceedings had to be submitted to the court of aldermen, and the wardens could be fined for recalcitrance. Internal discipline – always difficult in a voluntary association – was thus supported by municipal sanctions; approval of ordinances by mayor and aldermen brought with it their power to enforce the penalties laid down, and city and craft together could impose a close monopoly on a trade. But there was always a tendency for a craft to be treated as a branch of civic administration, and though the grant of a full set of ordinances brought recognition as an organised community capable of self-government, it brought also a degree of dependence that could be troublesome. The way out was to seek the support of a still higher authority, that of the crown, and the next step was to obtain a charter of incorporation from the king, and hence full legal powers. Thus was born the livery company, of the same general form but with many variations.

The freedom of London

Every freeman or freewoman[15] of a craft could – and by ancient custom was expected to – become free of the City of London. Besides being essential to a craftsman, since only freemen were allowed to practise their trade, the freedom brought other privileges such as immunity from market-tolls throughout England, exemption from impressment into the armed services, and the right to vote in ward and parliamentary elections; it was an essential qualification for high civic office and for admission to the livery of a company. There were also responsibilities: as well as having to live in the city, freemen were taxed for municipal expenses and were liable to be called upon for municipal duties.

Admission to the freedom of the city, like that of the companies, could be by servitude, patrimony or redemption, and by the beginning of the fourteenth century all three methods were in use: in the three-year period 1309–12 some 250 were admitted by servitude compared with 650 by redemption.[16] The admission of freemen was a duty of the city chamberlain,[17] the first name having been recorded in 1282. By 1319 the freedom was strictly controlled: it was laid down by Edward II that no stranger should be admitted without the backing of six men of a mistery or of the whole commonalty.

In the early days all the freemen turned out in a common livery such as red and white (still the city's colours) or red and black, each craft wearing its distinctive badge or ornamentation. Historically, over many centuries they were staunch upholders of independence against the encroachments of the monarchy. It should be remembered however that they were only a small proportion of the working population, the others ranging from churchmen and other professions to unskilled workmen and labourers; the 'London mob' (*mobile vulgus*) was an excitable crowd who provided a radical element in the city. At the beginning of the fourteenth century citizen families formed no more than a quarter of the total, and by Tudor times not one in 20 of the inhabitants was a freeman. Non-citizens were described as 'foreigns' if English, or 'aliens' if from overseas.

Apprenticeship

Of the three paths to the freedom, only servitude could guarantee the ability to practise a craft. The apprenticeship system, which dates from the thirteenth century, was designed to ensure a high standard of craftsmanship, though it was used later by some companies to limit the entry.

The London indenture (appendix 19) bound an apprentice to serve his master or mistress for seven years without payment. In return the master undertook to teach him 'the art which he useth' and to provide him with board, lodging, and all other necessaries. There was a binding fee, and the indenture had to be enrolled by the chamberlain. At the end of the term completion was enrolled by the master at the Guildhall, and the apprentice was admitted to the freedom of his craft, thus qualifying for the freedom of the city and the right to follow a trade. He was now a highly skilled artificer and could either hire himself out as a journeyman or set up on his own as a master-craftsman. Before being sworn before the mayor a would-be master had to have sufficient capital and must produce, if required, an expensive proof-piece or 'master-piece'.

An apprentice received both technical training and social education. Besides working in his master's shop he lived with the family and was subject to many rules of behaviour. Among forbidden pleasures were the haunting of taverns and playhouses and gambling 'to his master's detriment', which were banned by the indenture, also peacock finery and long hair, wrestling in the sanctuary of St. Paul's, bowling alleys and tennis courts, cock-fighting and brothels. The rules were not always observed by apprentices nor by their masters, with the result that many youngsters were forced into crime and degradation. They were not allowed to marry, but many, on gaining the freedom, found that marriage with their master's daughter was a high road to success, Dick Whittington[18] being the legendary example; in fact, he was the son of a Gloucestershire knight and married a west-country heiress. The fourteenth-century apprentice appears to have been an independent and lively character. In the Peasants' Revolt of 1381 he rallied to John Ball, the apostle of 'Christian democracy', and in more peaceful times, according to Chaucer, he was a keen pageant-follower:

> When there any ridings were in Chepe,[19]
> Out of the shoppe thider wold he lepe;
> And till that he had all the sight ysein,
> And danced wel, he would not come again.

Wax craft

The business of a wax chandler[20] was to process and sell beeswax and to make and sell candles and other wax products. Chemically speaking, the most important constituents of beeswax are wax esters (chiefly myricil palmitate $C_{30}H_{61}OH$), wax acids (such as cerotic acid $C_{25}H_{51}COOH$), and hydrocarbons. The honey-bee converts part of its sweet liquid food into wax from which it builds a honeycomb, domestic bees using wax foundation provided by the beekeeper. After collection with the honey from the hive, the wax is reclaimed, and under good conditions a surplus is available for commercial use. It is separated from the impurities by rendering and refining and is usually bleached, becoming white and translucent without scent or taste.

Wax appears in Greek legend as an unsatisfactory adhesive for the wings of Icarus in attempting to fly the Hellespont. More practically it was used by the ancient Greeks and Romans for writing tablets and for modelling as well as for candles and seals, and these remained the principal applications in the Middle Ages. As early as the first century A.D. the younger Pliny described rushlights made by dipping the partly-peeled pith of the rush in wax, and candles in which threads of flax were coated with pitch and wax.

When the London wax chandlers began to function as an organised body, white beeswax was comparatively expensive. The price per lb. has been given as *6d.* in 1432 and *3d.* in 1490 – as much as a labourer could earn in a day (yellow, unbleached, wax was about half the price). It was also a negotiable commodity, some fines and taxes were payable in pounds of wax, and there was a great temptation to adulterate it with cheaper substances. Nevertheless, in thirteenth- and fourteenth-century England wax was used on a very large scale indeed, particularly in candles for the church and the nobility, torches for processions, and seals on official documents. For example, in 1243 Henry III offered 1500 'lights' in St. Paul's Cathedral on the feast of the Conversion, and in 1303 wax candles weighing 1200 lb. were burned at the obsequies of the Bishop of London, Richard Gravesend. At the regular Corpus Christi processions[21] there would be carried, according to Stow,[22] 'more than one hundred Torches of Waxe (costly garnished) burning light'. In 1313–4 a year's housekeeping costs for Thomas, Earl of Lancaster, then the most important man in the land,[23] included '1,870 [lb.] of lights for Paris candles, called perchers'[24] and 1,714 lb. of wax for seals, the latter costing £314 *7s.* 4½*d.* Beekeeping was of course practised, not only for the production of wax, but also for the honey, which was the only sweetening agent before the introduction of sugar and was used for making mead,[25] then a popular alcoholic drink, and in medicine.

In spite of the representations of honey-bees on early documents and plate, there is no evidence that the London wax chandler was concerned with the production of beeswax,[26] but he certainly had the exclusive right to deal in it. Among his principal products were the wax candles from which the craft takes its name.

Candles were used extensively, not only for lighting but also for decorative and symbolic purposes; in quantity they made a fine show for a great occasion. The alternative to wax was tallow, which was much cheaper, but the animal fat gave an unpleasant smell;[27] owing to its low melting-point tallow was more prone to guttering and burned more quickly. At the beginning of the fourteenth century a royal palace had sergeant-chandlers in charge of a chandlery; besides buying wax and wick for the candles used by the king and high officials, they would deal in tallow for the humbler members of the household.

Candles were an important part of the allowances to the great officers of state. At the death of Henry I in 1135 the chancellor[28] was receiving a salary of *5s.* a day, the highest in the household, together with loaves, wine and 'i fat wax candle and xl pieces of candle'; with the high price of beeswax, candle-ends were a valuable perquisite (and continued to be so up to the time of George III). Under Edward IV (1461–83) the lord steward of the household received in winter months 'i torch to attend upon himself, i tortayes (small torch) to set his livery bason ewer and towel by, iii perchers wax, vi candles wax, viii candles peris (Paris), and viii candles tallow'. An ordinary secretary was allowed daily in winter 'i torch, i percher, ii wax candles, iii paris candles' and also red wax for sealing documents; 'when he has need of much writing' says the rule-book, he could have more perchers of tallow and smaller paris candles.

Wax candles were always a luxury article, used by kings and noblemen – and, for the glory of God, by the church. In Christian worship the candle typifies Jesus Christ, the

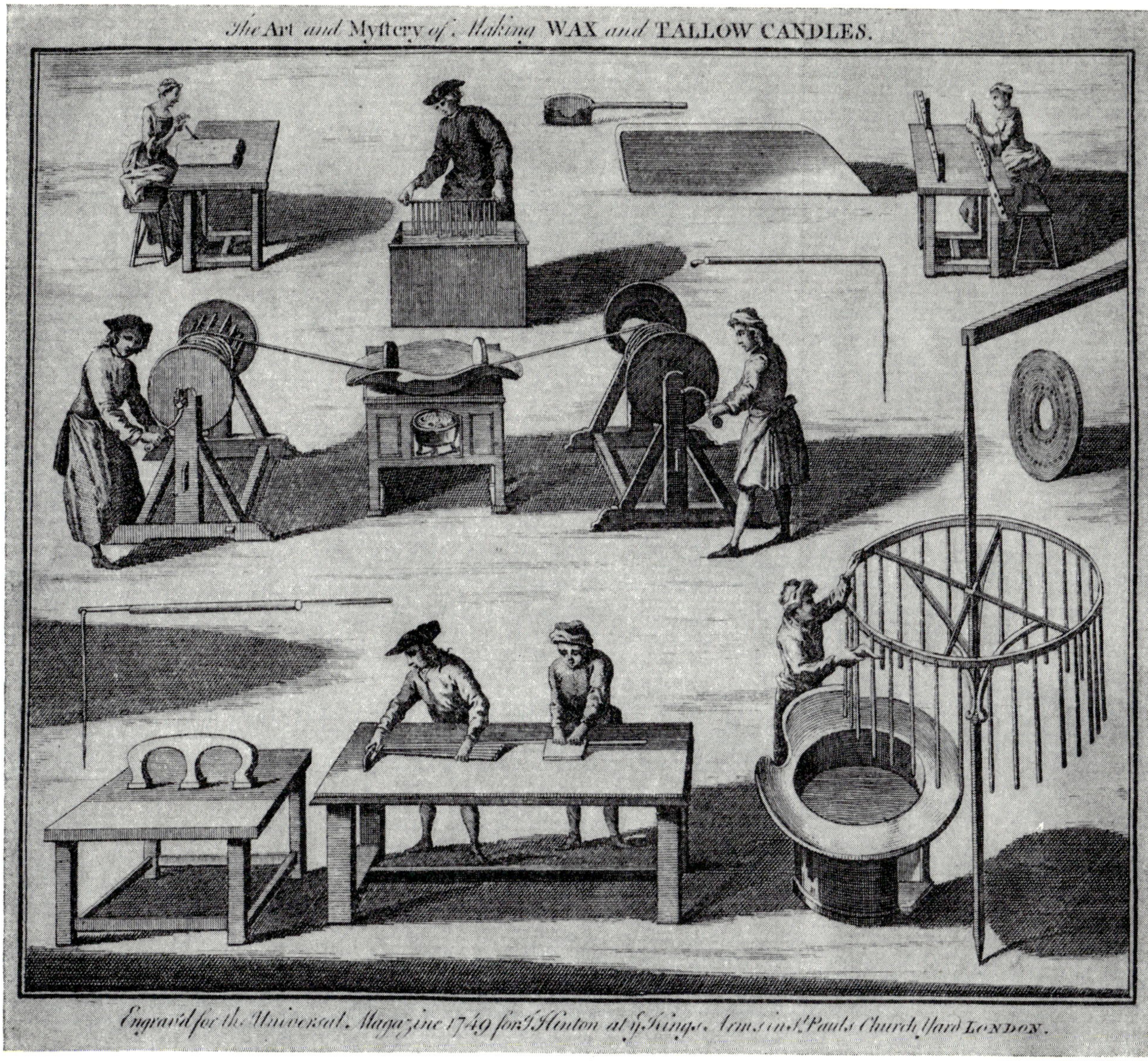

1. The chandler's craft: making candles by hand.

In the centre is a reel of taper wick being passed through a bath of molten wax and graduated draw-plates. At bottom right wax is being poured over vertical wicks; these candles were kept warm and soft in a feather bed before rolling to uniform thickness. Also shown are ancillary processes: threading the wick through iron sleeves and cutting wicks to length (top left and right), and rolling the candles and trimming the feet (bottom centre). A 'walnut-tree table', perhaps for stacking and bundling, is at bottom left. Tools illustrated are a ladle, cleaning knife ('coulter'), and draw-plate.

At top centre is a tallow chandler dipping his wicks in a mixture of mutton and beef fat.

light of the world: the wax represents His spotless body,[29] the wick His soul, and the flame His divinity. The candle also represents prayer and sacrifice. Before the Reformation, candles of pure beeswax were used at all liturgical services and ceremonies, and it was essential to have lighted candles of bleached wax on the altar when celebrating mass. Only at masses for the dead were yellow, unbleached, candles allowed. The year's supply of church candles was blessed at Candlemas,[30] the traditional day when Simeon hailed 'a light to lighten the Gentiles'.

In the earliest days candles were made by servants and monks, and it was perhaps the twelfth century before the wax chandler emerged as an independent craftsman and a flourishing trade began. His wicks were made of twisted cotton, flax or hemp, and the beeswax was usually purified to give the best light and least smell and bleached for good appearance. Candles could be formed by dipping or drawing a wick through molten wax, by basting a vertical wick or building it up with soft wax, by rolling a wick in wax and adding layer on layer, or by stretching a wick through a mould or metal tube filled with wax[31] (fig. 1); moulding was not very suitable for pure beeswax, which cooled and contracted too quickly. Though the socket type of candlestick was known in the fourteenth century, most early candles had the thicker end hollowed out for impaling on a spike or 'pricket',[32] the easiest method when they were relatively soft and, if made by pouring, of variable thickness.

Besides the standard domestic candle, many special types were made, ranging from slender tapers, sometimes in long coils called 'trindles',[33] and small round 'sizes' to large square 'quarerres' for funerals and tall stately 'perchers' for altars and ceremonial displays.

Wax torches or 'flambeaux'[34] with their scintillating flame were more impressive than candles, particularly for outdoor use; made of twisted tow or cotton soaked in resin and coated with beeswax, they burned fiercely enough to resist wind and rain and were often carried on wooden staves in processions.

Sealing wax, which was widely used for the seals necessary to validate official and legal documents, had beeswax as its sole or main ingredient. The seal impressions, taken from metal or other stamps, were usually made from a mixture of beeswax with Venice turpentine and colouring matter such as vermilion or verdigris. Seals of individual design would be struck for kings, bishops and other dignitaries and also for corporate bodies. There were three royal seals, and impressions of the Great Seal of England are attached to the company's first charter and its subsequent confirmations.

The London wax chandlers

Though the early wax chandlers left few records behind them, the city archives and legal documents such as wills and deeds enable some persons to be named if little more. For instance, William le Sirger was described as a wax chandler in 1298, and Robert, William and John le Cierger, whose names are mentioned between 1277 and 1311, must have been regular customers at least, a cierger[35] being strictly a wax-candle bearer; in 1277, when all recognisances of debts had to be taken before the mayor, Robert 'acknowledged himself bound in the sum of £4 for 2 tuns of wine', and in 1281 William was one of the 'mainpernors' or sureties who went bail for 100*s.* (a substantial amount) for an offender. In 1311 (4 March) John de Benstede, late apprentice of John le Cierger of 'Kandelwickstrate',[36] was admitted to the freedom of the city, perhaps the first record of a wax chandler's admission; another of the family, Richard de Benstede, was named as a wax chandler in an assignment of 1325. In a will of 1342, John de Hynton of All Hallows, Bread Street, was described as 'wax chandler, *cererarius*'.

So far only a few individuals are known, but by 1330 a recognised mistery must have been in existence, for the wax chandlers' was one of 20 crafts invited to contribute to a 'present' for the king, Edward III. They gave 40*s.*, equivalent to perhaps £140 today, towards a total of 1000 marks[37] or £666; the city was accustomed to make loans to the crown to meet special expenditure, but Edward considered this amount so trifling that he would only accept it as a free gift. A similar offering was made and accepted in 1355, and also in 1363 when 32 crafts subscribed a total of £428 9*s.* 4*d.* 'for an offering to be presented to the lord the King of England' for the French wars; the mercers' and the fishmongers' crafts gave £40 each, and the wax chandlers their 40*s.* as before.

At this time some control of the trade must have been in the offing for in 1343 four wax chandlers – William atte Noke, John Froyle, Roger de Wodhull and William Clerich, *cirgiarii* – were appointed to investigate the mixing of fat with wax and were sworn before the mayor. In 1358 it was put on a firmer footing by the issue of a series of by-laws or ordinances (appendix 1) on the authority of the mayor and aldermen. All wax chandlers within the city or suburbs, either citizens or outsiders, who made torches, tapers, prickets, great candles and the like, were to make them of as good wax within as without; they were not to put tallow or resin in wicks, or any kind of rubbish, and wicks were not to be so heavy as to sell wick for wax. An offender was to have all faulty goods on his property burnt before his door, and would be imprisoned till he paid a fine, at the discretion of the mayor and aldermen, for damage done to the common people; for the second offence he would be set on the pillory, and for the third he would have to forswear both city and occupation. Two or four of the best qualified people of the mistery were to be sworn before the mayor to present defaults. In the first year of these ordinances William Samkyn, Walter le Rede and John de Notyngham condemned a torch 'falsely made by John Donat, a Lombard': he was fined 20*s.* and committed to prison, a quick success.

In 1364 the crafts were ordered to elect four or six masters, who were to oversee their fellow craftsmen and the goods they made or sold, and present them to the mayor to be sworn. This order does not seem to have benefited the wax chandlers, for in 1371 they complained to the mayor and aldermen of bad government and much abuse in the city because, unlike other crafts, they had no masters appointed to watch for defects. They went on to ask that four searchers should be appointed and to present a new set of ordinances for approval (appendix 2). In addition to the standard instructions to use only good wax and wick, fines were laid down on a rising scale (from 6*s.* 8*d.* to 20*s.*) for the first three offences, but the pillory was omitted; prices were fixed for the hire of tapers and torches for funerals and for making chandlery with customer's own wax, and everyone was ordered to have a mark to set on his work, unmarked goods being forfeit. The ordinances were duly approved, and the first masters or overseers sworn – Walter (le) Rede, who had previously been appointed to inspection duties in 1358, and John Pope, who was later to represent the craft on the common council. Among later appointments as masters were –

1377 John Maynard, John Campioun	1428 Thomas Galiot, John Mayho
1421 Henry Gowe, William Burtone	1432 Richard Bury, Nicholas Boyly
1423 John Peryn, James Coterell	1438 Roger Wyllys, William Underhill
1424 John Broke, Richard de Bury	

Of these early masters, Rede's will made in 1375 includes a bequest to his servant John of '2 hoods of the livery of St. Giles and St. John', fraternities in the church of St. Giles, Cripplegate, with which he must have been connected. Pope and Campioun are mentioned as creditors (for 10*s.* 9*d.* and 13*s.* 6*d.* respectively) in an inventory made in 1391 on the death of Richard Tokey, a Grocer. Pope, in his will of 1402, provides a good example of a testator's care for the welfare of the dead as well as the living. He left his tenement[38] in Candelwykstret to Elizabeth his wife for life, the reversion to be sold to William Fynch, wax chandler, and the proceeds to be devoted to the good of his soul, the souls of his three late wives, the welfare of Elizabeth his wife and the souls of his daughter, father, mother *et al.*

On the other hand, 'John Maynard, wax chaundeler', appears with 'other misdoers of his covin' or conspiracy to have been a source of trouble and expense to the city authorities. In 1377, they were involved in a scuffle with Thomas of Woodstock, Earl of Buckingham, who was John of Gaunt's younger brother: 'Upon Cornehille in London' they 'made assault upon the servants of the said Earl, and beat and wounded them, and pursued them, when flying to his hostel, and broke and hewed down the doors of the same with axes and other arms, the said Earl being then within and lying in his bed, and, by reason thereof, no little alarmed; to the grievous damage of the said Earl, and so pernicious an example to the whole realm'. The misdoers were to be 'arrested and detained, until they and their sureties should have made sufficient compensation', but the outcome is not known.

Fifteenth-century wax chandlers of whom we have some slight knowledge include William Turner, John Fynche, William Terrell, John Orford, and John Ropkyns. Turner, who died in 1400, had a monument in the church of St. Michael, Wood Street, until it was destroyed in the Great Fire of London. Fynche figures in the exchequer roll of owners of lay property in the city[39] for 1412 as 'Joh'es Fynche Wexchaundeler . . . . iiij *li*'. Terrell, when making his will in 1418 (before his own craft was incorporated), bequeathed a tenement in Tower Street to the Merchant Taylors, the income to be used to keep an anniversary for the soul of John Creke and others in the parish of Our Lady of Abchurch.

Orford in 1466 was supplying the Pastons, the Norfolk family whose correspondence sheds much light on contemporary life and manners: 'to John Orford, wax chandeler for xii torches and one candell of 1 lb, lv*s* ii*d ob*',[40] i.e. 55*s*. 2½*d*. Ropkyns in 1474/5 was being sued by Christopher Goswell, Vintner, for debt and by Elizabeth Blount, single-woman, for trespass, and petitioned the Chancellor of England for help in defending these actions. Apparently Goswell had put Blount to board with Ropkyns for 16*d*. a week, but after 18 weeks she had departed leaving behind her 16*s*. arrears of rent and 'one harnessed girdle'; Goswell had claimed the girdle as his property, but Ropkyns would not give it up until the debt was paid.[41]

Civic duties

Though records dating from before incorporation are scanty, some firm evidence of an established position comes in the period 1376–84 when members of the common council were nominated by the crafts instead of the wards: the wax chandlers were among the fifty or so to send representatives – Roger Elys (Elles) and William Hatfield in 1376, and John Pope and Richard Saveray in 1381/2. Elys, who was elected alderman of the Aldersgate ward in 1377 and a sheriff in 1395, was a substantial property-owner; in his will he ordered his shop with houses over it and other shops in Gutter Lane to be sold, after the death of his present wife, for various 'pious uses', such as prayers for himself and Alice his dead wife and for his kinsman Dom Martin Elys, a minor canon of St. Paul's, and to provide dowries for poor virgins.

The veil can be lifted to some extent by considering the standing obligations of the crafts to the mayor. These included their contributions of money or men for the king and his wars and their compulsory attendance at royal and civic ceremonies. Examples have been given of money gifts from the wax chandlers between 1330 and 1363, and it can safely be assumed that they played their due part in enabling the city to meet the king's demands, a custom that went back to 1194 when the crafts provided some of the 150,000 marks required to ransom Richard I.

Triumphs or 'ridings' were regularly held to welcome the sovereign on return from war and to celebrate a coronation or a marriage, and each craft would be represented by some or all of its members. In 1415 when Henry V came to St. Paul's with his prisoners to give thanks after Agincourt, he received a stupendous welcome. The mayor and aldermen with representatives of all the crafts rode to meet him at Blackheath, and the streets were lined with mounted craftsmen to the number of 15,000 or more; houses were hung with tapestries, flags, streamers and decorated boughs, and fountains ran with wine. Though the wax chandlers must have been there, the first record of their attendance on royalty comes in 1463, when six of the craft rode out to meet Edward IV coming from the north, and two years later when they sent a further six to attend his queen to her coronation; the largest contingent was 24. In 1483 four wax chandlers were among the 400 citizens who, dressed in gowns of murrey (mulberry-colour) rode out to meet the young Edward

V in May and Richard III in November, the latter having consigned the boy-king and his brother to the Tower. No doubt representatives had also been present in the previous June, when Richard, having accepted the crown from the Duke of Buckingham, 'left Baynard's Castle and proceeded with a greate company of lordes and Gentilmen, wt also the Mayr and the Craftes . . . . . . unto Westmynster, and there toke possession of the Regalite sitting in Westmynster halle'.

Royal funerals, which were similarly honoured by the city, had a special interest for the wax chandlers on account of the large quantities of wax tapers and torches required. The burial of Anne of Bohemia, queen of Richard II, in 1394 was conducted with unparalleled pomp, and the illuminations were so exceptional that 'Abundance of wax was sent from Flanders to make flambeaux and torches'. For the funeral of Henry V in 1422, said to be the most impressive for 200 years, the procession, two miles long, was met at Blackheath by bishops, abbots and an army of priests carrying 1,400 wax tapers, and from Southwark to St. Paul's it passed between ranks of citizens, every fifth man bearing a torch; every householder from London Bridge onwards had a servant holding a lighted torch at his door. The mayor, aldermen, and crafts went on to Westminster – after further masses and feasting – the next day. The total number of official torches was 211, to which the wax chandlers' contribution was six. There must have been substantial orders for individual members of the craft: for instance, the Brewers bought eight torches using 138 lb. of wax for 51*s*. 9*d*., though they sold the residue (112 lb.) for 28*s*. later. But this pales into insignificance beside the contract obtained by one wax chandler, Simon Prentot: the bill – 'for divers hearses provided by him at Dover Canterbury Hospryne Rochester St Pauls London and Westminster . . . 300*li* 12*s* vj*d*' – represents an almost incredible sum, say £15,000 today. However, a few years later it seems that wax chandlers (not only in London) were overcharging for workmanship; they had been selling 'candles, images, figures and other works of wax for offerings' at four times the price of the plain wax, and in 1432 a statute[42] was passed limiting the increase to 3*d*. in the pound.

Besides attending the mayor at royal welcomes and royal funerals, the crafts took part in his yearly procession to Westminster[43] for royal approval, and his attendance at St. Paul's Cathedral on the seven great festivals of All Hallows, Christmas, St. Stephen, St. John, New Year, Twelfth and Candlemas. From 1453 it was usual for the mayor to go by road to one of the city wharves and continue to Westminster by river, London's only broad highway; the crafts accompanied him on horseback or in barges, and minstrels[44] were in attendance. The crafts also held a mayor's feast, eating and drinking being necessary adjuncts to ceremonial and taking up a great deal of time and money; the wax chandlers' bill for October 29, 1478 has been preserved:[45]

	s.	*d.*
A Loin of Beef		4
A Leg of Mutton		2½
Two Loins of Veal and Two Loins of Mutton ...	1	4
A Goose		6

	s.	d.
A Capon		6
A Pig and A Rabbit		6
A Dozen of Pigeons		7
A Hundred of Eggs		8½
A Gallon of Wine		8
A Kilderkin[46] of Ale	1	8
	7	0

All these processions and pageants were very popular in the late Middle Ages, perhaps because their bright colours and excitements helped to offset the tedium and squalor of everyday life. The various crafts were placed in strict order of precedence, though this seems to have varied considerably, perhaps with their relative fortunes. In 1422 the wax chandlers were 15th out of 31 crafts represented at the funeral of Henry V, and in the same year they were listed among 111 crafts 'exercised in London from of old' by the Brewers' clerk 'in case it may in any wise profit the hall and Company' – perhaps by hiring their hall for meetings or feasts. Between 1463 and 1465 their position seems to have varied between 19th and 23rd.

The crafts had the further duty of providing men and equipment for the standing and marching watches that policed and guarded the city. Nightly throughout the year, from sunset to sunrise a standing watch of citizens helped the constables to keep the peace; the normal street lighting was from 'cressets', or fire baskets burning pitch, and from lanterns containing tallow candles. Twice a year from about 1385 there was held a 'midsummer watch' or military muster of citizens, marching in procession from St. Paul's to Aldgate and back. This took place on the vigils of St. John Baptist (June 24)[47] and St. Peter & St. Paul (June 29),[48] and on these nights each house had to hang up a lantern and, in view of the profusion of torches, put out a tub of water as a fire precaution. The wax chandlers were scheduled to provide 21 men for a watch in 1470, and in 1485 (the Grocers sent 220), but these were special occasions – the first a troubled time with Henry VI enthroned as Warwick's puppet and able-bodied citizens called out to prevent disorder, and the second a few weeks before Richard III fell at Bosworth Field. The craft's normal contribution was probably three men, as in 1483.

A personal link between the wax chandlers and St. Paul's Cathedral[49] seems to have been established towards the end of the fourteenth century, when certain members of the craft made it their duty to maintain the taper candelabrum at the rood or crucifix above the north door, perhaps the most famous of the cathedral's many shrines. This spontaneous expression of devotion was later made official by an instruction that every wax chandler should give a pound or more of new wax each year on the feast of the Cross.[50] The text of the order, which has been inserted in the company's first ordinance book on the same folio as the ordinances of 1371[51] reads:

In the worschip of oure Lorde Jesu Criste and of oure Lady Saint Marie and all ye holy company of heven and the Holy Cros that Jesu Criste oure Lorde suffrede on payne and passion for all man kynde, a companye of the craft of Wax Chaundelleres of London ys sterid to devocion and assentid to susteyne a certyne taper braunched reall of a certeyne weghte beyng a forne ye rode atte north dore in ye chirche of Poules of London: and begonen was this devocion by pore men of the same company in the chirche of Seynt Poule of London aforeseyde, in the daye of ye fest of the cros the yere of grace a thousande thre hundred and [[52]], for the more helpe and savation of her sowles and for to nourisch love and frendschip among hem everlastyng in fulfillyng and susteynyng of devocion. The companye of the same craft aforeseyde have ordeyned that agaynes the tyme of the foreseyde taper schall be made and renewed that every man of ye same company schal gyf 1 pounde of new wex at the lest, and sum men more after the company aforeseyde wyll ordeyne.

The taper 'braunched reall' was probably a giant candelabrum for slender candles, 'bra(u)nch' meaning a branched candlestick and 'reall' being used in Mss. of about 1400 for 'royal', i.e. splendid. The 'rood of northern' or *crux borealis* was a miraculous crucifix said to have been carved by Joseph of Arimathea, and was the scene of many personal dramas of the Reformation; here on Shrove Tuesday 1527 six Lutherans, one carrying a lighted taper weighing five lb. and the others symbolic faggots, did penance before Wolsey on his throne and consigned Wyclif's tracts and testaments to the flames.

The supply of wax to St. Paul's presumably ceased in 1538 with the destruction of the rood at the Reformation, but the spirit behind it was revived after the 1939–45 war by the company's undertaking to provide candles in perpetuity for the new high altar. At a typical London parish, St. Mary-at-Hill, a reprint of the churchwarden's accounts for 1477–9 shows the 'Costs of the wax chandler' as –

	s.	*d.*
Item, paid for new wax bought for the use of the church as in beamlight[53] tapers, prickets and candles, weighing 92 lb, price every lb, 4½*d.*	34	8
Item, they received in old wax of store of the church, as in beamlight old tapers, within these two years 191 lb. Total of new wax and of the old 283½ lb by the small hundred.[54]		
Paid to Roger Middleton,[55] wax chandler, for making of the said new wax and old wax made in tapers for the beamlight and other tapers, prickets, and tenebrae candles,[56] for every lb, a halfpenny.	11	9
Item, paid to the said Roger, for making of the Paschal taper[57] by the said two years, each weighing 30 lb for every lb a penny, 5*s.* and for the waste[58] of the same in two years 5 lb, for every lb 4½*d.*, 22½*d.*	6	10½
Total	53	3½

In 1479–81 they paid only 22*s.* 11*d.* for 'all the wax'.[59]

A royal charter

By 1484 the wax chandlers had become sufficiently prosperous to obtain their first royal charter. This was an expensive matter – only 22 of more than 100 crafts had been incorporated – and not essential for a craft already in possession of civic ordinances and empowered to wear livery. But it brought considerable prestige, the independence and security of legal sanction, and the many practical advantages of becoming a corporation with the right to perpetual succession, to use a common seal, to make its own by-laws, to acquire and hold land, and to take legal action.

Incorporation was granted by letters patent dated 16 February 1484 (appendix 3). Stripped of legal verbiage the Wax Chandlers of the city and suburbs were authorised to choose one master and two keepers or wardens 'after their custome', to maintain standards of material and workmanship, and to search for faulty goods and bring offenders to the mayor for punishment. They were also empowered to acquire land and other property to the value of five marks[60] or 66*s*. 8*d*. a year; this was the usual exemption from the statute of mortmain,[61] *De Religiosis*, which forbade gifts of property to perpetual corporations such as the church except with the consent of the feudal superior, since it would then escape feudal dues. The low limit on the purchase of property is in sharp contrast with the fee of 25 marks[60] paid to the exchequer,[62] no doubt in addition to incidental expenses. Two typical features of the text – the opening fanfare and the homage to spiritual values – may be quoted here :

> Richard by the grace of God King of England and of France and Lord of Ireland[63] . . . to our well-beloved faithful and liegemen the freemen of the mistery or craft of wax chandlers of our city of London.
>
> Pray for the good state of us while we live and for our soul when we shall depart from this life, for the souls of all our progenitors, and for the benefactors of the said mistery and the souls of them when they shall depart from this world.

The original document (plate 1) is still in the company's possession. It is inscribed in Latin on vellum measuring 21 × 12 in., beautifully illuminated and complete with the Great Seal of England on its original cord. In the large initial 'R' are shown the arms of Richard III, last of the Plantagenets. The shield carries the fleurs-de-lys of France quartered with the lions passant of England, ensigned by an arched crown and supported by two silver boars tusked *or*; above the crown is the motto *loyaulté me lie* (loyalty bindeth me). The floral border is a design typical of the period, and the bees on many of the flowers recognise the source of all wax chandlery. For his Great Seal, which was kept by the lord chancellor and used to authenticate royal documents, Richard employed a matrix of his predecessor's, altering *Edwardus* to read *Ricardus*; the wording was *Ricardus Dei gra' Rex Fra'cie et Anglie et Dominus Hibernie*. On the back of the charter are notices of enrolment in the exchequer and at the Guildhall, prior approval by the court of aldermen being required by an act of 1437.[64]

A constitution for the company begins to take shape with this charter, which was confirmed by later sovereigns and remained in force until 1663. Rule by a triumvirate of master and wardens and their election by the freemen of the company are clearly set out. However it was another 30 years before a court of assistants would be set up, and liverymen are not mentioned; authority for the Wax Chandlers' livery rests on custom and not on any royal or aldermanic grant, so that there is no limit, in theory, to the number on the cloth.[65]

For use on their common seal the Wax Chandlers needed a coat-of-arms. Their grant-of-arms, complete with mantle, helm and crest, is dated 3 February 1485 and is one of the very few company grants to survive from the fifteenth century. Sir Thomas Holme, Clarenceux king-of-Arms, directs it to the 'gode, sadde, worshipful and weldisposed personnes the maister and wardennes of the ful honorable craft and ffraternitie of wex-chaundeleres . . . with al the holl bodi of the same' – the first time that 'worshipful' is used in connection with this or perhaps any other craft (by 1530 it had become a 'worshipful company'). Thomas Stone was master, and Thomas Bell and John Asshe the wardens.

The 'blazon' reads as follows:

> Asur thre morteres royal gold Upon a Cheveron silur thre Roses goules seded gold. The creste upon the helme A mayden kneling a monges dyuers ffloures in a Surcote cloth of gold ffurred with Ermyn making a garlond being in hir hand of the same ffloures sett withinne a wreth gold and goules. The mantell Asur furred with Ermyn[66]

The 'morteres royal' on the shield (plate 4) are a form of candlestick and the only direct reference to the trade of the wax chandler. As the name suggests, a mortar[67] (the more usual spelling) was originally a bowl holding wax or oil with a floating wick; the epithet 'royal' in conjunction with the elaborate design may imply a mortar of more than common splendour (*cf* battle-royal). The choice of red for the roses on the chevron may have been a predilection of Holme's as a Lancastrian:[68] he had a chaplet of roses on his own arms. The maiden crest is probably symbolic of the purity which it was the wax chandler's duty to maintain in his materials. A later version of the crest has the maiden kneeling in a 'Roseyare' or rosebush (F *rosier*): *la couronnement de la rosière* is a custom of great antiquity in some French villages, *la rosière* being a maiden to whom is awarded a wreath of roses for virtuous conduct.

In the initial letter the king-of-arms is represented as usual in his tabard[69] pointing to the coat-of-arms with his sceptre, and the bee is included in the floral background. The original arms were without supporters, which were not granted until 1530, and the motto 'Truth is the Light' was also added later.

Blue and gold, both prominent in the coat-of-arms, seem to have been adopted by the Wax Chandlers for their livery colours, and in later accounts there are frequent references to the purchase of streamers and other items in 'blue and yellow'.

> *Instead of dirt and poison we have rather chosen to fill our hives with honey and wax; thus furnishing mankind with the two noblest of things, which are sweetness and light.*
>
> SWIFT

Notes on Chapter I

[1]Gild: society for mutual aid or common object, the members paying towards a common stock (OE *gild* payment, G *geld* money). *Cf* Danegeld.

[2]Here and throughout 'religious' and 'secular' are used in their general sense, not their medieval (and Roman Catholic) sense, in which, for instance, the secular clergy were parish priests as opposed to the regular clergy who belonged to a monastic order.

[3]In York there were 41 approved craft gilds in 1450, but most towns outside London preferred a single 'merchant gild'; the Elizabethan martyr, Margaret Clitherow, long venerated as the Pearl of York and recently canonised, was the daughter of a wealthy wax chandler of that city.

[4]Mistery: either from L *ministerium* occupation (*cf* F *métier*), or from L *magister* master, via F *maîtrise* mastership. The words 'art' and 'craft', either of which denoted a trade or occupation, were also applied to the body that practised it, and in this sense craft seems to have superseded mistery for general purposes.

[5]Livery: F *livrer* to bestow, from L *liberare* in the special sense 'to distribute'. *Cf* livery stables and a chauffeur's livery. It originally signified the food and clothing allowed to dependants of great households, monasteries, colleges or gilds; later it was applied to a badge worn by a baron's partisans as a pledge of support in return for maintenance, and then to a type of clothing denoting the allegiance of the wearer and forming a badge of service and protection.

[6]Journeyman: workman paid by the day (F *journée*).

[7]No connection (except that both were intermediate grades) with yeomen in the usual sense of a class immediately below the gentry.

[8]Prime warden is still the title used by the Basket Makers, Blacksmiths, Dyers, Fishmongers, Goldsmiths and Shipwrights; the Shipwrights have a permanent 'master', an honorary position held by H.R.H. Prince Philip, and the Saddlers have changed over to prime wardens at times when members of the royal family were 'perpetual masters'. The Weavers are exceptional in preferring an 'upper bailiff'.

[9]For instance, towards the end of the fifteenth century it was laid down that no-one could be permitted to wear a livery unless he had attained the degree and estate of an 'esquire' or attendant upon a knight and, in heraldry, had ceased to be a gentleman; a general edict prohibited the wearing of the hood by those under the degree of an esquire of the king's household.

[10]7 Henry IV, *c* 14.

[11]12 Henry IV, II, *c* 167.

[12]'Lord Mayor' (*dominus maior*), the customary though unauthorised title, appeared in Latin in the thirteenth century, and during the sixteenth century it came into general, though not exclusive, use. 'Mayor' is still retained on precepts, leases etc..

[13]The mayor had the distinction of being the only commoner among the 25 signatories responsible for enforcing its terms.

[14]It will be understood that the word 'livery' may denote either the clothing itself or those who are entitled to wear it; in the latter sense the livery of the crafts and companies are *ipso facto* the livery of the city.

[15]Though sex was no bar to the freedom, women were and have continued to be in a very small minority

[16]Many of the redemptioners may have been fully qualified men from outside the city.

[17]His principal function being that of city treasurer and accountant.

[18]Richard Whittington (*c* 1358–1423), thrice elected lord mayor, became a wealthy Mercer who financed three successive sovereigns. In 1411 he occupied the Leaden Hall, a mansion and estate that was later used as a great market (a purpose it still serves) and an armoury and granary for the city.

[19]Chepe, first mentioned as Westceap (Estchepe was in another part of the city), is the usual medieval form, but Chepsyde occurs in the fourteenth century. Exceptional width made it the principal market-place (OE *ceap* price or purchase) and the natural location for civic pageantry and public penance; it possessed in 'Goldsmith's Row' the finest shops in the country.

[20]Chandler originally meant one who made or dealt in candles (OF *chandelier,* L *candelarius* from *candela* a candle). By 1583 the sense had been extended to cover other retail trades.

[21]Such processions are still maintained by the Skinners' Company, but bouquets are carried instead of torches. The feast of Corpus Cristi was established in the fourteenth century in honour of the Eucharist and celebrated on the Thursday after Trinity Sunday with processions and miracle plays.

[22]John Stow, the chronicler and antiquary whose famous *Survey of London,* 1558 and 1603, is a fascinating and invaluable source of information on customs and topography. In 1720 it was revised and brought up to date by an ecclesiastical historian, John Strype.

[23]After Bannockburn, he became leader of the baronial opposition to Edward II, but was defeated at Boroughbridge and beheaded in his own castle of Pontefract.

[24]Percher: a tall candle of wax or tallow, especially the bigger wax candles set on altars (originally for placing on a shelf or perch). Often called Paris (peris) candles.

[25]Mead is mentioned in Celtic and Anglo-Saxon literature as the drink of kings.

[26]Much wax was imported, principally from the Continent.

[27]Though Shakespeare may have exaggerated in *Cymbeline,* i.6 –

> Base and unlustrous as the smoky light
> That's fed with stinking tallow.

No disrespect to our fellow-craftsmen, who supplied a different market and with whom, despite occasional brushes, we would not normally have been in competition. The Tallow Chandlers' Company, incorporated in 1462, ranks next after the Wax Chandlers' in order of precedence.

[28]The chancellor had already risen from his original position of chaplain to that of the king's chief secretary and confidential adviser; later he was to become 'secretary of state for all departments'.

[29]Originally in imitation of the pagan mythology in which the bee was a virgin producer of offspring, or because the extraction of the wax from the flower typified the Virgin Birth.

[30]The spring purification feast of the Romans was converted like the pagan Easter into a Christian festival, the Presentation of Christ in the Temple, later called the Purification of the Blessed Virgin Mary; it was celebrated on 2 February by processions and the blessing and distribution of candles.

[31]All these methods are still used, though wicks of plaited cotton soaked in a mordant obviate the necessity for snuffing and give slower burning. The moulding process is mechanised, using highly polished moulds of tin or tinned alloy.

[32]The pricket survived in rural areas until the last century, and multiple prickets or 'hearses' are still used in Roman Catholic churches.

[33]Trindle: roll or coil of wax taper used for lighting in medieval churches, or a round cake of wax.

[34]Torch: F *torche,* perhaps from L *torquere* to twist. A flambeau (F from med. L *flambellum*) usually denoted a torch consisting of thick wicks dipped in wax.

[35]F *cierge,* a wax candle or taper, especially a large candle used in religious ceremonies.

[36]Probably a corruption of OE *candelwyrhta*, a candlewright, superseded by F *chandelier*. In 1348 another member of the craft, Thomas Fraunceys, had a tenement here; it became Cannon Street before 1666.

[37]1 mark = 13*s*. 4*d*.

[38]Tenement: dwelling house or piece of land.

[39]Among the largest property-owners were our neighbours the Goldsmiths', whose annual rent was valued at £46. 10*s*. 3½*d*. and the priory of St. John of Jerusalem, our future landlords, at £99. 19*s*. 7*d*.

[40]*Ob:* halfpenny (L *obolus* a small coin).

[41]Among the wills proved in the London Commissary Court between 1396 and 1483 were those of 27 wax chandlers; one of them, John Baldulc, in 1431 left 6*s*. 8*d*. 'to the fellowship of my craft' for attendance at his funeral.

[42]11 Hen. VI, *c* 12.

[43]The Palace of Westminster, from being a royal residence since Edward the Confessor, had become the legislative and judicial capital of the country. Apart from being the official title of the Houses of Parliament, it survives only in the Jewel Tower (part of the private quarters), Westminster Hall, and the crypt and cloister of St. Stephen's Chapel.

[44]Minstrels (OF *ménestral*, L *minister* servant) were professional musicians; in London they had a gild of their own.

[45]*Harleian MS 4778* (British Museum). Substantial though it looks as if the fare could not compare with that enjoyed by the wealthier crafts, for instance the goldsmiths who spent £26. 17*s*. 4*d*. for their feast on St. Dunstan's day 1473.

[46]Kilderkin: 16–18 gallons.

[47]The festival of his nativity, his martydom being commemorated on 29 August.

[48]The traditional anniversary of their common martyrdom, but with the instititution of the feast of the Conversion of St. Paul, this day became confined to commemorating St. Peter.

[49]Old St. Paul's, 'a Gothic glory of medieval London', was 585 ft. long, compared with 530 ft. for Westminster Abbey, and its steeple reached to 493 ft. above the ground, 89 ft. higher than Salisbury's.

[50]Holy Rood day: celebrated either on 3 May (The Invention of the Cross), the traditional date on which in A.D. 326 the Empress Helena discovered the True Cross, or on 14 September (The Exaltation of the Cross), when she dedicated a new basilica enshrining the relic in Jerusalem.

[51]*MS 9495*, fol. 8r.

[52]The exact year is left blank, both in the text and in a marginal note; the index to *MS 9495* gives 1371, but it would appear to have been compiled in the sixteenth century.

[53]The equivalent of the modern floodlight?

[54]100; a long hundred was 120.

[55]Middleton had their custom in 1477–93, and Robert Bale in 1498. Garret Burton was their wax chandler in 1552.

[56]For services on the last three days of Holy Week; they were timed to finish at dusk (L *tenebrae* darkness), and the candles were extinguished in succession.

[57]At Easter, in the western church, a large taper or candle was placed at the north side of the sanctuary, lit on Holy Saturday, and extinguished on Ascension Day.

[58]Waste: material consumed or used up; the churchwardens also paid 'For the wast of ij tapres at Caustons obite, iiij*d*.' There was no implication of useless consumption, or waste in the modern sense.

[59]Tallow candles were sometimes used in church, presumably to save money; in 1477–9 they paid 6*s*. 5*d*. for six dozen lb. of tallow candles 'spent in divine service . . .'.

[60]Today 5 marks would be roughly equivalent to £200 or more and 25 marks to £1,000.

[61]Mortmain: F dead hand. The act was passed under Edward I in 1279 to ensure, for instance, that the king would not be deprived of the valuable rights that came to him on the death of a tenant-in-chief. Subsequently many exceptions were made in favour of bodies such as universities and hospitals, but it was 1888 before the statute was repealed.

[62]The king's court of revenue, headed by the lord high treasurer.

[63]The French and Irish titles were high-sounding but illusory. 'King of France' persisted until it was dropped by George III.

[64]15/16 Henry VI, *c* 6.

[65]Nowadays the number of admissions to the livery is limited by practical considerations, such as the capacity of the hall for company functions.

[66] asur = blue goules = red surcote – a robe or jacket.

[67]Mortar later denoted a large candle and, in Victorian times, a night-light or dish-heater (mortar-light), in which the wick was anchored at the bottom.

[68]The Wars of the Roses (1455–85) were fresh in memory.

[69]Herald's coat bearing the sovereign's arms.

CHAPTER II

Around the Reformation: 1485 - 1603

THE ACCESSION of the Tudors found the Wax Chandlers a fully fledged livery company. They had a royal charter and a coat-of-arms and were soon to be associated with a sister gild in the Jesus chapel at St. Paul's. During the next 50 years they were to build and occupy their first hall, receive confirmation of their precedence as the twentieth of some 60 crafts, and have their arms upgraded by the addition of supporters.

Despite these symbols of prosperity and status, the future was clouded by the Reformation, which, on its doctrinal rather than political side, made radical changes in the religious activities of the companies and robbed them of any pickings from religious trusts. The Wax Chandlers lost the support of the gild of Jesus, which was suppressed, and forfeited some of their trust income, but more damaging financially was the prohibition of wax candles, tapers and images in the church. The ban on these staple products must have been a grievous blow to the trade. Moreover the companies were increasingly harassed by demands from the government, which required men, money, and equipment both for overseas wars and for home defence, and there were also demands from the city for money for poor relief, principally by laying up stocks of corn. The obligation to attend the mayor at state and civic ceremonies was an additional burden. In all these public duties the Wax Chandlers took their part, even when it meant borrowing the money or selling their silver plate.

Within the company a firm administrative basis was laid. New and more comprehensive ordinances were introduced, reinforcing control of the trade and strengthening the organisation generally. New officers – assistants, clerk and beadle – were appointed to support the master and wardens, and regular records began to be kept. Account books starting in 1528, court minutes from 1584, and a search book of 1574–1664 have been preserved. From these and from various legal documents one can picture the day-to-day activities of the leaders of the company and, to a lesser extent, of the ordinary members. It is a happy coincidence that the early accounts should date from the most interesting period of the company's history: no longer a loosely-knit body of craftsmen, it had functioned for half a century as a chartered company, maintaining a closed shop and enforcing quality control – the guardian of the craftsman and, incidentally, of the customer.

From this period three masters of the company survive in more than memory. Two were early benefactors – John Thompson, whose bequest of 1526 is commemorated each year by gifts of overcoats, and William Kendall, whose bequest of 1558 still provides annual gifts of money to the sick and needy. And an Elizabethan Wax Chandler and his family can still be seen, portrayed in brass, in the pre-Fire church of St. Andrew Undershaft.[1] Described by Stow[2] as 'a faire gilded plate in the wall', it commemorates Simon Burton, who died in 1593, having been three times master of the company, a common councilman for Aldgate, and a governor of St. Thomas's Hospital; he is depicted with his two wives and four children in an attitude of prayer (fig. 2).[3]

The first hall

For some years after incorporation the company seems to have had no permanent headquarters, but in June 1501 a group of Wax Chandlers whose names deserve to be remembered – John Monk (Munke), Stephen Warde, John Asshe, John Strange, Thomas Caphurst, and William Bateman – acquired for £36[4] a property in the ward of Cripplegate[5] with a view to providing a 'common hall'. The site (which was conveyed by release to 'John Shepard, Master of the Mystery of Wax Chandlers, William Baynard and Thomas Cressy, Wardens, and the Commonalty of the Mystery' on 9 May 1544) has been occupied by the company ever since, becoming its most valuable possession.

The new property was situated at the corner of Maiden Lane (now part of Gresham Street[6]) and Godrun[7] (now Gutter) Lane, and apart from losses due to street widening and minor adjustments there has been little change in its area. With a frontage of 50 ft. and extending 61 ft. down Gutter Lane, it was occupied by a 'brewhouse'[8] called The Cock on the Hoop[9] and two shops. A quit rent[10] of 20*s.* a year was payable to the prior of the hospital of St. John of Jerusalem[11] – the knights hospitallers – in Clerkenwell.

The first mention of the site is contained in a deed, undated but probably about 1293 when the prior, William de Totehale, on behalf of the brothers granted a plot of land in the Parish of St. John Zachary to Adam de Hallingeby (a future sheriff) for a quarterly payment of 20*s.* Later it was owned by Henry Yevele, the greatest architect of his day, designer of the naves of Westminster and Canterbury and a remarkable combination of artistic skill and business ability: he bought the brewhouse and five shops adjacent in 1367 and disposed of them together with 'all his new shopes with solars[12] built above' in Godrun Lane in 1396.

When the Wax Chandlers came into possession of the buildings, much reconstruction work was necessary. Temporary accommodation was available in Aldersgate Street, where John Monk and four of his colleagues[13] had bought a property for £20 from one Elizabeth Eustace: they leased it back to her for life on condition that the new owners with the master and wardens should have free entry 'to have theire semble and communicacion as often and as large as it shall please them and that she should keep out of the way whilst they were therein and be only in such place as they should specify'.

However by 1525 a hall had been constructed on the Maiden Lane property, apparently by adding a timber superstructure and wooden staircase to the stone-built[14] 'yelehouse'

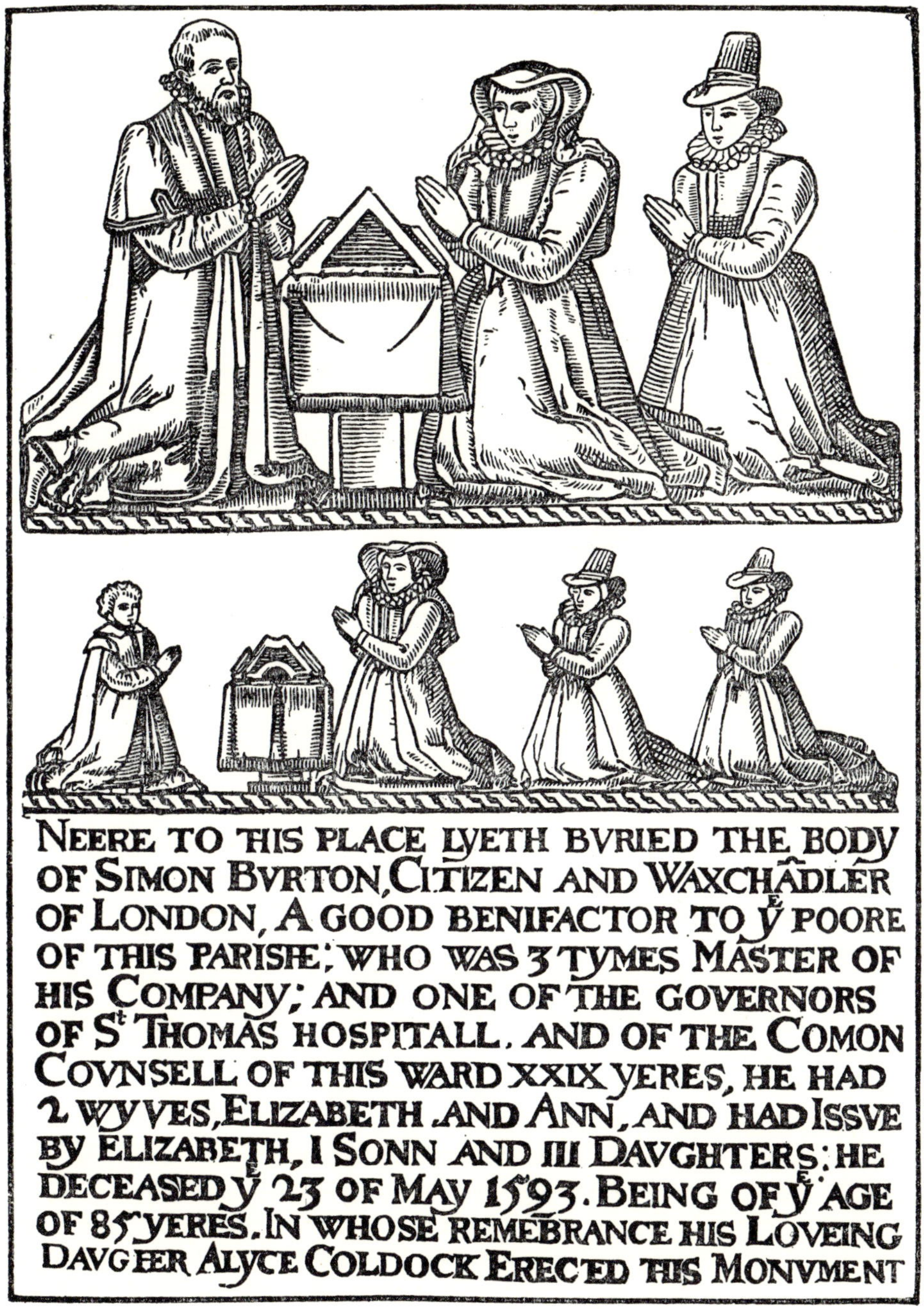

2. An Elizabethan Wax Chandler with his wives and family: Simon Burton, twice married, was master in 1562, 1570 and 1586.

or ale-house at the back of The Cock (which, as the residential part, was leased out separately). It appears to have had an open-rafter roof, which was tiled – a better fire-risk than thatch – and timber-framed walls, which were 'pargeted' or plastered externally; lattice windows occupied most of the wall space. A paved kitchen and a buttery were provided, and also a parlour for business and a chamber above it for social occasions. The buttery had a bay window, as did also a little chamber or garret and a bedroom for the beadle, who was not only a general factotum but also the hall caretaker, his wife acting as cleaner. There were four stained glass panels, probably quite small (say 1 ft. square), set in clear leaded lights: the Assumption of the Virgin Mary and the Transfiguration of Christ in the parlour and chamber respectively, and the arms of Henry VIII and his queen of the day in the buttery. Beneath the hall itself, which extended to the south-west corner of the site, was a cellar with stone staircase, and outside was a wooden lead-covered gallery on a timber support. The buildings were grouped round a small paved yard, approached by a covered entry from Maiden Lane and containing a well; this was a statutory requirement for brewing, which used more water than could be supplied from the public conduit, and it was soon filled up.[15]

No illustration of the hall or surroundings is known to exist, but a picture-map dating from the 1560s (fig. 3) shows the cluster of buildings on the site, and some idea of the probable building style[16] can be gained from the restored frontage of the upper floors at Staple Inn and the dining hall of Barnard's Inn, both in Holborn.[17] The usual type of construction employed a timber framework with the openings filled either with windows or with panels of wattle and daub; thick plaster on the outside and either cloth hangings[18] or a wainscot (wood panel) lining might be added to keep out the weather.

Further details can be gleaned from the accounts, which for the next ten years or so, show a series of alterations and repairs. In 1529–30 there was a payment 'to a playsterer for mendyng of our hall', and in 1530–2 an 'Itm payd to Jamys Jefferey Glasier for makyng clene of the glasse Wyndows abought the hall and for xvij quarelles and for mending of the Assumpcion of our lady in the parlour x*s*', presumably lattice windows (quarrels were the small panes of glass) and stained glass respectively. An earlier 'Itm payd for bred and drynke for the Carpenters because they went not home at drynkyng tymes xij*d*' suggests an overtime bonus. In the following year the accounts show payments for quantities of timber and ironmongery, and an item 'for the timber work of the beadle's Bay window ix*s* ij*d*'. In 1536–8 there was a substantial bill for 'Reparacions don Upon our hall and the tenement calld the Kok xxxij*l* iiij*s* ij*d*', but gifts from senior members must have lightened the load. Master Lane gave the glass window in the new little chamber 'with the Transfyguracion that late dyd belong to the kok', master Baynard all the glass windows in the buttery with 'the Kings Arms and Queen Janes' and the hanging of the hall with 'clothe of Arresse', master Hull 'the new ledyng over the South syde of the yeard of our hall', and Cressey (because 'he could not be master the space of vj yeares') the 'new ledding of the gallery abought the yeard'.

3. The city from St. Paul's Cathedral to the Guildhall in 1562.

The buildings at the corner of 'Goutter lane' and 'Mayden st.' contain the first Wax Chandlers' hall. Not far away in Noble Street is the company's parish church, St. John Zachary, with its tower numbered 17. The church near the hall is St. Michael Wood Street. Part of Christ's Hospital is on the extreme left of the picture, Aldersgate is seen on the city wall, and Cheapside has its Eleanor cross, one of those erected by Edward I to mark where his queen's body rested between Lincoln and Westminster, and St. Mary-le-Bow church.

In later years the hall continued to be a drain on the company's funds, though no doubt it was thought to be worth while: in 1587–8 for instance the accounts show payments 'for the Chamber over the Parlour £87 19 2. 1500 bricks 100 tiles, the Mantelltree of Stone 10/-, 1 pair of Crossgarners and one Casement; 36½ feet of glass'.

In 1602, near the end of Elizabeth's reign the queen's arms were ordered to be carved 'in wainscott' by one Rys Rogers dwelling in Southwark; they were to be 'rich and royal' with arches supported on 'Dorick Pyllers'.

A full inventory for the hall buildings is available for the year 1550 (appendix 8). It shows that the 'haule', which was reached by a wooden staircase, had its walls hung with 'grene saye (serge)', which was 'bordered aboute with picture of IHS'[19] – perhaps a tapestry design based either on the monogram or a picture of Christ himself. There was a plank floor, and the roof boards were probably painted. Furniture was principally trestle tables, the 'hier table' being 5 ells[20] (18 ft. 9 in.) long, a higher settle of 6 ells, benches (some set into the walls), and stools. Much of this was of superior quality, being joiner's work, not carpenter's, and having the parts framed up and fitted together. The tables would have had solid oak tops on heavy pedestals arranged for easy dismantling and storage between feasts.

The parlour, which had a door to the gallery, was 'wainscotted' or wood-panelled at a cost of £13 in 1552 and had hangings on each side of 'redd saye bordered with Scripture'; the windows were curtained. The furniture included two 3-ell tables, a 4-ell and a 3-ell form, and two 2-ell 'joyned' forms. There was probably a master's chair, for in 1544–6 a future assistant, Elles Martin, was paid 1*s*. to provide 'two scutcheons of our Arms that stood over the Chair'. But perhaps the most interesting item was a deed-chest described as 'the Shipp Chest that cam of St. blazes brotherhoode[21] and on the same Chest two banners there conesaunce is the Bee hives'. Blasius, an early bishop in Asia Minor, had been widely adopted as patron saint by wax chandlers and other trades. According to legend he was a physician, specialising in the throat and lungs (perhaps using honey) and doing many miraculous cures; in the Middle Ages the 'blessing of St. Blaise' would be celebrated by holding two crossed candles of beeswax touching the throats of the faithful.

The chamber above the hall was hung with tapestries telling the story of Jacob and his sons. It was furnished with a settle of 'Joyner's work' 6 yd. long, a plank table 3½ yd. long, and an aumbry; the buttery or larder house had another aumbry[22]. There were two 'Shipp chestes' containing title-deeds, account books, the charter and other necessities. Later, in Elizabeth's reign, the chamber was temporarily divided off from the hall and leased separately.

The kitchen contained the usual equipment of spits, jacks, and a set of brass weights. In 1544 it seems to have been threatened by some building work next door, and the company was all set to fight:

> Paied the xxix th of January for a quartern of ffaggotts when Mr. Kendelmas made a Sellar in the next house to oure Hawle and made boaste that he wolde have as mutche roome in oure Kitchen as sholde

make a paire of Staires to go up and downe to fetch them drincke, and wee by the advice of our lerned Counsell made water seething hott ready to poure on their hedds yf they had undermynded oure Kytchen, vj*d*.

Also kept in the kitchen were a small stock of armour and weapons, and six cressets in the cellar.

The plate[23] used by the company in 1550 included many interesting pieces, for example a silver-mounted mazer or wooden drinking bowl with a medallion of the Virgin in the bottom. There were also ten spoons resulting from the custom by which each new liveryman had to give a silver spoon as well as paying the usual 'fine' or fee on admission; in 1530 when Richard fford and William Kendall took the livery, each paid 'A spone and in mony vj*s* viij*d*', and in the following year six more did the same. In 1531 'Misteris Bateman for her husbondes bequest' gave 'A standyng Cupe gylt with a Cover gravyn abought wth Scripture', and in 1587 a past-master, Robert Thrower, who retired to Long Melford, Suffolk, left the company £340 and a silver-gilt cup and cover 'of the value of £1'. In about 1600 a gift of plate was received on condition that it would be sold if required to pay for future repairs to the hall.

Silver was an easily realisable investment and was frequently used by the companies as a means of raising funds. More than once did the Wax Chandlers pawn or sell their plate; for instance, the accounts for 1532–4 show –

Itm payd to Mr. Lane in parsell (part) of the mony that the plate of the Crafte ley in gage for xij*l* iiij*s* vj*d*
Itm payd to a gold Smyth for weying of all our plate in our hall iiij*d*.

and again –

Resceyttes for plate that was Sold & of Whete mony[24] that was lente
ffyrst Rec for iij maser bondes[25] when they were clensyd weyng xxv oncz & a quarter at iiij*s* ob the onc Summa Cij*s*
Rec for a white pote a smale Salte parsell gylte vj Spones & a flate pece all weyng xxviij onces at iij*s* vij*d ob* the once Cj*s* vj*d*
Rec for vj Spones wt lyons[26] weyng viij onces iij quarter diskante at iij*s* x*d* the once Summa xxxiiij*s*
Rec of the Chamberleyn of London for the half porsion of the mony that the Crafte lente to bye whete with x*li*

Summa rec of the plate & whete mony xxj*li* xvij*s* vj*d*

In 1538 the plate was sold once more, this time for £40, but it was bought in by warden Baynard.

As well as silver, both pewter and tin were replacing wood for eating and drinking, and the company had three 'garnishes' (36 place settings) of pewter – platters, dishes and saucers.

In addition to its use for normal business, the new hall was the scene of much feasting, the cost of which appears regularly in the accounts. Payment was made not out of a general fund but by contributions from individual members. For instance dinners for two years (1530–2) cost the master 40*s*., the wardens 26*s*. 8*d*., and the livery 4*s*. 8*d*.; others paid varying sums down to 2*s*. each. The money was not always paid promptly or in full, witness the accounts for 1528–30: 'Itm M[aste]r Rogers beying Mr. owith for his dynner the last Yere xx*s*'. In 1529 the cost of the election feast was shown as 'Itm payd on Jesus evyn for our dynner and sopper a Ribbe of beff a brest of veale a nek and a brest of notton (*sic*) wth vj conys . . . ij*s* xi*d*'. At this period Londoners were accustomed to dine at noon and sup at five or six o'clock.

A bill for food and drink for a dinner in 1531 (pages 154–5) was as follows:

	£	*s*.	*d*
A Buck and Fetching of Another	0	16	2
A Rump of Beef	0	1	0
Half a Lamb	0	1	0
6 Marrow Bones	0	0	9
7 Shoulders of Mutton and Suet	0	4	8
18 Pike	1	1	0
2 Fresh Salmon and a Salmon Trout ...	0	16	10
A Ling and a Side of Salt Fish	0	1	4
3 Barrels of Ale	0	11	3
A Kilderkin of Beer	0	1	0
For Wine at the 'Cardinal's Hat'[27] ...	0	18	8
	4	13	8

That such fare was appreciated by the company's guests was vouched for by Henry Machyn,[28] a Merchant Taylor who kept a lively diary from 1550 to 1563; in 1562 he noted that the 17 August was 'the Waxchandler fest for ther was good chere'.

One dainty that is missing from this menu is roast swan even though swans were kept by the company under a royal grant and, traditionally, fattened in the hall. In 1483 a statute[29] was passed limiting their ownership to persons of substance – owners of freehold land to the value of 5 marks a year – but nevertheless grants multiplied rapidly: by 1496 a Venetian diplomatist could write that there were 1,000–2,000 swans on the Thames, '*bella cosa vedere*' (a beauteous sight to see). In the early part of the sixteenth century the Wax Chandlers, as the Dyers and the Vintners still do, were making regular 'swan-upping' expeditions to take up their birds and mark them by nicking the beaks; in 1530–2 payment to the swan-herd, hire of boat, and cost of meat and drink for the company's representatives totalled £1 0*s*. 1½*d*. Roast swan was considered a great delicacy and indispensable to any large banquet;[30] the company's accounts for 1535 show 'payd for ij Swannys xi*s*', perhaps for lack of their own birds. However, a game of swans, being freehold property, could be a good investment, and on April 1 1606 the Wax Chandlers sold their 'mark and game' to Walter Wyllford, a city merchant and received '£14 of good money of England', worth perhaps £200 today.

The Gild of Jesus

Unlike some other companies the Wax Chandlers did not start as an offshoot of a religious fraternity, but by the beginning of the sixteenth century, if not before, they were associated with the Gild of the Holy Name of Jesus in St. Paul's Cathedral. The Jesus chapel, long a vital centre of devotion, occupied the east end of the crypt,[31] which at 100 ft. wide and nearly twice as long, was the largest and finest of the Gothic period in England. In this chapel the company held its election day service and its annual 'obits' or masses for the dead, and later its shield of arms was to occupy a place of honour near the gild officers' stalls. The accounts for 1530–2 show 'payd to a kerver for settyng the Armys of the crafte in ij grete clowde Angelles at powlles next to the Masters of Jesus pewys ii*s* iiij*d*'; these were probably wood carvings of angels with outspread wings, rising out of clouds and bearing heraldic shields.

The Gild of Jesus was incorporated by Henry VI in 1459 on the feast of the Conversion of St. Paul. It was to be managed by a rector – the dean of the cathedral – and two lay wardens elected every year and was empowered to acquire landed property to the value of £40 a year and to maintain an establishment of chaplains, clerks and boys for the services. In 1507 when statutes were drawn up the rector was John Colet[32] and the wardens 'William Bromewel, Mercer and John Monke, Waxchaundeler'; appropriately enough, Dean Colet, when founding St. Paul's School, stipulated the use of wax candles, not tallow.[33] It was ordered that the feast of the Transfiguration of Christ (6 August) and both the vigil[34] and the feast of the Name of Jesus (7 August) should be celebrated by full sung services led by the dean, 12 minor canons, 8 chantry priests, 6 vicars-choral, and 10 choristers from the cathedral staff;[35] on Jesus day there was also to be a requiem for the souls of the departed brethren. Six waits[36] with banners inscribed IHS were to sing through the streets to give warning of the Jesus day services, and on the vigil of the feast a 'bonefire' was to be lit in the churchyard, where the charnel house would have provided ample fuel.[37] The crypt was to be garnished with boughs and herbs, and cakes and ale were to be provided for those attending and for the poor.

Each of the gild feasts was important to the Wax Chandlers: on Transfiguration day they elected their officers, no doubt after attending mass in the chapel, and on Jesus day they held their obits for deceased members. *Transefiguracio Domini* and *Festum Nominy Jesu* have been inserted on the August page of a late fifteenth-century liturgical calendar[38] (plate 2) bound in with the company's first ordinance book *MS9495*. The only secular event entered in this calendar is at 13 February: *Decollata fuit Katerina Regina infra turrim Lond. Ao Dni* 1541. Thus was recorded the beheading of Catherine Howard in the Tower (the historical year was 1542); possibly the company or the gild intended to pray annually for the soul of the unfortunate queen.

The Transfiguration may have had a special meaning for the sole purveyors of light to the church: in St. Matthew's account 'Christ was transfigured before them: and His face did shine as the sun, and His raiment was as white as the light'. In 1532–4, 40*s*. was received from William Hull 'of his one (own) gyfte for the newe Banner of transfiguracion', perhaps to carry in procession to St. Paul's and bear witness to the company's religious connection.

The Wax Chandlers were accustomed to make regular payments to the gild for its ministrations, and they defrayed many incidentals. 'Expensis at poulles for ii yeres' 1534–6 were as follows:

to the Masters of Jesus Brothered in poulles for ii yeres	xl*s*
to the Clerke of Jesus brothered for ii yeres	ij*s*
to the iiij poremen[39] that waytith in the Chapell for ii yeres	v*s* iv*d*
to the Candel lyghter for ii yeres	ij*s*
to ij poremen that kepe the Cosshyns for ii yeres	iv*d*
to the preste that sayd Deprofundis[40]	ij*d*(*sic*)
for ij tapers and Caustykes[41] for ii yeres	ij*s*
to them that bere the Cosshyns to Poulles	iv*d*
for takyng downe and settyng up and makyng of Jesus lyght for Collers (colours) gold fyer mete and drynke for ii yeres	viij*s* vj*d*
for newe Wax for the Renewyng of Jesus lyght for ii yeres for xxxiij lb. of Wax	xvj*s* vj*d*
for Stuf and Weke for ii yeres	vij*d*

Summe lxxvij*s* ix*d*

The 'Jesus lyght' stood before 'an image of Jesus of silver and gilt' on 'a fote of tree overgilt' – a gilded wooden pedestal – in the chapel. The work, which was supervised by the company's beadle, included the painting and gilding of the wooden frame holding the candle; firing and food were provided for the workmen. The Wax Chandlers saw to their own comfort and warmth by bringing cushions for the pews and rushes for the floor; these gave warmth on earth, stone or tiled floors, though they have been described as 'noysome' in summer unless changed regularly. The company also entertained the officers of the gild: in 1529 there was an 'Itm payd at the gote[42] in Chepe when we bad the Masters of Jesus vij*d*'.

But the benefits were not all on the side of the gild. Its eighteenth statute laid down not only that 'Against Transfiguration liveries of gold and silver' should be given to the gild brethren, sisters and wardens, and to the city waits, but also that 'the ffeliship of Wexchaundelers' should 'yerely have their conysaunces and liveries over and beside the seid sume'. In 1533–4 for instance they paid 7*s*. 4*d*. for 'liveries given to the Waxchandlers and other the brethren and sisters', presumably allowances of money, not clothing. The gild must also have been a good customer, for the same accounts show a payment 'for Wax spent in the said Crowdes iii*li* iii*s* vi*d*', a year's supply.

The Gild of Jesus was suppressed in 1547, under Edward VI, and the chapel is said to have been used as a wine cellar; the company's 40*s*. continued to be paid, at first 'to the Masters of Jesus for their Pension' and later to the '3 Segesters of Jesus', the official sequestrators of the property. In 1556 under Mary the gild was revived 'to the use of the parish church of Seynte Feythes',[43] and given a new charter; this set up a more elaborate organisation (the Dean of St. Paul's was no longer the rector) and increased the licence in mortmain to £100 a year. Two years later, on Elizabeth's accession, the property reverted to the crown, and the Jesus gild disappeared for ever.

The church of St. John Zachary

The hall site was in the parish of St. John Zachary, the church in Noble Street near the corner of Maiden Lane. First mentioned in 1181 as St. John Baptist, it was granted to one Zacharie, a monk, in the twelfth century by the canons of St. Paul's 'in order that he may visit the church regularly' and on condition of certain payments. A rebuilding of 1390 lasted until the Great Fire, but apart from Stow's reference to a 'fayre church, with the monuments well preserued', almost nothing is known of it, though the tower is clearly shown on the picture-map in fig. 3.

After the Reformation, the Wax Chandlers transferred their election service to this church.[44] In 1560 for instance they 'paied to sent John Sacres churche to the queer for syngging of sarvys on Ihesus Daye, vs', and in 1586 the court regularised existing practice by ordering that on the election day 'the hole lyverye of the wax chandlers shalbe att ther haule by j of the clocke or ij at the fardest in their best lyveryes & there attend vppon his Mr & Wardens vnto the Church commenly called St. Jhon Sackaryes & ther heare Dyvyne servyce & a sermon to be preched by some learned devyne in the after none before the choyce be made'.

Parish dues[45] would have been payable by the company from 1500 when the hall site was purchased: the 1530–2 accounts show 'Payde to the parson of Seynt John Zacharies for his tythes[46] for ij yeres, xiij*s* iiij*d*; to the Churche Wardens ther for the Clerkys Wages, iiij*s*, and to the Skavengers for ij yeres, ij*s* viij*d*'. Taxes collected through the parish included the subsidies levied on all landowners, nominally 4*s*. in the £ on lands and 2*s*. 8*d*. on goods or personalty; typical payments by the company were £6 17*s*. 6*d*. and 8*s*. 1*d*. in 1544 and £8 and 32*s*. in 1597.

No doubt the Wax Chandlers took part in midsummer festivities connected with the parish: in 1559, according to Machyn –

> The xxiiij day of June ther was a May-game . . . and sant John Sacerys, with a gyant, and drumes and gunes [and the] ix wordes (worthies), with spechys, and a goodly pagant with a quen c[rowned] and dyvers odur, with spechys; and then sant Gorge and the dragon, the mores (morris) dansse, and after Robyn Hode and lytyll John, and M[aid Marian] and frere Tuke, and thay had spechys rond a-bowt London.

The same May-game went the next day to play before the queen and her council at Greenwich – a command performance.

Relations between parish and company were not always so friendly. The parish owned property to the south of the hall, and in 1544 it brought an action against the Wax Chandlers for trespass. The detailed 'costes and charges' (appendix 7) for the company's counter-action totalled no more than £7 13*s.* 0*d.*, but they tell a complicated story; after many negotiations, usually in a tavern, and the hire of a boat to Westminster, judgement was given in the company's favour. In 1566 the parish brought another action against the company, apparently for trespassing on its land by installing kitchen ovens and erecting a brick wall; a 'view' or survey (appendix 9) established that the claim was well founded and that the parish was entitled to possession of four small shops and a small house adjoining the company's property.

Charitable trusts

The medieval belief, later branded as superstitious, that welfare after death was dependent on the prayers of the living, led to innumerable bequests of property in trust; the revenue from the rents was devoted to the maintenance of chantries[47] where priests sang daily masses, anniversary services or 'obits',[48] and lights before shrines. At the beginning of the fifteenth century St. Paul's provided accommodation for no less than 70 perpetual chantries and 111 obits besides countless occasional masses. In addition to religious rites, provision was usually made for gifts in money or in kind to the poor, and 'potations' for all concerned. City companies being perpetual corporations conducted by successful businessmen were ideal as managers, and two such trusts or 'uses' came to the Wax Chandlers in the first half of the sixteenth century.

A property in the parish of St. Michael, Queenhithe,[49] consisting of two messuages[50] or tenements in Thames Street and six cottages in Sugar Loaf Court, was received from a past-master, John Thompson, under his will made in 1527; the income was to be used to set up a chantry priest in St. Michael's and to provide coals and clothes for the poor and alms on Sundays. In the words of the will Thompson provided for 'the founding of a priest for 3 years to say daily a mass for the soul of his wife, father and mother, and all christian souls at £3 sterling yearly . . . to expend yearly at an obit 20*s.* for the priests attending . . . certain moneys to the master and wardens, . . . coals and clothes, torches at the mass, alms to 13 poor persons on Sundays . . . and in default gift over to the Parish and Churchwardens of St. Michael, Queenhithe'; the Wax Chandlers were all to attend the obit wearing their livery. Of the beneficiaries, the men were to receive their clothing on St. Thomas's day, and the women theirs on Good Friday. The normal distribution was 60 qrs. of coal and 50 yds. of black cotton at 6*d.* a yard, but the cotton material was later replaced by finished goods – two coats and four gowns for the poor of St. Michael's and three coats for poor men of the Wax Chandlers.[51]

In 1543 some houses and land in Coleman Street, known as the Horsehowe, were bequeathed to the company by their owner, Robert Brockett, a Baker; the revenue was to be used to keep an anniversary for the founder's soul in the church of St. Benedict, 'Gracioustrete'[52] and for other purposes. The Coleman Street property had previously belonged to a Grocer, Robert Spicer, who left it to two trustees (one a Wax Chandler.

Richard Lynd), providing annuities for his wife and sister-in-law, Margaret and Agnes (Brockett's sisters) and for an obit to his benefactor, Lawrence Stockwood;[53] eventually the property was to go to some 'honest craft or fellowship in London'. In 1530 Brockett bought out the women and conveyed the property to the Wax Chandlers via two members of the company (Thomas Darsy and John Davell) as trustees, stipulating that they should keep up the obit and the annuities; the latter were to be paid half-yearly on Lady day and Michaelmas day between 1 and 3 pm. 'at the fonte within the cathedrall churche of Seynt Paule'.[54]

Prayers for the souls of benefactors such as Thompson and Brockett continued until an attack on the chantries was launched by Henry VIII. So profitable had he found the suppression of the monasteries[55] in Thomas Cromwell's hands, that in 1545 he made a similar assault on the smaller religious foundations; 'colleges, chauntries and free chapelles'[56] were named as liable to have their revenues taken over, so helping to pay for the war with France. When Edward VI, with the protector Somerset, came to implement his father's plan he introduced a new element – the reformation of doctrine. By a statute of 1547 all soul-masses, obits and lights were condemned as superstitious, and their endowments were vested in the crown. 'All manner of corporations, gilds, fraternities, companies and fellowships of misteries or crafts' had to pay to the king those rent-charges[57] or parts of them that had been devoted to superstitious practices; the Wax Chandlers were the poorer by 30*s*. a year, which had been used to maintain the obits for Thompson and Brockett.

As the total income gained by the crown was insufficient for its purposes, being only £939 a year, the companies were next compelled to buy back the rents and rent-charges at 20 years' purchase, and this produced a capital sum of £18,744. The Wax Chandlers paid a total of £64, which included quit rents for the hall and the Queenhithe property; since the dissolution these had been paid to the king. The list as given in the Calendar of Patent Rolls was as follows:

> 10*s* from a messuage called le Horsehowe in Colmanstrete in the parish of St. Stephen there to an anniversary in the church of St. Benedict in Gracioustrete for the soul of Robert Brocket.
>
> 20*s* from a messuage at Quenehith for the anniversary of John Thompson in the church of St. Michael at Quenehithe.
>
> 14*s* from messuages in the parish of St. Michael Quenehith to the late priory of St. Mary Overy.[58]
>
> 20*s* from a messuage called le Cokk alias Waxchandeler Hall to the late priory of St. John of Jerusalem in England.

The companies were thus reinstated in their trust possessions freed now from the superstitious obligations. That they made good use of the revenue, supplemented from their own funds, can be seen from a table drawn up in 1587; the Wax Chandlers' account is given below:

	£	s.	d.
They purchased of the Kinge in Rente, per annum ...	03	04	00
They sould tenements to buy the same		*nihil*	
Payments yerelie out of the Rents purchased			
In Pensions to poore Bretheren	06	13	04
In Almes	02	00	00
Sum	08	13	04

This table was for presentation to Elizabeth and her council, following an allegation in 1574 by an informer, ostensibly on behalf of the crown, that many companies had omitted from their returns some of the rent-charges that were liable to forfeiture; thus the property they acquired was more than was covered by the rent-charges bought back.[59] In fact it was often difficult to draw the line between money used directly on superstition, and that used for feasting the members after the service or for gifts to the poor, since recipients were expected to pray for the soul of the departed.

After the Reformation superstitious provisions were omitted from bequests. For instance, William Kendall, a past master, who died in 1558, bequeathed to the Wax Chandlers his property in Old Change[60] in the parish of St. Mary Magdalene, Old Fish Street:[61] profits were to go to the poor of that parish, of the parish of Bexley in Kent where he owned some land, and of the company itself. In his will dated 31st January 1558, Kendall bequeathed his houses –

to his son and in default of issue to the Company on condition that they should yearly disburse £8 of lawful money of England

	£	s.	d.
To the Poor of St. Mary Magdalene in gowns and coals ...	3	18	0
To the Churchwardens		2	0
To the poor inhabitants of Bexley	1	18	0
To the Churchwardens		2	0
To the poorest men and women of the Company	1	15	0
To the Master and Wardens		5	0

And the rest of the profits to go to the repair of the houses and tenements.[62]

This may be the same William Kendall[63] who, with 24 workmen, was engaged in making plaster moulds employing beeswax for the walls of Nonsuch Palace, Henry VIII's show-place and Elizabeth's favourite residence, near Epsom. Nonsuch was famous for its moulded decorations, which were used in great profusion on the outer walls, and they remained a feature of the facade until the palace was destroyed by Barbara Villiers, a favourite of Charles II, at the end of the next century. The Nonsuch building accounts[64] also show that beeswax was mixed with resin (or pitch) and used instead of cement in places where mortar was unsuitable because of excessive dampness; the beeswax cost 6½*d.* a pound, and the resin ½*d.*

Wax and the church

A much heavier blow to the Wax Chandlers than the raiding of superstitious trusts was the loss of one of their principal markets, the church. The tendency of the Reformation to simplify religious ceremonies had led Cromwell in 1538 to issue injunctions ordering the clergy to preach a quarterly sermon against offering candles or tapers to images and relics and to 'suffer from henceforth no candles, tapers or images of wax to be set afore any image or picture'. In 1547 they were further ordered to 'take awaie, utterly extincte, and destroy all . . . candelsticks, tryndilles or rolles of wax', and commissioners appeared at St. Paul's to see that the council's edicts were carried out: the cathedral had already discontinued the use of candles on Candlemas day. In 1594 altar lights were prohibited. The curate of St. Botolph, Aldgate, sold off his candles to one of the few women in the craft: the churchwardens' accounts include, among 'sales of Papisticall material' the receipt on 21 December 1547 'of Jone Sawkens wyddow waxchaundeler for a lees of a stocke of waxe the which dedd apperteyne to the churche, xl*s*.'

The overall value of the trade so suddenly extinguished is not known. It is said that the city companies alone were spending between £50 and £60 a year on wax lights at their own altars and shrines, and this must have been only a fraction of similar expenditure by churches, religious houses and private persons: as Stow says, the Wax Chandlers were 'much used in times of superstition'. For the festival decoration of their private altar at All Hallow's, Lombard Street, in 1525, the Pewterers supplied their Wax Chandler with 'old wax with 4 effigies, 4 Angels and the pins or sticks, weighing in all 21 lb', and received 'in new wax 5 tapers, 4 effigies, 4 Angels with the bowls (mortars?) and Symon (cement) – 25½ lb; also tapers of 2 lb each'. The bill read –

For labour on 21 lb at 1*d* a lb,	21*d*.
For 6½ lb of new wax at 8*d* a lb,	4*s*. 4*d*.
For painting,	3*d*.

In 1510 the churchwardens of St. Martin Outwich paid 'to Randolf Merchaunt, wexchandiler, for the Pascall, the Tapers affore the Rode, the Cross Candelles, and Judas Candelles,[65] ix*s* iiij*d*'. The Tallow Chandlers, like everyone else, bought wax candles for use in church: in 1519 they paid 'to the waxchandler for makyng of the light at Seint Botolphis vij*d*' and 'for wax at the sowle mas iiij*d*'.

A company might appoint an official 'wax-man' to collect members' payments towards the provision of candles, torches and tapers for funerals. Individual Wax Chandlers followed the usual custom of making provision in their wills for torches to be given to specified churches and religious fraternities; for instance, in 1525 William Bateman bequeathed a torch apiece to his parish church, St. Botolph, Bishopsgate, where he was to be buried, to the brotherhoods of St. Oswald and St. Lawrence in the same church and of our Lady in Shoreditch, and to the churches of 'St. Alborw's Within Bishopsgate' and 'St. Peter the poor'.

One victim of the suppression of the monasteries was Charterhouse, the great Carthusian priory, whose last prior, after resisting the king's demands, was executed at Tyburn in 1535 and for which the Wax Chandlers appear to have maintained a taper – in what connection is not known. The accounts of 1534–6 include –

Itm payd for lxvj lb of wax for the Charterhouse taper for ij yeares	xxxviij*s* iij*d*
for leyngnyng of the Charterhouse bason wt boltes & lynkes	xxi*d*
for a Case for the Charterhouse taper	viij*d*

The gloom was lightened, if only for a few years, by the return to the Roman dispensation under Mary. In 1558 a gigantic Paschal candle weighing some 300 lb. was set up at the newly restored shrine of Edward the Confessor in Westminster Abbey. Machyn, the diarist, wrote 'The xxj day of Marche was the Paskalle for the abbay of Westmynster mad ther the wheythd of iii C of wax . . . the master and wardens of the Waxchandlers [with] xx more at the makyng', and after a 'grett dener'; evidently the whole court attended to ensure a perfect product and to feast accordingly.

With the death of Mary, candles disappeared again, though not altogether. For example, according to Machyn, 'Master Thomas Grennell (Greenhill),' wax chandler to Cardinal Pole,[66] was buried at St. Giles, Cripplegate with the usual funeral trappings – 'iiij gylt candyllstykes and iiij grett tapurs . . . whyt branchys and xvj stayffe torches and the [Company of] the Wax-chandlers; and he gayff to ys compene [for to] make mere'. Elizabeth affected little regard for the religious significance of candles and torches, though she kept the altar candles in her private chapel; at her first state opening of parliament, when the abbot of Westminster and his monks met her with lighted tapers, she cried 'Away with those torches for we see very well'.

In lay circles, wax candles remained in favour with those that could afford them. In 1502 the expenditure from the privy purse of Elizabeth of York, queen of Henry VII, included –

Itm the viijh day of Marche to John Hynsted of London wexchaundeler for iij rolles of white wex of iij lb price the lb xv*d*, iiij*s* and for iij rolles yelowe wax of iij lb price the lb viij*d*, ij*s* by him delivered to the Quenes use, Summa vj*s*.

Item to the same John Hynsted for iiij rolles white wex of iiij lb price the lb xv*d*, summa v*s* iiij*d*, and for viij rolles yelowe wex of viij lb price the lb viij*d*, v*s* iiij*d*, Summa x*s* viij*d*.

A 'lady of honour' to Catherine of Aragon was allowed 'at our chandlery bar in winter, every night one pricket, and four sises of wax, with eight candles, white lights and one torch'.[67]

In 1570 when Queen Elizabeth was to visit and name the new Royal Exchange, prospective tenants were offered a year's rent-free tenancy (40*s*.) of as many shops as they could furnish, fill with luxury goods and light with wax candles.

Crown and country

Under the Tudors the heaviest financial burdens on the companies were due to emergency taxation imposed by the crown. The monarch's ordinary income – the national revenue – came principally from crown lands, customs, and feudal dues. When this was not sufficient it was supplemented by direct taxation. On the one hand there were 'benevolences' (nominally free gifts) and forced loans or compulsory investments at interest; on the other hand there were parliamentary grants of 'fifteenths and tenths' (in shires and towns respectively) of real estate, and these might be supplemented by two-part 'subsidies' or taxes on owners of property. In the event of war the crown, without calling parliament, would go to the towns for fighting men and equipment and for money to pay and equip mercenaries, there being no standing army.[68] London, by far the largest and richest, had to make the main contribution, either by loans from a few wealthy merchants, by levies on the wards, or by assessment on the companies: many of the livery would have been involved on all three counts.

When the supply of men or money was to be organised through the companies, the mayor would issue his precept[69] giving each of them a quota to fulfil, and though the records are incomplete, it is often possible to establish their individual contributions. There is plenty of evidence that the Wax Chandlers were not behindhand in their participation.

Soon after his accession Henry VII obtained loans of £2,000 and £4,000 from the companies for wars against Scotland and France followed by a benevolence of £9,000 in 1492, probably in connection with the siege of Boulogne. Henry VIII was supplied with 300 'harnest' men for the force that won the battle of the Spurs in 1513, a few days before Flodden: their total cost was £405, of which £6 came from the Wax Chandlers. For an invasion of France in 1522, the target was £100,000, and the companies were required to surrender their money and their plate: despite the power of Wolsey, the king had to be content with £20,000, and the plate valued at £4,000 was not handed over, though some had to be sold. Though forced loans of money were in anticipation of revenue and were meant to be paid back, an act of 1529 freed the king from this obligation; one result was that the Wax Chandlers received a gilt cup in lieu of the money left by William Bateman in his will made in 1525 – 'I gyve unto my company of waxchaundelers iiij *li* which was lent to the king and promysid to be paid ageyne as it apperith by a byll and well knowen in our hall and they to have it to pray for me'.

At the time of the Pilgrimage of Grace, the Roman Catholic revolt of 1536, the companies provided a force of 264 bowmen and billmen, all 'honest and comely persons, well horsed and arrayed in jackets of white with the cross of the City'; they were to meet Henry VIII at Moorfields. However the rising collapsed early in 1537, and the two men-at-arms equipped by the Wax Chandlers never set out. The cost to the company was still substantial:

The Charges for the two men that shuld have gone in to the North parties

ffirst payd for a horsse xlvi*s* viij*d*
Itm payd to Mr Hull the Costes & Charges of his horse x*s*
for ij Sadylles & Bridelles wt all thynges therto x*s*
for the same horsemete iiij*s*
for the Suyuge (*sic*) of the same ij horsis xiiij*d*
for meate & drynke for the same ij men for iiij days & a half iiij*s*
for ix yeardes of white Cotton at vij*d* the yeard v*s*iij*d*
for Red Cloth & the makyng of the same ij Cottes xvij*d*
for ij Gerkyns ij*s*
for ij mens harnesis xxvj*s* viij*d*
for ij Swerdes & ij Gerdylles vj*s*
for ij daggars ij*s* viij*d*
for ij payer of Bottes v*s* iiij*d*
for ij payer of Sporis x*d*
for ij dossen of poynttes iiij*d*
for ij Cappis & ij hattes ij*s* viij*d*
for a bowe ij*s*
for a Sheff of Arrowes iij*s*
for a Byll ij*s*
for Bowe strynges ij*d*
to them for ther prest mony (recruitment bounty) xiij*s*
to the same men when that they cam home agene xx*s*
Summa of the Charges for the ij men viij*li* ix*s* ij*d*.

The first horse was sold later for 26*s*. 8*d*., a loss of £1; the second seems to have been the upper warden's. For the force that captured Boulogne in 1544 a total of 800 archers and billmen were supplied by the companies; as usual the Wax Chandlers provided two men, by name Richard Matravers and Anthony Pavier.

In 1553 under Mary the companies contributed both men and money to put down Wyatt's rebellion and defend the city. They set watches and sent 500 men with eight pieces of ordnance to Rochester, where they seem to have deserted, leaving the ordnance to the rebels. However the queen encouraged the loyalists with a rousing speech at the Guildhall, the citizens were mobilised, and when Wyatt marched on London (with Lady Jane Grey's father) the gates were held against him; within a few weeks he and many of his men had followed Queen Jane to the scaffold. In 1557 the companies raised 1,000 'good sadd and hable men to be souldgears', and in 1558 another 1,000 of 'the handsomest and the best picked' after the fall of Calais in January. In the same year the queen asked for 100,000 marks (over £60,000) to renew the war in Flanders, but £20,000 only was lent at 12% on the security of the crown lands; the Wax Chandlers contributed £30 towards this sum, which provided the force that won the land battle of Gravelines.

In Elizabeth's reign it was the same story, for her traditional fixed revenues[70] fell steadily in value owing to the inflation inherited from Henry VIII and the import of precious metals from the Americas. Demands were more for men than for money (though that came later). In 1560 a total of 1,350 soldiers and sailors were required to counter the French support of Mary Stuart; the last 200 were to be 'men of the Tallest and Beste picked persones', and the Wax Chandlers supplied one to this specification. In 1562 the companies provided 600 men for coast defence; the Wax Chandlers sent two 'good and hable soldiours meete for the Warre', one with corselett and pike, the other a 'Harquebussher'.[71] In the next year 1,000 men were required for a heroic attempt to hold Le Havre, and in 1574 a further 400 for the 'Queen's Ships'; in 1569 men were mustered and equipped in order to assist in quelling the rebellion of the northern earls in defence of the old faith, but once more the rising had collapsed before they set out.

For Ireland the city provided men and equipment to suppress a rebellion by the Earl of Desmond, and some years after Desmond's murder in 1583, an attempt was made to colonise his estates by the 'plantation of Munster'. To this the companies seem to have contributed for the Wax Chandlers have a receipt dated 1587 'Mem paid by the Company to the Chamberlain for our lands given the company in the year above written £5'; a note has been added – 'Enquired what estates the City had from the late Queen Elizabeth for the money that was paid', but no answer has survived. In 1593 rebellion broke out again and the colonists were driven out, thus ending the settlement scheme. Soon afterwards, when the O'Neill headed a revolt in Ulster, the city was called upon for a loan of £20,000 to which the Wax Chandlers contributed £40, and a further £60,000 on mortgage.

When a Spanish invasion was expected in 1585, the companies sent 4,000 men to the city militia, where they were reviewed and addressed by the queen; the largest contingent was 395, the Wax Chandlers sending four men, two for shot and two with pikes. In 1587 two contingents were sent to the Low Countries, one of 600 men at a cost of £50 to which the Wax Chandlers contributed 1*s.* 7*d.*, and one of 250 men for which the Wax Chandlers and the Upholders supplied one man between them. In April 1588 with the Armada ready to sail, the city undertook to equip 16 ships and four pinnaces at a cost of £30,000, thus making a substantial contribution to Lord Howard's fleet which, three months later, won the decisive battle off Gravelines; the money was provided by 17 of the wealthier companies, but this did not prevent their poorer brethren from taking part in the victory celebrations.

In 1591 when the *Revenge* fought single-handed against massed galleons off the Azores the companies gave £8,000 to provide six warships and a pinnace. In 1595 they sent 4,000 shotmen, pikemen and halberdiers[72] from their own members for an unsuccessful expedition to the West Indies under Drake and Hawkins, both of whom died at sea. In the following year there were further demands from the queen, and when the city authorities demurred, pleading general scarcity and want, they were quickly told that the companies should forgo their feasts and give half the savings to the poor. But eventually £3,500 was given towards the provision of 1,200 men, 12 ships and two pinnaces 'to annoye the King of Spaine', the Wax Chandlers taking their usual share (£6); this was the expedition under Essex and Raleigh that surprised and captured Cadiz. In the same year £6,000 and 200 soldiers were provided for Flushing, one of the 'cautionary' towns that were held as an insurance against the Netherlands concluding a separate peace with Spain. Two months before the great queen's death in 1603 her government was supplied with two ships and a pinnace 'for the suppressing of the Dunkirkers', notorious as pirates.

'Musters' or assemblies of able-bodied men were frequently held in the presence of Henry VIII and of Elizabeth. In 1539 (when convocation acknowledged Henry as Supreme Head of the Church in England and catholic Europe was threatening war) the king ordered a great display of military power, including a general muster throughout the country: 15,000 London citizens met at Mile End and marched through the city to Westminster for a grand review. In 1559, under Elizabeth, a muster of 1,400 was assembled in Greenwich Park before the queen and the ambassadors of the Empire and of France; the Wax Chandlers sent a 'Harquebusier', two pikemen and two billmen. In 1572 the companies were ordered to equip and train 3,000 Londoners as 'pike-men and shot' (musketeers) for review at Greenwich, and in 1578 they paid the expenses of 2,000 arquebusiers and 2,000 citizens for training; the latter had to be 'of agilitie and honest of behaviour . . . to be trayned for harquebusseshott, every one of them having a murrion,[73] a sworde and a dagger, and a caliver,[74] with sufficient furniture for the same, and one half pounde of powdre, besides towche powdre'. These were the famous London 'train-bands', which were under the command of the mayor and had been started at the time of Wyatt's rebellion; from 1585 they were trained by the Honourable Artillery Company, whose 'artillery' included every kind of missile. For home defence there was also a statutory obligation on all persons of means – worth £15 a year or more – to provide themselves with arms and armour for use in emergency, and every livery company had to keep stocks of arms and ammunition available.

Elizabeth's chronic shortage of money led to new methods of fund-raising such as the sale of monopolies[75] to the queen's servants or courtiers; these, and the resulting abuses, affected the business of nearly all the companies. There were also the public lotteries, whose prizes were often long delayed or non-existent. In 1567 the first prize was £3,000 sterling with plate and tapestry worth another £2,000, but much of the money is said to have been appropriated by the queen for her own use; in 1596 the prizes were 'rich and costly armour, guilt and engraven'. The lotteries were supported by the companies, who collected from their members and subscribed under the customary pseudonym – a short verse or 'posy'. Other ventures in which many companies took shares were Raleigh's privateering excursions against the treasure-ships of Spain. One such, in 1592, realised a total of £141,000 the greater part of which went to the queen, but in the following year when there was a major outbreak of plague from which 15,000 died, the companies were told to put a third of their net gains to building a pest-house for the infected poor.

State processions, the customary displays of royal power, continued to be attended by the companies, the livery either riding with the aldermen on horseback or lining the route. The streets would be decorated (according to one account) with banners bearing the royal arms, the silk 'ancients' of the companies, streamers in their colours, and pendants of their arms; the liverymen wore their best gowns and hoods, and often a representative body would ride out to greet a distinguished visitor.

In 1485 when Henry VII brought the captured standards from Bosworth Field and two years later following the defeat of the pretender, Lambert Simnel, the 65 crafts were represented by 400 horsemen clothed in velvet, 4 riders coming from the Wax Chandlers. On the marriage of Catherine of Aragon to Henry VIII and their coronation in 1509 there were the usual processions from the Tower to Westminster; railings were set up from Gracechurch Street to Chepe, and the companies lined the way, 'beginning with base and mean occupations and so ascending to the worshipful crafts'.

Henry's second marriage – to Anne Boleyn – was so unpopular that the wardens were urged by the mayor to order their journeymen and servants 'and, a still more difficult task, their own wives' to cease murmuring against it, but for her coronation in 1533 there was a great procession by river from Greenwich Palace;[76] all the companies had their barges with their sides decked with targets[77] and 'such seemly banners and bannerets as they had in their halls or could get . . . and every barge had a minstrel'. The Wax Chandlers accounts show:

at the Coronacion of Quene Anne our hall taxid at vij*s*vj*d*

for hire of a barge when Quene Anne was fetched from Grene Wyche to the Tower at the Coronacion xvij*s*

for the Carpenters fframe that was made in Cornell for the lyverey to stond uppon when the Quene came by x*s* vj*d*

for Carpettes to Cast over the fframe before the lyverey xij*d*

payd to Writhocke the paynter for the iij newe Banners for Sylke gold ffrenge and workemanship and the mendyng of iij old Banners and payntyng of the Stavys cxvj*s* viij*d*.

payd for a newe Banner Staf and mendyng of another viij*d*

payd for a Box to lay the Banners in ij*s*.

Among other royal occasions the companies turned out for the coronation of the boy king, Edward VI, in 1547, when wine flowed from the street 'conduits' or standpipes, and for Mary's coronation, when St. Paul's steeple was to have been illuminated by torches; the evening breeze from the river blew them out, but many sightseers lit 'tapers made of most sweet perfumes', some of which were wafted on to the queen. The coronation of Elizabeth on 15 January 1559 was preceded by a great procession in which the queen in an open litter drawn by two mules was accompanied by 1,000 citizens on horseback. From Fenchurch Street to Cheapside the streets were lined with liverymen, standing behind wooden rails draped in cloth and hung with tapestries, velvet, damask, satin and silks, while rich banners and streamers waved from the windows; halts were made at frequent intervals for pageants, tableaux, and dramatic representations or interludes.

The destruction of the Spanish Armada was celebrated by a triumphal procession to St. Paul's. The queen's route was lined by the companies with their standards and streamers, the livery taking up their positions at 8 a.m.; after the service, she dined with the preacher, the Bishop of Salisbury, and the companies returned to their places to cheer her back to Somerset House.[78] In 1602 the companies were ordered to send the 'most grave and comelie' of the livery to escort the queen from Chelsea to Westminster, and the Wax Chandlers provided four to this specification. Throughout Elizabeth's reign there were levies for royal pageants such as the yearly 'mayings' or May-games in Greenwich Park.

Also honoured by the city were the processions held for great princes of the church. In 1515 when Wolsey was made a cardinal, his hat was attended by 'the aldermen on horseback and the gilds on foot' from Blackheath to Westminster, and in 1554 when Pole was finally admitted as papal legate he was received in the same way.

State funerals were done on a lavish scale, and the extensive use of candles and torches must have meant good business for Wax Chandlers. At the lying-in-state of Elizabeth of York in 1503, 10,000 torches lighted the way, and 500 tapers and candlesticks were placed round the bier. For the funeral of Henry VII six years later there were 600 servants in black liveries carrying torches. The procession was met by the mayor at Southwark and conducted to St. Paul's, and the next day to Westminster; at each resting place the body was placed in a stately 'hearse'[79] or candle-stand blazing with light, 1,557 lb. of wax being used at the cathedral and 3,606 lb at the abbey. One company alone, the Drapers, spent 114*s.* on 'xij torches . . . weying ccxx lb and 1 quartr, whereof was wasted xxxij lb, at iiij*d* le lb and xij*d* for making of eury torche'. The Wax Chandlers supplied gowns, hoods and torches for six mourners, a comparatively high number.

City and citizens

London was growing apace: the population is thought to have expanded from 50,000 to at least 150,000 during the second half of the sixteenth century. The authority of the city over the companies continued to increase, and in 1512 the court of aldermen began to regularise their order of precedence, declaring it to be 'sett, ordeyed and agreed . . . as in John Shaa's day' (the mayor of 1501–2). On 31 January 1516 they listed 48 craft gilds in order 'for their Goynges as well in all processions as all other goynges Standynges & Rydynges for the busynessys & causes of this Citie'. The Wax Chandlers were 20th, their present position, and the first twelve included the same companies as today and in the same order. Perhaps more important, since liverymen formed both the parliamentary and the city electorate, the wearing of livery became a matter of direct concern to the civic authorities, and in 1560 the aldermen assumed the right to grant liveries to such companies as did not enjoy them already, either by 'prescription' (as with the Wax Chandlers) or by specific mention in royal charters.

Frequent precepts from the mayor demanded participation in civic functions and in improvement and welfare schemes, and these expenses are a regular feature of company accounts. Perhaps the most spectacular occasion – apart from the midsummer watch – was the mayor's annual procession to Westminster. This took to the water at Three

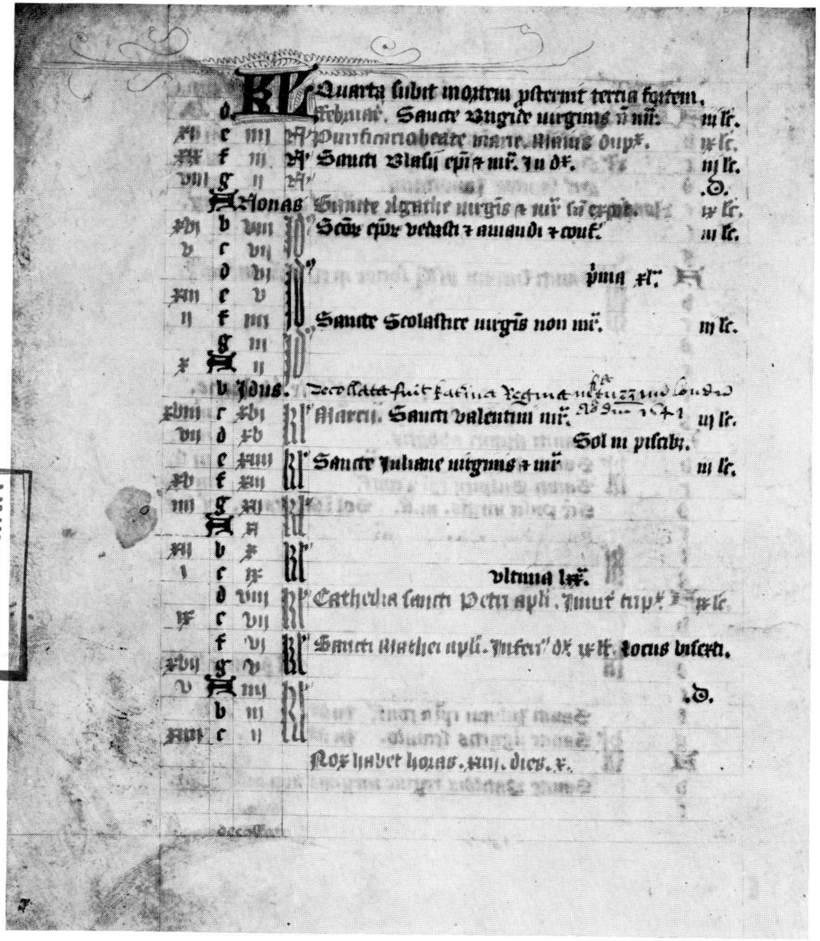

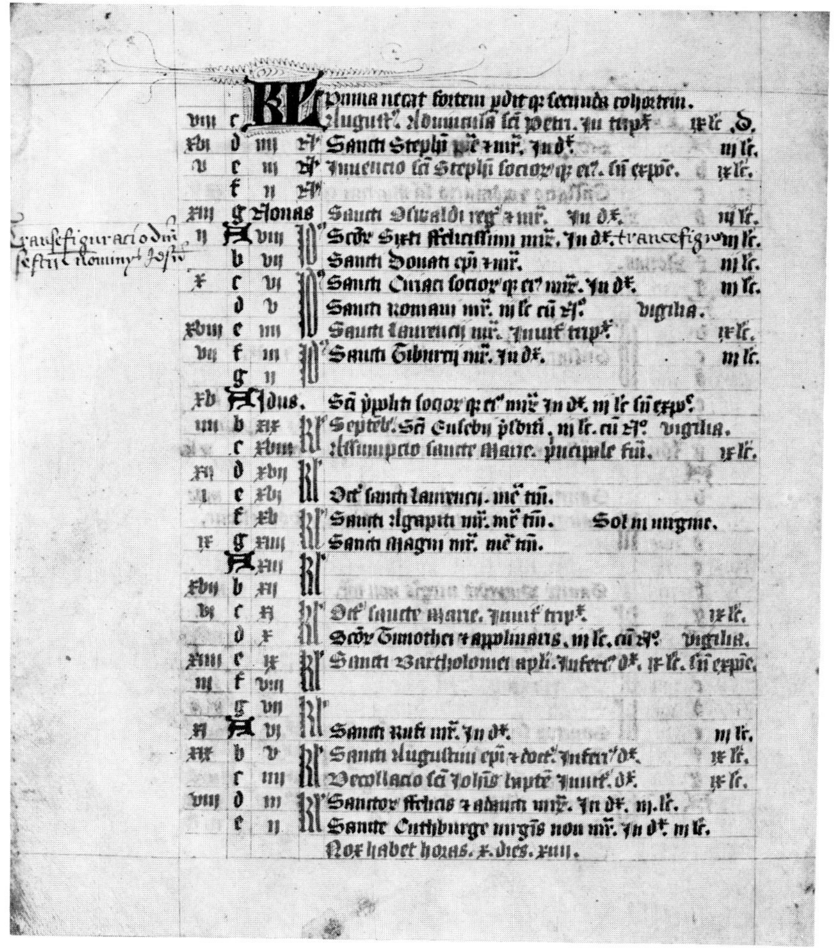

2. Leaves from a 15th-century liturgical calendar.

This calendar (in Latin) is bound in with the company's earliest ordinance, oath and evidence book. On the February page (left) the execution of Catherine Howard was recorded in 1541/2, and on the August page the company's feast days have been entered in the margin.

Besides the St. Paul's Use information, column 2 of the calendar gives the Dominical Letters, which determine the day of the week for each day of the month, and columns 3 and 4 give the day of the month in the Roman calendar; at the foot of each page are the average hours of darkness and daylight.

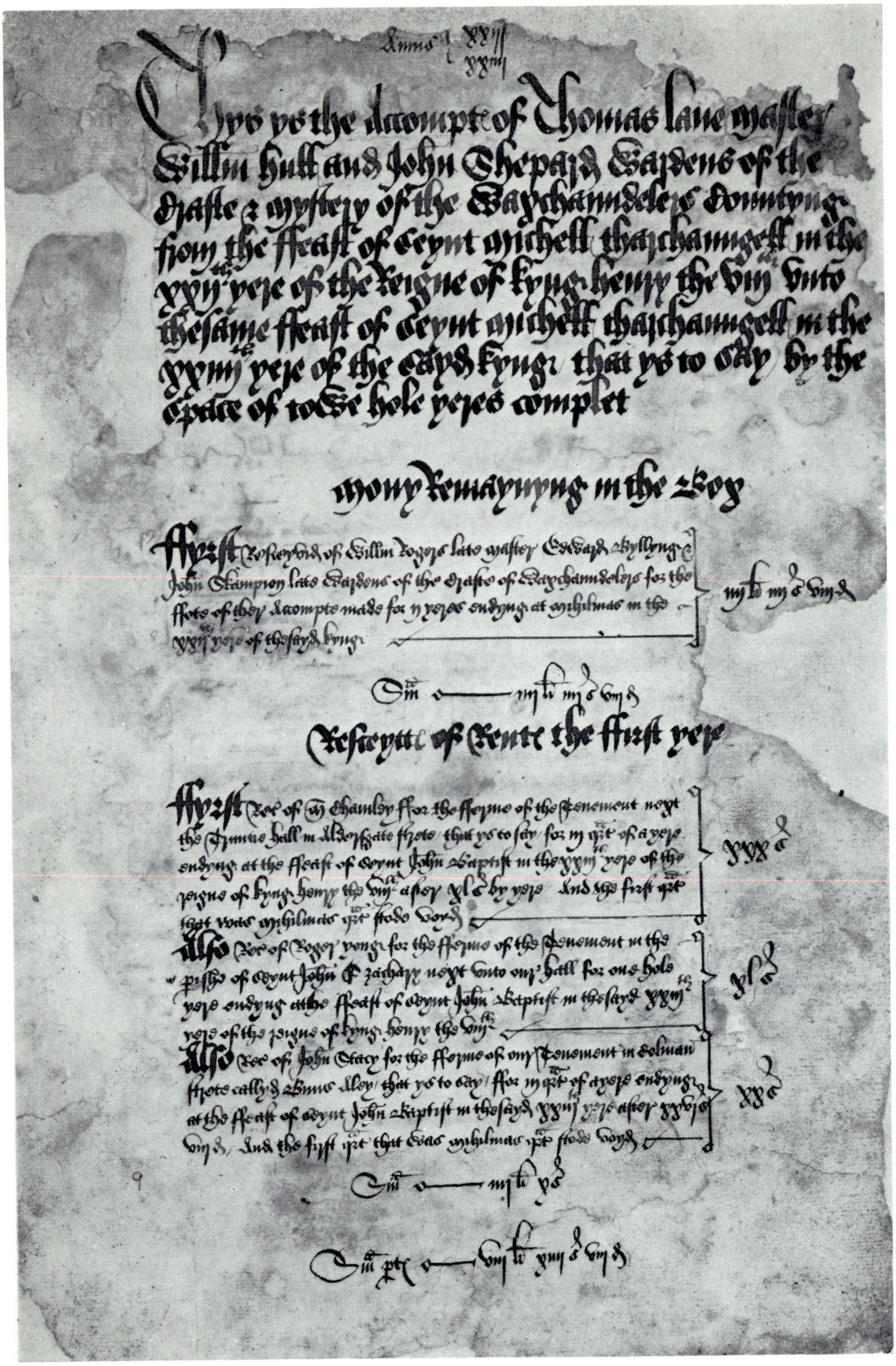

Thys ys the accompte of Thomas lane master Willm hull and John Shepard wardens of the crafte & mystery of the Waxchaundelers conteynyng from the ffeast of Seynt Michell tharchaungell in the xxij yere of the reigne of kyng henry the viij unto the same ffeast of Seynt Michell tharchaungell in the xxiiij yere of the seyd kyng that ys to sey by the space of towe hole yeres complet

Mony Remaynyng in the Boxe

Resceyte of Rente the ffirst yere

3. The first page of the renter warden's accounts for 1530–2.

'Thys ye the Accompte of the Crafte & Mystery of the Waxchaundelers . . . by the space of towe hole yeres complet.'

The account starts with the surplus handed over from the previous two years and the rents received from tenants. A full transcription is given in appendix 6.

Cranes Stairs at the end of Queen Street, where a famous tavern sign, known to Ben Jonson and Pepys, showed three birds in punning allusion to the wine-hoists on the wharf. The mayor's stately barge was preceded by the barges of his own company and followed by those of the other companies, forming an elaborate water spectacle; there was a land pageant on the return journey to Guildhall. At first the emphasis was almost all on the mayor's company, which bore the expense and organised the procession, but later a general trade pageant was added. Machyn, writing in 1553, says that the mayor was accompanied to Westminster by the 'craftes of London . . . with trumpets blohyng and the whets (waits) playng'. In common with many others the Wax Chandlers were in the habit of hiring a barge and decorating it with their own banners and streamers'; their accounts for 1532–34 show –

Hire of barge for Lord Mayor for ii years	xxij*s*
Rushes for the barge of Lord Mayor for ii years	viij*d*
Watermen of barge for Lord Mayor for ii years	xvj*d*

and those for 1530–2 –

Hire of barge to Westminster when the Lord Mayor made his oath xxj*s* iiij*d* and wages of watermen and drinkes to them.

Senior members of the companies were accustomed to attend the mayor's admission feast,[80] which was at first held in Grocers' or Taylors' hall but was transferred to the Guildhall when kitchens were built in 1501; by 1529 it was also attended by great officers of state. The Wax Chandlers sent 11 'masters' and livery to dine in 1531 and 15 in 1536.

Of the civic functions that were practical as well as ceremonial the midsummer watch continued with ever greater elaboration and expense, something like 2,000 taking part. In 1518 the court of aldermen ordered 47 companies to provide 204 bowmen each year: the quotas ranged from two to eight, the Wax Chandlers providing four. In 1530–2 their 'four men for the Musters' cost 33*s*. 2*d*. and in 1536–8 the cost to the company was £1 15*s*. 4*d*.; in 1542 they paid 2*s*. for 'painting and gilding sixteen scutcheons (ornamental shields) at midsummer'. Suits of armour were kept at the hall and scoured by an armourer before use; in 1550 the company had two 'Almayn revets',[81] a popular type of half-suit, and six iron cressets with staves were kept in the cellar. From 1540 Henry VIII prohibited the main extravagances and confined the march to its original function of a military muster, and, after a brief revival in 1548, the watch was continued on a more economical plan; in 1584 it was held in conjunction with a muster of 4,000 citizens for review by the queen in Greenwich Park.

Apart from its practical value (which may be questioned), the midsummer watch was a popular festivity, akin to a military tattoo, in which everyone took part. Stow's description, perhaps heightened by nostalgia, conveys the magic in the air:

In the Moneths of Iune, and Iuly, on the Vigiles of festiuall dayes, and on the same festiuall dayes in the Euenings after the Sunne setting, there were vsually made Bonefiers in the streetes, euery man bestowing wood or labour towards them: the wealthier sort also before their doores neare to the said Bonefiers, would set out Tables on the Vigiles, furnished with sweete breade, and good drinke, and on the Festiuall dayes with meates and drinks plentifully, whereunto they would inuite their neighbours and passengers also to sit, and bee merrie with them in great familiaritie, praysing God for his benefites bestowed on them. These were called Bonefiers aswell of good amitie amongest neighbours that, being before at controuersie, were there by the labour of others, reconciled, and made of bitter enemies, louing friendes, as also for the vertue that a great fire hath to purge the infection of the ayre. On the Vigil of Saint Iohn Baptist, and on Saint Peter and Paule the Apostles, euery mans doore being shadowed with greene Birch, long Fennel, Saint Iohns wort, Orpin, white Lillies, and such like, garnished vpon with Garlands of beautifull flowers, had also Lampes of glasse, with oyle burning in them all the night, some hung out braunches of yron curiously wrought, contayning hundreds of Lampes light at once, which made a goodly shew, namely in new Fishstreet, Thames streete, &c. Then had ye besides the standing watches, all in bright harnes in euery ward and streete of this Citie and Suburbs, a marching watch, that passed through the principal streets thereof, to wit, from the litle Conduit by Paules gate, through west Cheape, by ye Stocks, through Cornhill, by Leaden hall to Aldgate, then backe downe Fenchurch streete, by Grasse church, aboute Grasse church Conduite, and vp Grasse church streete into Cornhill, and through it into west Cheape againe, and so broke vp: the whole way ordered for this marching watch, extendeth to 3200 Taylors yards of assize, for the furniture whereof with lights, there were appointed 700 Cressetes, 500 of them being found by the Companies, the other 200 by the Chamber of London: besides the which lightes euery Constable in London, in number more then 240 had his Cresset, the charge of euery Cresset was in light two shillinges foure pence, and euery Cresset had two men, one to beare or hold it, an other to beare a bag with light, and to serue it, so that the poore men pertayning to the Cressets, taking wages, besides that euery one had a strawne hat, with a badge painted, and his breakfast in the morning, amounted in number to almost 2000. The marching watch contained in number about 2000 men, parte of them being olde Souldiers, of skill to be Captains, Lieutenants, Sergeants, Corporals, &c. Wiflers, Drommers, and Fifes, Standard and Ensigne bearers, Sword players, Trumpeters on horsebacke, Demilaunces on great horses, Gunners with hand Guns, or halfe hakes, Archers in coates of white fustian signed on the breast and backe with the armes of the Cittie, their bowes bent in their handes, with sheafes of arrowes by their sides, Pike men in bright Corslets, Burganets, &c. Holbards, the like Bill men in Almaine Riuets, and Apernes of Mayle in great number, there were also diuers Pageants, Morris dancers, Constables, the one halfe which was 120 on S. Iohns Eue, the other halfe on S. Peters Eue in bright harnesse, some ouergilte, and euery one a Iornet of Scarlet thereupon, and a chaine of golde, his Hench man following him, his Minstrels before him, and his Cresset light passing by him, the Waytes of the City, the Mayors Officers, for his guard before him, all in a Liuery of wolsted or Say Iacquets party coloured, the Mayor himselfe well mounted on horseback, the sword bearer before him in fayre Armour well mounted also, the Mayors footmen, & the like Torch bearers about him, Hench men twaine, vpon great stirring horses following him. The Sheriffes watches came one after the other in like order, but not so large in number as the Mayors, for where the Mayor had besides his Giant, three Pageants, each of the Sheriffes had besides their Giantes but two Pageants, ech their Morris Dance, and one Hench man their Officers in Iacquets of Wolsted, or say party coloured, differing from the Mayors, and each from other, but hauing harnised men a great many, &c.

All these ceremonial affairs must have been highly profitable to individual Wax Chandlers. For the funeral of their mayor in 1513 the Drapers paid 'To Stephn Ward, wax chandler, for 24 torches, of 24 lb a piece, 4 tapers, of 14 lb a p'ce, and two branches (candelabra) of white wax, goodly made, together with iiij myghtie highe standard candylsteks, clene gylt' 54*s*. 4*d*.; for a midsummer pageant in 1522 they paid 'Willam Wakefield for xij staf torches' 30*s*. 4*d*. and he was to have 'all that was left unspended of the wax'. For the mayor's pageant in 1566 another wax chandler, Richard Sharpe, furnished torches that were 45 ins. long and cost 15*s*. a dozen; on this occasion there were 20 boats, music from a 20-piece band, and fireworks. At midsummer something like 1,000 torches might be required, and one of the company's ordinances emphasises the necessity of good order on this occasion.

The companies were also the main source of money for purposes of direct benefit to the city and its inhabitants. Besides improvements such as building operations at the Guildhall, for which the Wax Chandlers paid £3. 6*s*. 8*d*. (compared with £40 from the Mercers) in 1501–2, there were many municipal welfare schemes of which the most important was the provision of corn for sale to the poor in times of scarcity or famine; to this the companies subscribed regularly for well over a century.

It was in 1521 that the city first borrowed £1,000 to stabilise the price of corn, and from 1543 similar sums were raised almost every year for purchases; in 1532–4 for instance the Wax Chandlers lent £20, £10 of which was repaid later. In 1578 when the companies started to buy themselves, they provided a total of 5,000 qrs. of wheat at 20*s*. a qr. In 1587 55 crafts provided 10,000 qrs. according to a fixed quota: at the top of the list were the Merchant Taylors with 936 qrs. and the Wax Chandlers (with four others) were 36th, contributing 20 qrs., 1/5 of 1% of the total. The city had its common garner in the Leaden Hall up to 1520, and then in the Bridge House at the south end of London Bridge; this was equipped with water-driven mills and ovens for grinding corn and baking bread. By 1596 so much wheat and rye had to be imported that the companies were told to provide granaries at their halls.

A company might obtain the money for corn by levies on the members, or certain individuals might cover the risk, using their own funds and dividing the profit on the sale. In 1586, 34 Wax Chandlers took shares of 2*s*. 6*d*. or 5*s*. each, £5 in all; the clerk entered in his minutes *A Posy for the Lottery in the Corn:*

As the Bee them stings that honey brings
Out of the hive or bower,
By my consent be true content
To take the sweet with sour.

In poor relief generally London can claim to have been a pioneer. Before the Reformation religious foundations such as monasteries, gilds and hospitals had been the main source of assistance, and, private and civic benevolence notwithstanding, their closure led to large numbers of the poor and the sick being thrown on the streets. Accordingly the city petitioned the king to allow the re-establishment of three of the five 'Royal hospitals'[82] – those of St. Bartholomew, St. Thomas, and St. Mary of Bethlehem; the common council decided in 1548 that the companies should provide a total of 500 marks a year for Bart's, and the Wax Chandlers paid 2 marks (26*s*. 8*d*.) by quarterly instalments. In the last years of Elizabeth a comprehensive poor law act[83] established a national system of relief in which 'overseers of the poor' took over the responsibilities of churchwardens to see that no-one need starve, but it did not put an end to poverty, which continued to contrast with the splendour of the court and the affluence of the merchants. In London from 1599 the company halls were taxed for the benefit of the poor in their parishes, and in 1602, following many years of hardship due to bad harvests and high prices,[84] the city imposed a small levy to form a fund for the poor; this totalled only £78. 14*s*. 8*d*., the Wax Chandlers' quota being 4*s*. payable by quarterly instalments. A personal concern for those in prison was shown by one Wax Chandler, Stephen Ward, in his will of 1527: he left 20*d*. each in bread to the poor, and often starving, prisoners of Newgate, Ludgate and the two sheriff's prisons. In 1566, the city collected money for 'the Setting at worke of the worke-folkes in Brydwell', which had been opened as a 'House of Correction and Occupation'.

Administration and discipline

Following the grant of a royal charter, new ordinances were approved by the mayor in 1488 (appendix 4), and, though comparatively limited in scope, they show the problems of the day. For instance, obedience to master and wardens and attention to their summons were made obligatory, no-one from outside the city and no aliens were to be taken on as this affected the intake of apprentices, and young men who would not work for reasonable wages were to be punished; the scale of fines for selling faulty products was doubled, and makers' marks were required to be registered with the master and wardens.

However in 1514 a more comprehensive set of ordinances (appendix 5) was submitted, this time for royal as well as civic approval: the former had become necessary under a statute[85] of 1504, which ordered that 'no Master . . . of a mystery or fraternity' should 'do anything touching the king's prerogative... or the common profit of the people', thus encroaching to some extent on the city's control of the crafts. The signatories[86] on behalf of the crown included William Warham, Archbishop of Canterbury and Chancellor of England (he preceded Cranmer and Wolsey, by whom he was humiliated in the one post and ousted from the other), and Thomas, Duke of Norfolk, Treasurer of England. The original exemplification in English, now replacing Latin, has an illuminated initial letter containing the royal arms, and a border of roses with golden hips and a golden bee at each flower. The preferred designation for the company is fellowship (in various spellings); occupation and craft are used occasionally, but mistery and company never.

The new ordinances began by laying down procedures for company elections and obits and went to to deal with discipline and behaviour, giving a scale of penalties for disobedience, abusive language, and enticement of another man's servants and providing for the recovery of fines by distraint. Members were to pay a quarterly subscription or 'quarterage' and to use a maker's mark; the practice of the craft was restricted to contributing members working in their own houses. There was to be a two-yearly audit of accounts, and a quarterly reading of the by-laws to the whole company at the common hall. But the text of some of these ordinances is so informative that they must be considered in more detail.

The first ordinance prescribed the holding of elections on the feast of the Transfiguration, clearly because of the company's connection with the Gild of Jesus:

> Bee it ordeined and established that everie two yeears once the said master, wardens and fellowshipp after ther wonted manner and laudable custom shall assemble att their comon hall, that is to say in the day of the ffeast of the Transfiguraton of our lord god and then and there to elect and chuse one maister warden and two other wardens associate unto him to rule order and governe the same fellowshipp for two yeares then next and ymediatlie ensuing . . .[87]

A supplementary ordinance[88] of 1584 enlarged on the qualities required of the wardens and gives the impression that the master was *primus inter pares* rather than a supreme authority:

> The said company shall once in everie two yeares . . . . choose and elect three of the moste honest, wise, substantial and grave persones for master and wardens, keepers and governors . . . and that the said three wardens whereof thone is called by the name of a maister and the other two wardens or associates shall contynue in their said offices fullie two yeares . . . .

It will be seen that by 1514 the annual election laid down by the charter had been dropped in favour of a two-year term of office; it is believed that the Bowyers' is now the only other company to hold its elections every second year. The officers were to be elected by the whole body of members, a democratic method that was in accordance with the charter but was later abandoned; the companies were not exceptional in becoming oligarchies, for boroughs, universities, colleges and inns of court all adopted the same sort of government. Wax Chandlers' elections, as has been seen, were preceded by a service, which took place in the Jesus chapel up to the Reformation, but by 1560 the company was attending the parish church of St. John Zachary, a sermon taking the place of mass. After the service 'according to the old custom' they returned to the hall to elect the master and wardens. A payment of 10*s.* was made to the preacher.

The second ordinance prescribed the holding of an annual obit on the feast of the Name of Jesus:

> And for the general obit the next day after the sayd feast of Transfiguration of our lorde god yerely from yere to yere the sayd master, wardens and fellowship do kepe an anniversary and obitt solempnely in they place accustomed for the soulles of the brethren and sisters of the same crafte passed out of this transitory lyffe . . .

The obit was held in the Jesus chapel until the gild was dissolved. Besides praying for their souls *en bloc*, the companies gave their deceased members fine funerals with feasting to follow. State palls or 'herse-cloths' were kept for use with the hearses or iron candlestands; around 1544–6 the Wax Chandlers bought a 'hustecloth' of cloth-of-gold for 10*s.*

Under the third ordinance six 'viewers and assistants' were to be elected for searches. Their primary function – the regular inspection of materials and products – was recorded in search books, one of which, starting in 1574, has been preserved. However the control of each craft by its company had become less effective for various reasons. The act[89] of Edward III restricting each freeman to one craft had fallen into disuse, and the 'custom of London' allowed freemen by patrimony to practise the trade of any other company than their own. The population of London, as it moved towards 200,000 was spreading beyond the city boundary and the companies' jurisdiction.

Our own viewers' hands were strengthened in 1569 when the master and wardens were authorised by the mayor to 'search and demand quarteridge of all such as sell Wax or other stuff ready wrought concerning the mistery of Wax Chandlers': they were to pay 3*s*. a quarter or go to prison. Control was further reinforced in 1581 by a parliamentary statute, which laid down new rules and penalties covering both wax and honey (appendix 10); this had national application, and 50% of the fines were to go to the crown instead of to the city. The statute was entitled 'An Acte for the true melting making and working of wax'; the Wax Chandlers accounts show that they paid a Mr. Owen[90] 3*s*. 4*d*. 'for his counsel about the Bill', and there is a marginal note, 'Money well spent'.[91]

No doubt the 'viewers and assistants' were the forerunners of a court, which was functioning regularly by 1530 and meting out punishment for disobedience to the ordinances; within a generation it had expanded to 23, still the maximum number. The minute books recording court proceedings from 1584 are extant, but they deal mostly with routine administration. An early entry shows an interest in further education: an exhibition was granted 'to one at schoole at Cambridge'[92] for four years at £2 a year, and there were later exhibitions to Oxford.

The fourth ordinance enjoins 'obedience of the occupacion', particularly in connection with lights for the Corpus Christi and midsummer celebrations and for funerals. Only a reputable body of craftsmen would be allowed to cater for these important events, and their lavish use of candles and torches must have been of great importance to the trade.

Under the disciplinary ordinances, the types of offences most prevalent are shown by the accounts. Bad work, illegal sales, working at prohibited hours, lateness or absence from functions, and simple abuse or disobedience were among the most frequent cause of money fines. Some entries dealing with trade offences are given below:

Thomas Grennell 'for Makyng of pascalles at ester of gomyd wax[93] fyned xx*d*'

William Kendall 'for over holying[94] of tapers at Candelmas vj*d*'
'for over holying xxx quarter tapers and xxxii obit candelles to lyght viij*d*'

Thomas Kempe 'for nawghty makyng of staf torchis xij*d*'

Thomas Pykeman 'for . . . vij quarter Roulles[95] beyng to sore chargid xvj*d* . . . for lynkes nastely made xij*d*'

William Symmys 'for the Sellyng of 1 lb of halpeny candelles at Candelmas to a woman of another occupation to Sell them Agen fyned xvj*d*'

Thomas Pykeman 'for brekyng of the price contrary to good orders ij*s* viij*d*'

John Roberts 'for making of Ill Red Wax for seals xx*d*'

Other misdemeanours are indicated by:

For 'Breaking of howers[96] iiij*d*'

Alyn Creswell 'for not coming to Court on the Court Day viij*d*'
'for goyng away at a Courte day vj*d*'

Thomas Day 'for none commyng to prosession xij*d*'

William Baynard 'for commyng late to powlys to the general obet viij*d*'
'for none commyng vi*d*'

Thomas Grennell 'for commyng late to poulles of procession ij*d*'

Richard fford 'for Revyling of the Master and Wardens iij*s* iiij*d*'

William Kendall 'for disabedyens aganst the Mr and Wardens iiij*d*'

William Baynard 'for his prentys more than the good order of the craft wold suffer[97] xl*s*'

'Itm payd for havyng of William Ormond to the Counter[98] because he came to prosession in nawghty Rayment and for Vngodly Wordes xij*d*'

There were also items concerning apprentices:

payd for xj yeardes of Canvas to make Cottes hoddes and Vyssers to the same for the Correccion of lewede[99] prentices v*s*

payd to Thomas Wolpytt for makyng of the same ij*s* viij*d*

Misdemeanours apart, many of those fined became a credit to the company. Ormond and Grennell were wardens in 1540, Baynard was the warden who bought in the plate when it was sold in 1538, and Kendall was master in 1554 as well as a valued benefactor.

The ordinances end with the oaths to be taken by master, wardens, freemen and clerk, each concluding 'So help you God and his saints'. This is the first known reference to a clerk; the necessity for a permanent official at a high level, no mere book-keeper as is indicated by the oath, may show the growth of company business. The writing up of the early accounts and deeds appears to have been undertaken by juniors or put out to professional scriveners. Examples of payments for secretarial work in 1530–2 are –

Pd John Lynd for writing three accompts in the new book and writing the Confirmation (of the grant of arms) iij*s* jv*d*.

Paid for bread and drink for him when he did write in our Hall vj*d*.

Paid to Mr. Wylford Skryvener xl*s* viij*d* for writing our Evidence (deeds) and preparing drafts for Mistress Spicers lands in Coleman Street.

and in 1544–6 –

Pd to Thomas Shepperd for the writing of Mr. Daies accompt into the Great Book iij*s* iiij*d*.

Day had been renter warden in 1538-40.

A beadle is not mentioned in the ordinances, but by 1529 'our officer' was appearing regularly in the accounts, for instance 20*s*. was paid for his new gown. In 1584 a court minute shows that the wages of the beadle, James Edmontes, were increased to 40*s*. a year 'during the life or widowhood of the widow Looman; also specified were his fees for services such as 'seiring (cering)[100] a dead Corps if Labour in it', and various perquisites including the hood of a dead liveryman.

The 1484 charter, which automatically expired with the sovereign, was renewed from time to time; we still possess the confirmation by Elizabeth in 1560 of an *inspeximus* by Philip and Mary, though the latter exemplification is lost. The fees paid are shown in the accounts for 1558:

> Expense of the suet to the queen's majesty for our company £3. 10*s*. 4*d*.
> For renewing of our corporation £7. 3*s*. 8*d*.

In 1530 the coat-of-arms was given supporters, a privilege generally reserved for the peerage. Thomas Benolt,[101] Clarenceux king-of-arms, confirmed the previous grant 'Rettiffyed with my hande' and added 'also I have devyssed and grauntyd to the same worshipfful company the Unicorns to Uphold theyre armes as they do apyer in the sayd margyn herin depyct': on either side of the shield he placed a unicorn argent gorged with a garland of various flowers proper, the horn wreathed or and gules (plates 4 and 18). The accounts show payments –

> to Mr. Clarencius for Alowyng of the Armes of the Crafte and Settyng to his hand . . . xiij*s* iiij*d*
> to Robert Porkelyn his servunte . . . ij*s*
> to the paynter for payntyng of the ij Vnicornes . . . iij*s* iiij*d*
> for a newe boke and for the translatyng of the boke of the confirmacion . . . xiij*d*

Unicorns may have been chosen because of the maiden crest: according to one legend this fabulous beast could only be trapped by setting a virtuous maiden in its haunts, whereupon it would lay its head in her lap and sleep. Another possibility is suggested by the reputed value of the horn as a protection against poison or other dangers. The colouring of the horns may have recognised their resemblance to the candles and tapers made by the Wax Chandlers.

Six years later the company requested elucidation of the original arms, the wardens considering that there were 'dyverce wordis so obscure and darkely wrettyn deffuse to be understande and also ther bests with ther crest not plainly nor ryght sett forthe in pyctur', and Thomas Hawley,[102] Clarenceux, was asked 'to over se peruse and corek the sayd wordys and the armes'. Hawley duly produced a new patent, but without any significant improvement unless his description of the unicorns as 'horned and pisseled [or]'[103] can be so regarded; there may have been a reference to the maiden legend and to the colour of wax candles. However, Hawley's blazon seems to have been suppressed for at the herald's visitation of London in 1634 when grants of arms were examined and checked, the 1485 patent with its supporters of 1530 was confirmed by Henry St. George, Richmond Herald, and this remains the authorised coat today. The motto 'Truth is the Light' was added to the exemplification at the time of this visitation.

The coat-of-arms: a modern painting based on the original grant of 1485 with the supporters of 1530.

The master's badge: a Victorian version of the arms in silver-gilt and enamel.

Finance, membership, and wages

The company's accounts[104] were the responsibility of the junior or 'renter' warden, who, besides collecting the rents, seems to have had many miscellaneous duties. The financial period corresponded with the two-year term of office, at the end of which there was an audit before handing over to the new master and wardens. In addition to showing the current financial position, the account books throw much light on the day-to-day business of the company and often reflect the social and economic conditions of the time. The earliest complete set – for 1530–2 – is printed in appendix 6; it is not quite typical because of a large amount of litigation before the mayor in carrying out the company's responsibilities to the city.

At this period the income was usually £75–80 (for two years). For 1528–30 there was a profit 'for the Box' of £4. 4*s*. 8*d*., and thereafter when there was a deficit senior members seem to have come to the rescue. In 1536–8, there were some exceptional expenses, and the plate was sold and bought in by warden Baynard –

Income	£	*s.*	*d.*
Rents	29	16	8
Quarterage	16	7	0
Fines (fees)[105]	1	13	4
Fines (penalties)	9	5	5
Levy on members for two horsemen	7	15	6
Sale of plate	40	0	0
Other 'forren' receipts[106]	10	7	8
Payments for first dinner	2	15	4
Payments for second dinner	6	12	8
	124	13	7

Expenditure	£	*s.*	*d.*
Quit rents on property	4	11	3
Wages to Alman 'our officer' and his wife as cleaner	4	4	0
Annuities (pensions)	7	10	4
Mass at Queenhithe[107]	12	5	0
Obit at Gracechurch St.[108] ...	1	5	8
At 'Poulles'[109]	3	5	8
Midsummer muster men	1	15	4
Mayor's feast		11	0
Court days ... ... Searches ... ... Taking actions before the mayor Coat-of-arms	46	13	0
Provision of two horsemen	8	9	2
Building repairs –			
Queenhithe, Coleman St. and Aldersgate St.	6	15	11½
Hall and 'Kok'	32	4	2
Cost of first dinner	3	8	3
Cost of second dinner	13	12	11
	146	11	8½[110]

For its regular income the company seems to have depended on rents, quarterage, and fines. A member who refused election was liable to a fine of 40*s*. for a master and 20*s*. for a warden; this recognised the frequent reluctance to incur the personal expense associated with office and could provide a useful source of income. Normal expenditure covered quit rents on property, wages, pensions, building repairs, masses and obits. Though the order of St. John was dissolved[111] by Henry VIII in 1540, a quit rent continued to be paid for the hall until 1550 when it was bought in from the king, leaving the site to be held freehold; payments for masses and obits ceased at the Reformation, and payments for church services began. There were also expenses in connection with civic ceremonies and taking actions before the mayor, often against working wax chandlers who lived outside the city or suburbs and were not freemen of the company; in 1528–30 two 'yeomen' were paid 6*d*. each to help the mayor's officer arrest a 'foreigne'. Miscellaneous payments include 14*s*. 10*d*. 'for keeping & clothing a certain Thomas Stone',[112] 12*s*. 2*d*. for his new gown and 7*s*. 6*d*. for burying him in 1532–4 – the first master had fallen on hard times; 3*s*. 'to the Wayettes of London for ther ffee for both yeres' (1532–4); 3*s*. 'for 4½ doz. of Liveries', which from the amount involved must have been badges rather than gowns (1542–4); and 2*d*. for carrying away 'the garbage that was made at the hawle on Jhesus Eve'.

The first indication of the size of the company comes in 1502, when there were 17 members on the livery; this compares with 84 for the Grocers and Merchant Taylors and 80 for the Drapers, the total number for all companies having liveries being 1458. In 1531 the Wax Chandlers had 54 members paying quarterage, and in this list (appendix 6), which is headed by 'Master Lane', eight names are prefixed with 'Mr', indicating a master-craftsman, and three names are prefixed with 'Mistress'. The women, like others whose names crop up from time to time, were probably widows of members of the company, though they may also have been Wax Chandlers in their own right; one, Mistress Nashe, had her son with her in the shop. In the same two years there were eight admissions to the livery at a fee of 6*s*. 8*d*. plus a silver spoon. In 1538 the membership had fallen to 34, according to a list[113] sent by the mayor to Thomas Cromwell in connection with the provision of armour and weapons for the defence of the city; the wardens (including the master) of each company were scheduled to provide four sets of harness and four halberds, the liverymen two of each, and the householders one. The Wax Chandlers names included Thomas Lane, who was serving his second term as master, Walter Sawlkin and Agnes Sawlkin, a widow.

It is only towards the end of the century that yeomanry are mentioned as a separate class, but the Wax Chandlers probably followed the general pattern, in which the journeymen who formed the first yeomanry were joined by the small masters, who eventually gained the ascendancy. Their chief function, often as a semi-independent body, was to represent the manufacturing master-craftsman against the mercantile interests of the ruling body, which often tended to become tyrannical. In the next century the original gild system in which the independent craftsman was only bound by the rules of mistery and municipality was to be replaced by merchant capitalism: thenceforward an entrepreneur would employ groups of men working in their own houses (often outside the city boundaries) and with their own tools – the 'putting-out' or 'outwork' system.[114]

During the early part of the sixteenth century apprenticeship continued on the traditional lines.[115] However, by the time of Henry VIII some payment not envisaged in the London indenture must have crept in, for it was found necessary to forbid it by act of common council. In 1563 the famous Statute of Artificers and Apprentices[116] limited apprenticeship to the sons of freeholders worth 40*s.* a year and confirmed the seven-year term; since 1555 a would-be master had had to wait a further three years before being sworn in. Though the Tudor gentry were in the habit of apprenticing their younger sons to a trade, thus helping to blur the dividing line between land and money, the London apprentice retained his independent character: on Evil May Day 1517 a curfew on the revels and the general resentment against foreigners led many apprentices into a rising that was severely dealt with. Dress was still an important matter, and flat woollen caps[117] with ties under the chin became the fashion for youthful citizens. Liverymen also may have worn a flat cap as headgear together with the gown and hood, the latter hanging down the back.

Working conditions in all trades were directly affected by the 1563 statute, which lasted for over 200 years. Its effect was to extend gild regulation of trade and industry to the whole nation and to override local municipal authority by national control. The Plantagenets, such as Edward III, had attempted to regulate wages and prices by their 'statutes of labourers', but under Elizabeth control was more wisely and effectively carried out.[118]

The wages of a working Wax Chandler are known from the control imposed by the Privy Council, which issued annual proclamations fixing wages for 'the best and most skilled workmen and journeymen and hired servants' in various trades. From 1563 a London Wax Chandler was to be paid by the year £2. 13*s.* 4*d.*, by the week 2*s.*, and by the day 6*d.* – all with meat and drink – or by the week 4*s.* 6*d.* and by the day 11*d.* if meat and drink was not provided; in 1589 the yearly rate, with meat and drink, was raised to £4, the other figures remaining the same. A tradesman did not get much more than a labourer, whose daily wage in 1589 was 5*d.* with meat and drink or 9*d.* without.[119]

O! she doth teach the torches to burn bright.

SHAKESPEARE

Notes on Chapter II

[1]So-called because the principal maypole in Cornhill was higher than the church steeple.

[2]The church also contains Stow's own monument with a fine effigy of the great chronicler.

[3]The brass was put up by Burton's daughter Alice; her monument nearby shows her kneeling figure and lists her three husbands – all Stationers – in order.

[4]The purchase price can be considered equivalent to £3,000 in today's money values.

[5]One of the less important gates or posterns (perhaps from OE *crepel*, a narrow passage); it was situated where Wood Street came up to London Wall.

[6]Gresham Street took in St. Anne's Lane, Maiden Lane, Lad Lane and Cateaton Street, all widened and straightened.

[7]Now thought to be an OE personal name rather than a mythical Dane.

[8]Brewhouse: a brewery, which might be combined with an alehouse or a tavern, the brewing plant being in out-buildings.

[9]'On the hoop' was a common feature of inn signs. Any place selling beer or wine would be marked by an ornamental bush, the ivy-bush being sacred to Bacchus, or by a crown, which was often made from a hoop covered with evergreens.

[10]Quit rent: rent paid by a freeholder or copyholder in lieu of service.

[11]Founded in the twelfth century to provide lodging for pilgrims to the Holy Land; the knights were a military order who in later years defended Rhodes and Malta and whose English contingent provided Henry VIII with his best cavalry.

[12]Upper rooms, originally open to the sun.

[13]Warde, Asshe, Strange and Caphurst.

[14]A will of 1425 refers to the 'stone wall of the brewery called le Cock on ye Hope'.

[15]Water for feasts was brought in by bearer. Many years later (in 1608) the well was re-discovered and presumably brought into use, since a pump was ordered for it.

[16]See also the 1639 view of Cheapside in plate 12.

[17]Both were originally 'inns of chancery' or residences for law students (OE *inn* a dwelling place).

[18]Tapestry had superseded painting in tempera as a wall decoration and was also used for warmth.

[19]Representing the first three letters of Jesus in Greek and in keeping with the company's connection with the gild of his Holy Name.

[20]1 ell = 45 in.

[21]A gild located near St. Paul's, but otherwise unknown.

[22]Aumbries: wall cupboards.

[23]Plate (Span *plata*, silver) denotes solid gold or silver articles; the earliest silver was often covered with gold, so that a goldsmith worked from the first in silver.

[24]A compulsory contribution to the city's supply of corn (page 49).

[25]Perhaps the silver bands from wooden bowls or masers.

[26]Perhaps a very early example of the *lion passant* mark, which is still placed on sterling silver.

[27]A well-known tavern in Lombard Street, near the church of St. Mary Woolnoth to which it was bequeathed in 1493.

[28]An undertaker by profession, his diary pays special attention to notable funerals.

[29]An Act for Swans (22 Edward IV *c* 6).

[30]A statute of 1572 fixed the price of a fat swan at 6*s*. 8*d*., a large fat goose 1*s*., and chickens 4*d*. each.

[31]The St. Paul's crypt was generally known as 'the crowds' (from Anglo-French *crudde*, a corruption of L *crupter* from Gk *kryptos* hidden) or 'the shrouds'; the western half, which was separated by a timber screen, formed the parish church of St. Faith-under-St. Paul's.

[32]The famous cleric whose words were compared by Erasmus to those of Plato. He entrusted St. Paul's School to the Mercers because, it is said, he had found less corruption among the London livery companies than anywhere else in high places.

[33]His foundation statutes stipulated that 'In noo tyme in the yere they shall use talough candill in noo wyse but allonly wax candill at the cost of theyre ffrendes'.

[34]The vigil in the early church was the night before the feast day; thus the vigil of Jesus would have been on 6 August after the Transfiguration services had been completed.

[35]For their attendance the canons were to be paid a total of 20*s*., the priests 8*s*., and the vicars (men singers) 9*s*.

[36]Waits were originally watchmen, who patrolled the streets and piped the watch, a ceremony perpetuated by the 'wakeman' at Ripon. The city waits (who were paid 13*s*. 4*d*. by the gild, and a further 2s. a year by the Wax Chandlers) were a town band using wind instruments, later supported by strings and singers; they appeared regularly on ceremonial occasions.

[37]The charnel house was demolished in 1549, and more than 1,000 cart-loads of bones were removed to Finsbury, this forming Bunhill Fields, later a dissenters' burial ground.

[38]Both feasts came to St. Paul's from the Sarum use, the Name of Jesus (see *Phil.* ii, 9–11) in the fifteenth century. This was a St. Paul's use calendar before it was superseded by Sarum.

[39]Laymen kept by the gild to attend mass and say prayers for the brethren.

[40]*De profundis*: The opening words (in Latin) of Psalm 130 in the Roman Catholic burial service.

[41]Very large candles used at funerals and masses for the dead?

[42]The Goat on the Hoop, a tavern in West Chepe, was bequeathed to the Drapers' Company in 1517.

[43]St. Faith's remained a parish church until Victorian times, when the parish was joined to St. Augustine's, and both are now incorporated in St. Mary-le-Bow. At the east end of Wren's crypt, the chapel corresponding to the old Jesus chapel was dedicated in 1960 to the Order of the British Empire. Immediately above is the apse of the cathedral, for which the name of Jesus chapel was revived in the nineteenth century; in 1958 it became the memorial to Americans who fell in operations based on Britain in the war.

[44]It was also the parish church of the Goldsmiths, and as far back as 1374 they maintained a St. Dunstan's light there, consisting of 12 wax candles and two torches weighing 18 lb. The parish, like all those in the city, was very small, covering little more than 2 acres; there were nearly 100 churches within the city wall.

[45]Under a statute of Henry VIII in 1546 citizens had to pay their parsons 1*s*. 4½*d*. yearly on every 10*s*. rent, but 'any Halls of Crafts or Companys' were excepted 'so long as they be kept unletten'.

[46]Tithes were levied at 10% on the profits of merchants and craftsmen as well as on country produce.

[47]Chantries were endowments for masses for the dead, usually the founder and his relatives. They increased greatly in number during the fourteenth and fifteenth centuries; each had (or shared) a chapel or altar, the richer chantries combining to form colleges of priests. In 1527 a Wax Chandler, Stephen Ward, left in his will 10*s*. for a trental (a set of 30 masses) and 'iiij*d* for bread and wine'.

[48]L *obitus* death.

[49]An important port, though on the wrong side of London Bridge. The church was destroyed in the Great Fire, but the churchyard and harbour remain.

[50]Messuage: dwelling house with outbuildings and land.

[51]Thompson's property was partly destroyed in the 1939–45 war, after which it was sold and the gifts redeemed by a cash payment, but the founder's memory is still kept alive by a distribution of overcoats (page 123).

[52]A common form of Gracechurch Street in the sixteenth and seventeenth centuries, and the pronunciation lasted much longer. St. Benet Gracechurch was burnt down in the Great Fire, but the churchyard remains.

[53]See also appendix 6, p. 149.

[54]Brockett's property was sold in 1955 to help defray the cost of rebuilding the hall.

[55]The Act of Supremacy of 1534 (26 Henry VIII, *c* 1) nationalised the church in England and trebled the royal revenue, bringing in some £200,000 a year that previously went to Rome; the subsequent sale of monastic and church lands brought in a capital sum of £1½m, besides giving the new owners a vested interest in Protestantism.

[56]Specially authorised by the king and therefore outside the diocesan jurisdiction.

[57]Rent-charge: a periodical charge on land etc., reserved by deed to one who is not the owner, e.g. a contract to pay so much from the rents in return for a sum down, and thus a form of investment.

[58]St. Mary 'over the river' was founded by Augustinian canons in 1106; the church is incorporated in Southwark Cathedral.

[59]The accusations cost many of the companies dear. In 1609 they were again attacked under James I, resulting in fines and a demand for £6,000 for arrears of payment, but a statute of 1624 stopped further action.

[60]*La chaunge* in 1297, it was named from the royal mint there.

[61]Later Knightrider Street, it was the site of an early London fishmarket. The church was burnt down in the Great Fire.

[62]This, the company's most important charity, was carried on in the original form for three hundred years but is now administered under a scheme settled by the high court in the late nineteenth century (page 108). The Old Change property was sold in 1913, and the money re-invested.

[63]The possibility of this identification was first mooted by C. G. Todd.

[64]John Dent, *The Quest for Nonsuch*, 1962.

[65]Judas candles: for fixing on wooden stocks or Judases, painted to match the candles and thus give a false impression of height.

[66]Reginald Pole, the 'English Cardinal', returned from exile as papal legate; his first act was to absolve the nation and receive it back to Rome, and he has been blamed for the subsequent Protestant martyrdoms.

[67]William J. Thoms, *The Book of the Court*, 1838.

[68]Armed men were generally hired mercenaries, except for the defence of the city when freemen were involved. In the accounts for 1536–8 is a payment 'to Benson the soldier 8*d*' for the standard day's wages.

[69]Precepts are still issued, for instance, for convening wardmotes.

[70]In the Armada year of 1588–9 the fixed ordinary revenue was £295,000 to which parliamentary taxation added only £88,000 – less than half the cost of setting up Tilbury Camp, the main stronghold against invasion.

[71]A harquebus (arquebus) was a portable gun, strictly an early type needing a support when fired. Firearms replaced bows and arrows by the end of the sixteenth century.

[72]A halberd was a combination of spear and battleaxe.

[73]Murrion: a kind of helmet without beaver or visor.

[74]Caliver: the lightest type of portable fire-arm (originally of a certain calibre).

[75]Royal patents of monopoly could give an individual or group the sole right, for example, to make or sell a commodity, issue a licence, or trade with a region. Commercial monopolies such as the great overseas trading companies were recognised as advantageous to the country; they might be joint-stock such as the Muscovy Company, which was operating in 1553, or regulated (each member taking his own risk and profit) such as the Merchant Adventurers, which was incorporated in 1553.

[76]Greenwich palace, the birthplace of Elizabeth I, was a favourite residence of the Tudor monarchs.

[77]Small round shields or shield-shaped ornaments.

[78]The palace started by the protector, the Duke of Somerset and, on his execution, forfeited to the crown.

[79]F *herse*, a harrow. Later hearses were mounted on wheels to form funeral carriages.

[80]On October 17 up to 1546, and October 29 thereafter (till 1751).

[81]They originated in Germany and were sold in England over the counter.

[82]These hospitals had been founded to provide houses of rest for travellers and homes for the destitute and sick, functions that were also a minor activity of the monasteries; the others were Bridewell, which was converted from a royal palace to a prison, and Christ's, which was founded in the house of the Grey Friars or Franciscans for the education of orphans. Though their primary function was the relief of the poor, Bart's and Thomas's provided some medical treatment, Bethlehem dealt with the 'distracted' (hence Bedlam), and Bridewell was a combination of workhouse and reformatory. It was not until the eighteenth century that other hospitals in the modern sense were built.

[83]39 & 40 Eliz. *c* 3, 4, 5; it consolidated much previous legislation and lasted, with revisions, from 1601 to 1834.

[84]The rise in prices originated in the debasement of the coinage under Henry VIII, when there was a 2/3 reduction in silver content, and the import of gold from the Americas; during the sixteenth century a wide range of prices rose six times while wages only doubled.

[85]19 Henry VII *c* 7.

[86]Two chief justices also signed, Sir John Fyneux of the king's bench and Sir Robert Rede of the common pleas.

[87]This and the following extracts are transcribed from an engrossment of 1622 (*MS*9496).

[88]Supplementary ordinances were issued in 1569, 1580, 1584, 1597 and 1599; those of 1584 include directions for the keeping of goods and chattels by the renter warden and the use of a chest with four locks. Two further ordinances, one giving an oath for the viewers and the other requiring official approval of maker's marks, are included in an ordinance book of 1622 (*MS* 9496) with a transcript of other early documents made for the master, William Sharpe.

[89]37 Edward III, *c* 5.

[90]Perhaps Thomas Owen, a judge of the common please from 1594.

[91]There were a number of expenses in connection with parliamentary matters from 1528 to 1542, for instance 'Item payd to the Speker of the parlement to have his counsell v*s*'. In this and the next two centuries nearly every official worth buying could be bought – an accepted practice, if done quietly.

[92]At the medieval university, a small room in college might cost 10*s*. a year.

[93]Adulterated with resin?

[94]Hollowing out the tapers so that they used less wax and burned down too soon?

[95]Rolls of wax? – and overcharging for them.

[96]Perhaps working at prohibited times, such as the mid-day break.

[97]Baynard's apprentice may have been unusually obstreperous or merely one more than his master was allowed, but the penalty was heavy – equivalent to say £100 today.

[98]A prison associated with the sheriff's court; 'compter' became the official spelling.

[99]Troublesome, not necessarily lascivious.

[100]Cering: wrapping in a waxed cloth or 'cerecloth' (L *cera* wax) as winding sheet before burial, *cf* cerements. In the Middle Ages all but the rich were wound in a cerecloth and laid in earth with no coffin.

[101]Like his colleagues Benolt led a public life that was much more active than most modern heralds: between 1514 and 1533 he undertook many diplomatic missions to foreign courts, particularly those of France and Scotland.

[102]Hawley bore the English challenge to the King of Scots in the Flodden campaign of 1513. His patent named Thomas Lane as master with William Howell (or Hull) and William Baynard as wardens.

[103]From the colouring on the grant.

[104]The account books have been preserved almost completely from 1530 to 1560. Most of the Elizabethan accounts are incomplete, and after James II they become very spasmodic, only recovering with the Hanoverians.

[105]The word 'fine' was used for any money payment, fees or other money dues as well as penalties for wrong-doing.

[106]Including gifts for the hall.

[107]For John Thompson; it includes the priest's wages.

[108]For Robert Brockett or Lawrence Stockwood?

[109]For the general obit and other services in the Jesus chapel.

[110]The deficit was given as £32. 19*s*. 1½*d*.; in spite of the audit, the figures do not always add up.

[111]The prior, who claimed to be the premier baron of England, was granted a pension of £1,000 a year. The modern revival of the English order has its headquarters in the gatehouse of the original priory and runs the St. John Ambulance service.

[112]A gown for him cost 16*s*. for the cloth and 20*d*. for the making.

[113]Edward Salisbury, *Middlesex & Herts. Notes & Queries*, 1897.

[114]Often called the domestic system, but the early craftsmen who had both industrial and commercial independence were also domestic workers.

[115]Though the earliest surviving register of Wax Chandlers apprentices does not start until 1596.

[116]5 Eliz. *c*. 4. The full title was 'Touching divers Orders for Artificers, Labourers, Servants of Husbandry & Apprentices'.

[117]They are mentioned by Ben Jonson, *Every Man in his Humour* (1598).

[118]And after the Reformation the number of 'holydays' had been reduced from nearly 100 to some 27, giving a useful increase in national production.

[119]Earlier in 1536–8, the company's accounts show that the wages of a bricklayer and a labourer together amounted to 13*d*. a day.

6. The Normansell cup, 1683.

Made for presentation to the company by its tenant in Aldersgate Street, and appropriately engraved (see fig. 4).

7. Early silver plate, 1653?–1737.

Tankard 1673, beadle's staff head pre-1664, taper sticks 1737, seal-top spoon pre-1653, trifid spoons 1681, and trencher salts 1675.

8. Silver plate, 1763–1856?

Rose-water dish (plated) pre-1856, caddies 1763, goblet 1808, gravy boat 1794, and chamber stick 1828.

9. Silver plate, 1773–1906.

Rose-water dish 1906, standing cup (German) 1897?, cake basket 1773, and standing cup 1897.

CHAPTER III

The Stuart Era : 1603 - 1714

UNDER the Stuarts and the Lord Protector the Wax Chandlers endured the Civil War, the Great Plague, and the first Great Fire of London. Like other companies they met the requirements of the government whatever its political complexion: from 1640 to 1645 they contributed over £600 – say £6,000 today – to king or parliament. Soon after his accession James I involved the city in costly schemes for colonising Ulster and Virginia, and Charles I obtained funds from the same source. But in the Civil War London supported the parliamentary side and supplied much of the money that proved so decisive; it also embodied the militia, the famous 'train-bands', who were to meet their finest hour.

After the Restoration the brilliance of court and society was marred first by the plague with its disruptive effect on life and trade and then by the fire which laid waste most of the city. Neither the cathedral nor the company halls were spared, and the Wax Chandlers had to replace the old Tudor structure by their first brick building; within four years this was ready for occupation, and it soon brought in an income from lettings. Feasting was resumed, wives being officially invited, and a start was made on the replacement of plate. From this period come some of the oldest pieces of silver in the company's possession, among them the Normansell loving cup of 1683, with its engravings of bees and bee-keeping, still gracing our banquets.

Under Charles II also the company obtained a new charter and new ordinances, and these are still in operation. The company's jurisdiction was extended to a radius of ten miles, and its maximum expenditure on land and property increased to £100 a year. The right of search was confirmed, but control of the trade became inevitably less effective with the growth of London and the movement of craftsmen to the outer suburbs.

However the trade in wax candles remained substantial – in 1663 Pepys was testing wax against tallow at the Admiralty[1] – so much so that by the time of Anne it was worth taxing. In 1710 duties were imposed[2] of 4*d.* per lb. weight on candles of beeswax (pure or mixed) and ½*d.* per lb. on tallow; they applied to imported as well as British candles and were to continue for 32 years with the object of raising £1,500,000 by a lottery. These were the first excise duties[3] on candles, but customs duties had been in force during the seventeenth century; they were reduced in 1650 and abolished in 1691, free export being favoured at that time.

For king or parliament

In the seventeenth century the government's demands on the city became ever more troublesome. The chief revenues of the Stuart monarchs continued to be drawn from crown lands and customs duties such as 'tonnage and poundage',[4] and normally these enabled public services to be maintained. In an emergency, extra money, if not granted by parliament, had to be obtained by loans in anticipation of revenue or by other expedients. Frequent calls were made on the city, and wealthy aldermen and merchants provided very large sums, as did the 'customs farmers' to whom (up to 1683) the duties and their collection were farmed out in return for a fixed annual payment to the exchequer. Deficiencies might be made up by the 'chamber of London' (the city's bank), but, as in the previous century, money was often collected on a wider basis – through the wards and the livery companies; where the companies were the channel, it would ultimately be the members who paid, and no doubt they were often liable to contribute as ward residents. Examples will be quoted of loans that were raised directly through the companies, the usual basis of assessment being the corn quota.

Early in the reign of James I the Wax Chandlers with most other companies were involved in the 'plantation of Ulster'. Following successful expeditions against rebel Irish chieftains and the submission of the Earls of Tyrone and Tyrconnel, the king decided to raise money by colonising their confiscated lands, and at his request the task of resettlement and the promotion of religious order and industry was undertaken, though unwillingly, by the city of London.[5] A committee – the Honourable the Irish Society – was set up to manage their estates. In 1609 an area corresponding to the present County Londonderry was granted to the 12 great companies for £40,000, later raised to £52,500.[6] The minor companies also were to subscribe (in accordance with the corn quota), and 1/16 of the Haberdashers' share between Londonderry and Coleraine was divided between the Founders, Turners and Wax Chandlers. The cost to our company was £80, which was paid in two instalments, and levied on the members. In May 1620 they received the first distribution – a total of £11. 15*s*. 8*d*.; a later payment was celebrated by the three minor companies spending 2*s*. 2*d*. at the Mermaid Tavern in Cornhill.

After successful early years the Irish Society ran into many difficulties, notably the rebellion of 1641, when the Wax Chandlers gave £15 to the poor of Londonderry; in the following year they sent corn to help the distressed Protestants, and in 1643 they invested a further £50 in the plantation. Thereafter accounting for rents became uncertain, and dividends fell into arrears. Eventually, in 1686, the Wax Chandlers with their associates sold all their land in Ireland, reserving their rights of fishing, hunting and mining to the Irish Society; the purchaser was Dame Catherine Beresford, and the price £500, the company's share being £192.[7] Before this there had been a period when the Haberdashers withheld the dividends due to the three minor companies, and no action could be taken owing to the destruction of records in the Great Fire. However a fortunate accident brought the necessary information to light, and in 1704 counsel's opinion was taken to the effect that the Haberdashers, who had claimed the Statute of Limitations, were liable to pay all the arrears. This appears to have led to a satisfactory settlement.

A scheme for the refounding of Raleigh's Virginia, the first English colony, was launched in 1607. A group of speculators – the Company of Adventurers and Planters of the City of London for the Colony of Virginia – was recommended by the lord mayor for support, and their second charter named 56 companies (and 659 individuals) as incorporators. It appears however that 41 of the companies, among them the Wax Chandlers, made no payment and took no direct part in the project. Later there was a request for money to entice some of the surplus population to emigrate, and in 1612 a lottery for plate in which all the companies including the Wax Chandlers participated.[8]

Money loans for James I began in 1604 when £15,000 was supplied by the companies, the Wax Chandlers contributing, and in 1614 the city softened its refusal to lend a further loan of £100,000 by a free gift of £10,000, half of which came from the companies. In 1620 the Wax Chandlers gave £20 towards the £5,000 sent by the city for the relief of the Rhenish Palatinate, whence the Elector Frederick and his wife, James's daughter, were soon to be driven by the Imperialists.[9]

For Charles I, at war with Spain and France, the city raised £120,000 in 1627–8 on the security of the crown lands. The Wax Chandlers contributed £120 and £40, but some companies offered stiff opposition and had their officers committed to Newgate; the city was covered with placards denouncing the 'Yield-all'. This loan was eventually repaid, but for a time the government's record was so bad that it could no longer borrow from the city. In 1635 the king added 'ship money' to other expedients, extending this tax, which was normally levied on coastal towns, to the whole country,[10] and a further windfall was to come. Ten years earlier he had embarked on the confiscation of the city's estates in Ulster, and now the Star Chamber gave judgement: the city was to pay £70,000, give up its lands, and forfeit its charter. Negotiations reduced the fine to £12,000, for which a new charter was granted though not before a further £2,355. 3*s*. 8*d*. had been paid to officials; £8,000 of the fine came from the companies, £125 from the Wax Chandlers, in 1638.[11]

In 1640, to avoid summoning the Long Parliament, Charles asked for £200,000 for the maintenance of his northern army; this was agreed in the face of strong opposition, but was finally whittled down to £50,000. The loan, which was on the security of 'the noblemen's bond' – in fact, of the customs farmers – was levied on the companies and was repaid some years later, the Wax Chandlers' contribution being £125. When the Long Parliament was convened in November, it introduced a poll tax[12] to provide money for the disbanding of the Scottish and English armies. This was levied on the whole population from dukes (at £100 each) downwards. In London the city officials and company members were assessed on a graduated scale; the mayor paid £40 and the masters of the first twelve companies £12 each. The other companies were divided into three groups, the Wax Chandlers being in the second: this was assessed at £3 for the master, £2 each for the wardens, £1 for the livery, and 1*s*. for freemen. In 1641 when the king returned from Scotland he was welcomed with the usual ceremony but no money, and in January 1642, when he made his celebrated raid on the House of Commons and precipitated the Civil War, the city provided safe refuge for the five members led by Pym and Hampden. Thenceforward, though high officials and some wealthy men adhered to the crown, London generally began to veer to the other side. But with Charles in flight to York and rebellion in Ireland, the parliamentarians took their turn in borrowing from the city. In June 1642, to obtain a loan of £100,000 at 8% for a year, a deputation from the lords and commons met the livery assembled in common hall: the money was voted with alacrity, but some companies were reluctant to support their members and there was still a large deficit six months later. The Wax Chandlers contributed £250, which they had to borrow; this loan was ostensibly for the relief of Ireland, and the companies were also asked to provide bread and corn for the Ulster plantation.

On the outbreak of civil war, London was fortified with the help of 50 trades. The first earthworks went up in 1642, and the main fortifications in the spring of 1643 in anticipation of a Royalist attack. Popular enthusiasm was so great that up to 20,000 men, women and children worked for their rations alone, 'clerks and gentlemen' alongside servants, the lady mayoress with the Billingsgate fishwives; the companies including 'the candle-makers' marched out with 'roaring drums, flying colours, and girded swords'.[13]

In January 1642 the train-bands had been put on a war footing; they were enlarged to 10,000 and re-equipped for review in Finsbury Fields. A further 20,000 men were raised for the Earl of Essex, the Roundhead commander-in-chief. By October twelve companies of train-bands were ready to defend the city, and in the following month they forced a Royalist retreat at Turnham Green. In the summer of 1643, with the fortifications completed and the livery companies' stocks of arms requisitioned, the train-bands were despatched under Essex to relieve the siege of Gloucester, perhaps their most successful operation. On the way back to London they fell in with Prince Rupert's horse at Newbury, where their pikemen and musketeers 'behaved themselves to wonder', foiling the Royalist attempt to take the capital.

In August 1643, in view of the possible approach of the royal army to London should Gloucester fall to the king, parliament was provided with a loan of £50,000 at 8% to which the Wax Chandlers contributed £125 or £150. By now individuals were impoverished, many companies had sold or pawned their plate, and some had mortgaged their halls; it was difficult to assemble a court without heavy fines on absentees. Nevertheless the parliamentary commissioners pressed their demands; in 1644 there was a levy of £30,000 to maintain the Scottish forces, and in 1645, the year of Naseby, the Wax Chandlers had to advance a further £150.

With this steady drain on their funds it is not surprising that in 1647, 'the times being bad', the Wax Chandlers increased the scale of fines, though the 'Ancients' and the past masters were given £5 each out of the common stock, and the renter warden £2; once again liverymen were ordered to supply a silver spoon on admission. In the same year the companies nominated a committee 'to sollicitt for ye Companies moneys lent to ye State', and the Wax Chandlers sent in their account as follows:

Theis are to certifie to whome theis presence (*sic*) shall concerne that the Companie of Waxchandlers of the Cittie of London have lent to the Vse of the State theis particuler sommes followeing viz

	£	*s.*	*d.*
In October 1640 upon ye Noblemens bond towardes ye raising of 50,000 *li* … … …	125	0	0
The Interrest whereof untill the 25 of March 1647 cometh to … … … … …	064	11	0
The 15 of June 1642 towardes ye raising of 100,000 *li* the somme of … … … …	250	0	0
The Interrest whereof untill the 25 of March 1647 cometh to … … … … …	095	0	0
The 28 of September 1643 towardes ye raising of 50,000 *li* then lent the somme of … …	125	0	0
The Interrest whereof untill the 25 of March 1647 cometh to … … … … …	035	0	0
	694	11	0
Rec ye 19 of November 1644 ye somme of … … … … … … … …	12	10	0
The Interrest whereof untill ye 25 of March 1647 cometh to … … … … …	02	6	8
Rec ye 16 of October 1646 ye somme of … … … … … … … … …	12	10	0
The Interrest whereof untill the 25 of March 1647 … … … … … …	00	8	11
The whole somme receaved with interrest cometh to … … … … …	27	15	7
Rest due to ye said Companie the 25 of March 1647 for Principall and Interrest ye Somme of	666	15	5

A later note adds:

Rec ye 25 of Julie 1651 in parte of the same debt ye somme of … … … … …	06	05	0

In 1647–8 the company paid £12 for six months assessment on the hall for the army under General Fairfax, and in 1649, to prevent demonstrations at Charles's execution, troops were quartered in city churches and company halls; the Wax Chandlers had prudently appointed a committee 'Uppon an imirgent occassion' to dispose of their 'treasures, goods, books and writtings' in suitable places. By the following year they had £240 in their treasury chest, but in 1654, with loan money still outstanding, they had to sell some land in East Meath for £90, and four years later they sold their plate for £55. 17*s*. 10*d*.

When the Restoration was agreed, the city raised £12,000 from the companies as a gift to Charles II and his brothers, the Dukes of York and Gloucester, and money to pay off and disband the 'new model army' and navy was raised by a further poll tax; assessments were on the same basis as in 1640, and more than £70,000 was received from the city alone. In 1664–5 naval and ordnance preparations were required for the war with Holland, and the city lent the government £200,000 at the usual 6% interest. This loan was secured on the payments for the hearth tax, which had been granted to Charles II in

1662 as a perpetual revenue, 1*s.* half-yearly being levied on all hearths not occupied by paupers; 'chimney money' for the hall amounted to 10*s.* a year.[14] Later the tax was farmed out to meet another urgent gap in naval supply, but the loan was eventually repaid. The first £100,000 was subscribed by individuals, and nearly half the balance was obtained from the companies, the Wax Chandlers providing £250; this they had to borrow, and a committee was appointed to get in the money and sell the plate. The companies also built and equipped the *Loyal London*, which cost £18,355, of which £13. 12*s.* 6*d.* came from the Wax Chandlers; this was one of the ships that defeated de Ruyter and Tromp in 1666, but in the following year she was burnt by the former's fleet when it sailed up the Medway.

In 1689 came the bloodless and therefore 'glorious' revolution, which put William and Mary on the throne, and there followed almost immediately requests for a loan, and also for regiments of horse and dragoons towards which the Wax Chandlers paid £25. While the manpower and arms of the city were needed to keep peace at home and hold off the Jacobites, its money was soon required for William's wars: in a period of five years over £1,000,000 was advanced, but on one occasion at least, when £200,000 was required in 1691, the Wax Chandlers 'could not contribute any sum'. However, the old system of forced loans was drawing to a close with the foundation of the Bank of England in 1694.[15]

Although the company was relieved of governmental demands for money, there was one Wax Chandler whose business relations with the crown led him into difficulties. This was William Warren, a supplier of sealing wax to the royal household, the departments of state and the law courts; the exchequer, for instance, would have been an important customer for green wax,[16] which was used for seals on the estreats and other documents sent to the sheriffs. In 1698 Warren appears to have borrowed £1,000 from Sir Stephen Fox,[17] who was head of the king's purchasing office or 'board of green cloth', and also a banker; this was to tide him over the wax bleaching period (from April to June according to the weather). In two letters[18] to Fox asking for deferred terms of repayment, Warren refers to his 'unspeakable griefe' and the need to preserve himself and his family 'from Utter Ruin' and ends with a plea to 'compassionate my Condicon' – it is not known to what effect. But the very large sum of money involved shows both the importance of the sealing wax side of the trade and the size of Warren's business that it needed so much capital.

Under the first Stuarts royal processions were attended by the companies in their usual splendour, the livery either standing or (from about 1625) sitting behind rails hung with tapestries, and so impressive was the scene that, on one occasion at least, Dekker, Webster and Ben Jonson were all moved to describe it in verse. In 1603 the companies welcomed James I on his arrival from Scotland and attended his passage with the queen from the Tower to Westminster for their coronation, £2,500 being raised for this occasion. In 1639, under Charles I, Marie de' Medicis, the exiled mother of Louis XIII and of Queen Henrietta Maria, passed through Cheapside, a scene depicted in a well-known engraving (plate 12). The king himself received a civic welcome on returning from Scotland in 1641, but this was the last honour the citizens paid him.

At the Restoration all the companies sent gifts or congratulations to Charles II. The Wax Chandlers gave £30 towards £120,000 demanded for his entry into the city. This was celebrated by a triumph involving 20,000 persons on horse and on foot; according to Evelyn, the diarist, all the companies were there in their liveries, chains of gold, and banners, and the procession took from 2 to 9 p.m. to pass through the city. The Wax Chandlers gave a further £15 towards the £6,000 raised for the coronation procession, a grand display, followed by celebrations from which Pepys (a Clothworker) got to his bed only 'pretty well'. For the reception of the Russian ambassador in 1662 and a royal entry in 1663, the companies sent 500 liverymen 'appareled in velvet coats with chains of gold, well mounted on horseback'. In 1697 William III was greeted 'with all pageantry' on the conclusion of the war with France by the treaty of Ryswick. The livery were ready in their stands at eight in the morning, 'well appareled' and with new banners of their companies before them; the streets were guarded by six regiments of train-bands, and the houses were bright with tapestry hangings.

The civic scene

The population of greater London (city, liberties and suburbs) rose to nearly 400,000 in the 1660s, after which growth slackened; by the end of the century the total was around 500,000, only half of whom resided within the city boundaries. In the time of James I the mayor's authority was at its height – he actually claimed to be master of all the companies – but the king was often wont to interfere. It was on his direct orders in 1611 that the mayor issued a precept giving the most precise details of clothing and ornaments to be worn by apprentices and maidservants; the penalty was imprisonment for 18 hours in the Guildhall's Little Ease, so-called because the culprit could neither sit, stand or lie down. As usual the companies provided the pageantry for the lord mayor's processions and also contributed to municipal services such as local defence and poor relief. In 1620 the livery attended a state visit to St. Paul's to hasten the subscriptions for repairs, a lengthy business towards which the Wax Chandlers were to pay £50 twelve years later.[19]

With the ending of the midsummer watch the lord mayor's show had become the main civic procession of the year. There were elaborate pageants in which songs, speeches and dramatic interludes with minstrels and fireworks – today's *son et lumière*? – reflected the great age of English drama: librettos composed by Peele were followed by those of Middleton, Webster, Dekker and Heywood. But with the Restoration the combination of poetry and pageantry gave place to pure spectacle, which continued until the time of George I.

On lord mayor's day, the mayor was accompanied by the waits of the city to the wharf, usually the Three Cranes, from which the river procession set out: the barges of the mayor and the companies were gaily decorated with canopies, banners and streamers, and there was music from drums and trumpets or fifes. The Wax Chandlers were in the habit of hiring a barge, paying in 1664 £6. 10*s*. 0*d*. for barge and watermen to carry 30 of the livery,[20] and in 1691 they paid £4 for hire and 5*s*. 10*d*. for '14 yards of blew and yellow ribbon' for the bargemen; a blue barge-cloth was kept at the hall. On returning to another wharf, Paul's or Baynards Castle,[21] the route led to the Guildhall where, the companies having returned to their own halls for dinner, the mayor held 'a Royal Banquet, Glorious to the Eye and Delicious to the Palate'. The pageant might be resumed at about 3 p.m., but in some years the programme read 'dinner ended and night approaching' and allowed him to go straight home.

For the land procession it was usual for the mayor's torches to be supplied by the Wax Chandlers', at first by members of the livery and yeomanry in rotation but later 'to prevent abuses . . . by four seniors at 16*s*. for great ones and 10s. for small ones'. Apart from those for the mayor, large numbers of torches were used in the procession and side-shows; in 1617 the Grocers spent £42. 3*s*. 3*d*. on torches and links[22] for their mayor's triumph:

Payde to William Uffington for 49 dozens of large staffe torches at 15*s* a dozen	£36	15	0
More to him for 10 dozen and ½ of small torches at 9*s* per dozen, and for 5 dozen and ½ of linkes at 2*s* 6*d* per dozen, for to light the pageant and other shewes from Leaden-hall over night to Carter Lane and other places appointed – *in toto*	£ 5	8	3
	£42	3	3

Municipal services provided by the companies included men and equipment for the militia, men for the standing watch (until 1693 when all the inhabitants, in theory, took their turn), and various forms of poor relief. Since the mid-sixteenth century or earlier each craft had provided men regularly for the defence of the city, and the important part played by the train-bands[23] in the civil war has been described. They had been included in a general muster with 6,000 men in armour in 1614, by which time their calivers had been replaced by muskets, and they turned out again for the Restoration celebrations and for a general muster in 1670. The companies continued to maintain their armouries with stocks of munitions, which were regularly reported to the mayor.

The corn levy continued, the assessments being reviewed from time to time. In 1638 the Wax Chandlers' contribution was raised from 20 to 25 qrs., perhaps an indication of growing prosperity; by 1664 they were putting their livery fines aside to pay for corn. After the Restoration in 1660 the common council demanded £12,000 'to be laid out in corne as a present to the king's majestie', the Wax Chandlers contributing their £30 share; however the city had often borrowed corn from the king in the previous century. The destruction of the companies' granaries in the Great Fire of 1666 foreshadowed the end of the corn custom, but precepts continued to be issued, though not always obeyed, for the next 20 years or so.

Some silver-gilt plate. Rose-water dish 1827 and ewer 1867, tankard 1650 (German), honey pot 1860 and tray 1810, and salt-cellars 1846.

The master's gown: a new design (with other gowns for wardens, livery and clerk) commissioned in 1969.

An important improvement in the city's finances was effected towards the end of the century through the 'orphans' fund'. By old custom the orphans of freemen were a civic responsibility, and any money due to them was held in trust by the chamber of London. When a considerable sum had accumulated, the orphans' fund would be raided for municipal purposes; for instance in 1381 the mayor took 2,000 marks from the 'Orphants Chest' and in 1577 £1,000 of 'Orphenage Monye' towards the purchase of corn. Under the Stuarts the fund was used to support loans to the government, and in 1694, when it had become greatly in debt, parliament enacted[24] that it should receive certain duties on coal and wine and other dues.[25] Among these was the apprentice binding fee of *2s. 6d.*, which was to be paid to his company for transmission to the chamberlain; the Wax Chandlers possess a 'Register of Apprentice Bindings with an account of Orphan's duty paid into the chamber of London 1694 – 1857'.[26]

Both the Great Fire and the Great Plague, which immediately preceded it, were disastrous in their effects on the city and the companies. The plague[27] alone claimed 100,000 victims and brought London's industry to its knees: according to the Bills of Mortality issued by the Parish Clerks' Company[28] it accounted for 7,160 out of 8,297 burials during the worst week and for 68,596 out of 97,306 during the year (to December 1665). The onslaught started – it is said in the slums of St. Martin or St. Giles in the Fields – in March, when a prolonged frost had already caused unemployment, to relieve which the mayor had ordered a collection to be taken from the livery. Soon the city made levies on the companies in order to assist those infected and provide coal for sale at cheap rates to prevent profiteering; each summer 8,000 chaldrons, perhaps as much as 16,000 tons,[29] of sea-coals were to be laid up, the Wax Chandlers taking their usual share – 19 chaldrons. In June further contributions were levied on the companies, and they cancelled all dinners, including the election feasts, and entertainments; they were ordered to devote a third of the money saved to the relief of members in need. Throughout the year they carried on under great difficulties, losing many members and some masters and cutting down their meetings; the Wax Chandlers found that 'a Court of Assistants was difficult to be got', and a committee was appointed to manage the company's business. In their own parish of St. John Zachary, no fewer than 54 out of 85 deaths in the year had been caused by the plague.

Then, from 2 to 6 September, 1666, came the Great Fire, which laid waste three-quarters of the city, taking few lives but causing damage amounting to some £10,000,000. Starting at Pudding Lane by London Bridge, the fire raged for four days through streets that were narrowed by encroachments and lined with houses mostly made of wood: when at last the wind changed, 13,000 houses and 87 churches were burnt out together with St. Paul's Cathedral, the Royal Exchange, and 44 company halls, including that of the Wax Chandlers. Valued at £150,000 but not to be measured in monetary terms was the loss of the booksellers' stocks from Paternoster Row: they had been deposited in the crypt of St. Paul's, only to burn for a week when the roof fell in. Pepys and Evelyn have portrayed the fearful spectacle of a city in flames, noting also that the king and his brother lent a hand with the fire buckets while the mayor bemoaned his inability to help. It was in fact owing to the king's personal direction that the rebuilding was carried out at a rapid pace.

Before the fire, craft restrictions and the burdens of office had driven many tradesmen to set up in the suburbs, and in 1673 the companies were ordered to make returns showing how many of their freemen were not free of the city, and how many were living outside its jurisdiction; the cost of the city freedom was reduced to 7 nobles,[30] say £2. 6*s.* 8*d.* In 1689 the mayor issued a stern reminder that all freemen of companies were expected to become free of the city.

A new charter

In 1652, under Cromwell, a Committee of the Commonwealth met at the hall and commanded that the charters should be delivered to the Committee of Corporations at Westminster; a replacement was solicited but without result. In 1662 however the company decided to lay out £100 towards a new charter[31], and this was granted on 23 November 1663. The actual cost was over £130, as detailed in the accounts:

Paid William Rutt for drawing up the charter	40*s.*
and other expenses	2*s.* 9*d.*
Mr. Johnson for the company's charter	£126. 9*s.*
Issure for his paynes	45*s.*
a box to put the charter in	18*d.*

An important change in view of the rapid expansion of London was the widening of the company's jurisdiction to a radius of ten miles. The composition of the court was specified, and procedures laid down for holding elections; the election day was secularised as the first Thursday in August, perhaps suggested by the fifteenth-century calendar of *MS* 9495 in which the feast of Transfiguration fell on a Thursday. Detailed instructions were given for searching for and dealing with bad wares. The limit on the purchase of property was raised from the original 5 marks (£3. 6*s.* 8*d.*) to £100. It was confirmed that the craft could only be practised by those who had completed a seven-year apprenticeship.

The charter master was named as Grace[32] Hardwyn, and the wardens William Rutt and William Burroughs. The text (in English) was generally less flowery and more practical than that of 1484, as will be seen from the abridgement[33] below:

> The King, on petition of the master, wardens and commonalty of the art or misterie of wax chandlers of the city of London, being an ancient societie or fraternitie for the better rule and government of all and every person and persons using or exercising the said art or mystery of a wax chandler within the city of London or ten miles of same, and for the benefit and advantage of the said art, and the reformation of inconveniences and abuses frequently used and practised therein, to the public damage, has confirmed to the said company all charters, liberties and privileges granted to their predecessors.

All persons using the said art or mystery in London or within ten miles thereof to be one body corporate and politic, by the name of master, wardens and commonalty of the art or mystery of wax chandlers of the city of London, to have perpetual succession, and to be able and capable in law to have, purchase, receive manors, messuages, lands, tenements, liberties, privileges, jurisdictions, franchises and hereditaments of any kind for term of life, lives, years, in fee simple or otherwise, also goods, chattels and other things.

Also to give, grant, demise, alienate, assign, and dispose of any of their manors, lands, tenements and hereditaments, and do other things.

Also they may plead and be impleaded, answer and be answered, defend and be defended in any court or place before any judges or justices in any actions, pleas, writs, plaints, matters and demands as other people and bodies corporate do.

They may have and use a common seal for their affairs, which they may change at will when necessary.

They may meet from time to time in any convenient place within the city to elect one of their number to be master of the said art or mystery and two to be wardens, also twenty to be assistants to assist the master and wardens in their business. Master, wardens and assistants, or a majority of them of which master and one warden must be two, may constitute, ordain, make and establish from time to time any reasonable laws, ordinances, orders and constitutions in writing which seem fit to them for the good rule, governing and correcting of the freemen and members of the company, and for the reforming, amending and bettering of the works and workmanships thereof, and to set and impose such pains, penalties and punishments by fines and amercements on all offenders as they or ma ajority of them may think fit. They may have, recover, levy, receive and take the said fines and amercements by distress and other lawful means to their own use without hindrance by the crown or rendering any account.The laws are to be observed as far as they are agreeable to the laws and statutes of the realm and the liberties and customs of the city of London.

Master, wardens and assistants for the time being or majority of them shall yearly for ever[34] on the first Thursday in August elect one warden or assistant for the time being as master of the company for the ensuing two years and thenceforward until another master is elected and sworn, such newly elected master shall take corporal oath well and truly to execute the said office; after taking oath the new master shall exercise office for two years and until his successor be chosen and sworn.

At the time of the said election, master, wardens and assistants or majority of them shall elect two assistants to be wardens for the next two years and until two more wardens be chosen; new wardens are to take corporall oath for due performance of office.

If master and wardens die or be removed in less than two years after election, the remaining master, wardens and assistants shall elect and swear a successor according to the foregoing rules, to serve until the following first Thursday in August and election of successor; on death or removal of an assistant, removal being by majority of master, wardens and assistants, the remainder or majority may choose a successor, master, wardens and commonalty shall nominate, elect, constitute and make a fit person to be clerk to the said company, and a beadle to be serviceable and attendant on master, wardens and assistants in all affairs of the company, to be removed for due cause. Clerk and beadle are to take corporall oath.

As great deceits and abuses are often used, committed and done by divers persons using the trade of wax chandler in the city of London, and others bringing and sending commodities of bad and insufficient stuff, and work them deceitfully, and as much white wax is brought from abroad which is mixed, corrupt and not fit to be wrought, made up or sold, all of which deceits and abuses are to the detriment of the public, for reformation thereof master and wardens, with two or more others, may as often as they think fit by all lawful means search houses, shops, etc. privileged or not privileged, have rule, correction and government by those who use said trade and are members of the company, having, bringing or putting to sale any such corrupt, mixed or bad wax as aforesaid, or make or sell any bad or corrupt wax lights, tapers, burning links, flamboys, prickets, hard wax, soft wax or any other sort of work in wax, such work to be seized and condemned.

Master, wardens and commonalty shall have full power to execute their lawful ordinances, orders and constitutions hitherto established, and to recover, levy and receive all fines and amercements imposed by distress or action for debt or in any other way according to law, to the use of the said company.

Besides property, value five marks yearly which they have bought under former letters patent, the company may buy other messuages, lands, tenements, rents, reversions, meadows, pastures, woods, underwoods, rectories, tithes and any other hereditaments within the realm, of any person, not exceeding £100 yearly in value besides all charges and reprisals, the Statute of Mortmain notwithstanding.

For the better discovery of faults, deceitful and insufficient works of things, wares and commodities belonging to the said art, it is ordained that henceforth no-one in the city of London or within ten miles of it may use and exercise the art of a wax chandler unless first he or they shall serve as apprentice or apprentices for at least seven years according to the statute of Elizabeth.

All justices of the peace, mayors, sheriffs, bailiffs, constables and other officers shall assist master and wardens or any two of them in carrying out the provisions of this patent. The present patent or enrolment thereof is to be good, sufficient, firm and effectual in law, and expounded and construed chiefly, beneficially and largely for the greatest profit, commodity and advantage of the company. If present patent or any clause of it shall hereafter be found contrary to law, prejudicial or inconvenient or not of public benefit or advantage, on declaration thereof such clauses shall be made void.

The use of the old phrase 'art or misterie', which is repeated in the subsequent ordinances, establishes this as the most formal title of the company.

The 1663 charter is still operative, but there was a period when it seemed likely to go into limbo. In 1684 Charles II, following the example of earlier kings when short of money and also wishing to show his power in the city, revived the *quo warranto*[35] procedure instituted by Edward I and had writs sent to nearly all the companies to show by what authority they used certain liberties and privileges. A contemporary record states that our master, wardens and clerk attended His Majesty at Windsor and were presented by the secretary of state, the Earl of Sunderland. On their knees they surrendered the charter, but the king having bade them rise, the clerk read a petition, which His Majesty said he would take care of and delivered to the Earl of Sunderland for safe keeping. The master and assistants knelt again and kissed the king's hand, an honour reserved for persons of distinction.

The Wax Chandlers had surrendered their charter on promise of a new one, but before this could be granted the king died, and it was nearly a year – January 1685 – before a charter was received from James II. This cost the company £161. 16*s*. 10*d*., which was raised by increasing the scale of fines, and it introduced some unwelcome alterations and limitations, including the dismissal and replacement of several members of the court. The officers and livery of the company were to hold communion with the Church of England, which James, though a Roman Catholic, had promised to defend, and the officers must have received the sacrament within six months before election; the livery must not frequent conventicles or unlawful assemblies, and they must also be approved by the mayor and aldermen. However, in 1688, the king, in a last effort to retain the throne, restored the *status quo* in the city and ordered the old charter to be handed back because its surrender was not enrolled – but it could not be found. James having fled the country in December, the validity of a contemporary transcript was confirmed by the attorney-general, Sir George Treby,[36] and in October 1689 the old assistants were able to resume their places. In the same year an act of William and Mary annulled the judgement on *quo warranto*, and the 1663 charter was officially reinstated.

Administration and finance

The new charter from Charles II was soon followed by a new set of ordinances, which were approved on 13 May, 1664, and confirmed on 28 June by Lord Clarendon and judges of the king's bench and common pleas.[37] The expenses involved amounted to nearly £50. Payments were made to:

The Lord Chancellor's secretary and clerks £10 6*s*.
The Lord Chief Justice's clerk 13*s*.
Counsel for viewing the Order 40*s*.
Lord Chief Justice Hyde for his hand and seal £7.
Counsel for examining the Order 20*s*.
Lord Chief Justice Bridgeman and his clerk £7.
The Lord Chancellor and his clerk's fees £12.
Mr. Pym for drawing the Order £3.
Mr. Rutt as appears by a bill £6. 13*s*. 11*d*.

The new ordinances covered much the same ground as in 1515, and it is likely that they reflect the practice of the time rather than introduce new ideas. Having never been superseded, they are in force today, but an escape clause is provided in the charter: the by-laws are to be observed only in so far as they are in accordance with 'the liberties and customs of the City of London'. Thus the ordinances do not stand in the way of change, provided that the city approves.

Procedures were laid down for the election of officers and for admissions to livery and freedom; those chosen for the livery were to be 'meet, honest, and of ability to be called'. Master and wardens were to be elected on the first Thursday in August 'every second year' for a two-year term. An 'honest, discreet, and fit person' was to be chosen as clerk, and another 'from the trade of waxchandlers' as beadle. Assistants, clerk, and beadle were to hold office for life. Searchers were to be appointed to assist the master and wardens on visits of inspection. All these officials were to take oaths in a prescribed form. Two stewards chosen from the livery were to provide a dinner for their brethren on lord mayor's day, and whifflers from the yeomanry were to act as constables and hold back the crowds.

Court meetings were to be held monthly or more often for normal business, and also quarterly (within 28 days of quarter-day) when the whole company was to assemble in the hall to hear orders read and pay their quarterage. Regulations were laid down for proper dress. Discipline and behaviour were to be dealt with, by expulsion if necessary. There was to be an annual audit of the accounts. Provision was made for the safe custody of valuables and for the payment of company dues (with distraint for failure to pay). A scale of fines was fixed for non-attendance, and a scale of charges for hiring the hall and bringing guests to dinner. Other rules covered place of work, qualifications of craftsmen, apprenticeship, employment of foreigners, and enticement of labour. Standards of quality were laid down and the use of a maker's mark was ordered.

Some summarised extracts from the ordinances are given below; for the text of the oaths see appendix 11.

1. Master, wardens and assistants, or majority of them, to assemble on the first Thursday in August every second year, at their common hall or other convenient place 'in decent and comely manner and in their livery gowns' to nominate persons for election as master and wardens; master, wardens and assistants then to elect one master and two wardens, who shall be sworn and shall hold and exercise office for the ensuing two years.

5. Each master, warden and assistant shall on election day on reasonable summons given or left in print or writing at his dwellinghouse or shop by the beadle of the society make personal appearances in livery gown at common hall by nine of the forenoon, and at court or meeting give his voice or hand in writing who shall be master and wardens for next two years or as required, and not leave without permission; everyone so warned and coming late to pay 2*s.* If one does not come at all to pay 5*s.*

6. Master, wardens and assistants may when they think fit make a livery or clothing in the society, and shall nominate and admit such freemen of the society as they think 'meet, honest and of ability to be called and admitted'; everyone so called to pay 30*s.* for admission, to be used as stock for corn to be provided by the society, by precept of the lord mayor yearly. Clerk to the society to have 2*s.* 6*d.* for registering and entering name; beadle to have 12*d.*

9. Masters, wardens and assistants shall when required elect an 'honest, discreet and fit person' as clerk, to give them advice and counsel in their affairs and business, to keep their courts, enter and register their accounts, etc; clerk shall hold office for life, taking all usual fees, profits and commodities, unless he be removed for good cause.

10. Master, wardens and assistants shall when required elect out of the trade of waxchandlers an honest, discreet and fit person as beadle to serve them and be attendant on master and wardens and at their lawful commandment concerning the affairs and business of the society and generally to do and execute what pertains to office; each person shall hold office for life and have customary fees, etc. unless he be removed for reasonable cause.

11. Master, wardens and assistants or majority shall keep in the common hall for quarter-day courts, within twenty-eight days of Michaelmas, Christmas, Lady day and Midsummer respectively, yearly for ever; reasonable warning to be given to every member of the company and all other persons using said art within city of London or ten miles round, left in print or writing at house or shop; freemen so summoned shall then and there pay quarterage and hear orders read; anyone absent without reasonable cause shall forfeit 1*s.* for every such default.

12. Master, wardens and assistants or majority, shall keep in the common hall once every month or oftener if necessary a court of assistants for handling, consulting, conferring, counselling and discerning articles, constitutions, orders and ordinances concerning society, and for deciding controversies, etc. and all freemen and others, if they shall have been duly summoned, and fail to attend without reasonable cause, shall forfeit 1*s*. for every such default.

13. Every person duly summoned to be at quarter-day court, court of assistants or other court to be at common hall or other appointed place for a morning meeting by 9 a.m. for an afternoon meeting at 2 p.m. and remain until court be ended; anyone coming late to be fined 8*d*., or departing early 6*d*. unless he has special leave.

14. Because decent and comely apparel is to be worn and used by the citizens of so noble a city as London, and meetings are to be in an orderly and comely manner, every master, warden and assistant shall sit at monthly and other courts in gowns and not in cloaks; everyone in livery coming to common hall for court or other reason shall come in a gown and not in a cloak; no one of the art shall come to common hall before master or wardens for court, assembly or quarter-day with his apron about him, all attending meetings are to come in decent and meet apparel; offenders to forfeit 1*s*. to master, wardens and society, those coming in aprons to pay 4*d*. to the beadle.

15. Anyone borrowing the hall shall pay 20*s*. each day for use of it to master and wardens, 10*s*. to beadle, except in case of a member of the company, when master and wardens have discretion as to charge.

16. No one shall bring a friend to dine in hall without leave of master on penalty of 2*s*. 6*d*; anyone dining in hall on quarter-day without paying a quarterage to pay 1*s*. 6*d*. each liveryman, 1*s*. for yeomanry; liverymen refusing to attend on lord mayor at dinner in Guildhall on lord mayor's day to be fined 10*s*.

18. Master and wardens or any two of them, with others, shall have authority to inspect anyone using the art of a waxchandler in the city of London or ten miles round, in matters concerning the said art, to discover abuses, deceits and falsities in workmanship and materials tending to the wrong and detriment of His Majesty's subjects and to the scandal of the said art by making wares and commodities of bad and corrupt wax or not making them of the weight, length and sizes appointed; the person aforesaid may enter houses, shops, cellars, warehouses, yards, gardens, orchards and other places used or occupied by persons using the said art, or selling products or selling English or foreign wax, in any place, to inspect wares and workmanship, to see whether they be 'well and sufficiently made and wrought and of good stuff and material, made without fraud and deceit' and of the length, weight and sizes required, a report to be made to master, wardens and assistants at next court of assistants, persons offending or failing to appear on summons to be fined not exceeding 5*s*., to be paid within ten days to use of society; anyone resisting search or refusing to pay the sums imposed to forfeit £5 for each offence.[38]

19. Persons of the company may not revile each other in open audience, if 'of the clothing', nor may those not of the clothing revile in open presence or audience any that are, offenders to forfeit 10*s*.

20. Wares and commodities of the art, viz, torches, tapers, prickets, flamboys, etc. shall be of good and perfect wax and good wick, not mixed or corrupted with turpentine, resin, tallow, etc. except the casting of torch staves which cannot be done without; every small torch to be a yard long in the wax besides a convenient snuff; every large torch an ell (45 ins.) long, with like snuff; every yellow link to weigh 1½ lb.; every black link 1¼ lb., both yellow and black to be a yard and a half-quarter long; all booke candles,[39] cearing candles[40] and soft wax to be made good and clean, all hard wax to be made of good stuff clean wrought and of good colour as good within as without, offenders to forfeit 20*s*. for each offence.

27. Every apprentice of a freeman shall within three months after his term has expired (if there be no reason otherwise) be made free of the company by presentation of his former master or mistress; persons so made free to pay 5*s*. 4*d*. to buy napery etc. for society, 3*s*. to clerk and 2*s*. to beadle: any delaying to present himself without good cause, or refusing or delaying to take oath or pay fees, to forfeit £10.

29. Yearly within thirty days after first Thursday in August the retiring master and wardens shall in common hall deliver to new master and wardens, in presence of assistants, or to auditors appointed a true plain and perfect account in writing of all receipts and payments during term of office touching the affairs and business of the company, and yield up accounts under auditors hands, as well as plate, jewels, ready money, charters, books, writings, goods, chattels, household stuff, keys, etc. in their hands belonging to the company, with a note of debts due to company; anyone refusing or neglecting to render account or deliver plate money, etc. to forfeit £100 for each offence.

30. Every one living in city of London or within ten miles thereof and using the art of a waxchandler shall have his own mark and set it upon his own wares and workmanships, except on all hard wax that is not 'perfect gumme'[41], and shall register his mark at the common hall of the company so that notice may be taken of it; anyone within the circuit aforesaid who shall neglect to set his mark on his own goods, or shall counterfeit or deface another's mark or set his own mark on another's goods or another's mark on his own or on any but the best sort of hard wax shall forfeit 40*s*. for each offence.

32. No one using the said art in the city of London or within ten miles thereof, or any other freeman of company, shall strike, beat, abuse or in any open audience jeer, mock, revile, misuse, slander, hurt or speak evil of any member of the society, on pain of forfeiting up to 20*s*. at discretion of master, wardens and assistants or majority of them, no member shall affirm anything in court that is not the truth, the whole truth and nothing but the truth, anyone refusing to give answer in any public Court on any matter coming before master, wardens and assistants for decision, or any refusing to give vote when required shall forfeit 40*s*. if he be an assistant or of livery, 20*s*. otherwise.

Throughout the ordinances emphasis is laid on the supreme authority of the court – master, wardens and assistants. 'Nine in the forenoon' was the usual time for court meetings, and for arriving late the fine was 8*d*., for leaving early 6*d*. Elections appear to have been by show of hands up to 1708, although by 1659 the company had a 'balloting box', probably the one still in use. A new scale of fines on acceptance or refusal of office or livery was laid down –

	acceptance	*refusal*
Master	£1. 0. 0.	£5. 0. 0.
Upper warden	2. 10. 0.	4. 0. 0.
Renter warden	2. 10. 0.	10. 0. 0.
Assistant	1. 0. 0.	5. 0. 0.
Livery	1. 10. 0.	10. 0. 0.

The assistant's fine on acceptance was later raised to £2. 10s., and the livery to £5. Stewards and whifflers were also liable to fines – £20 and 20*s*. respectively – on refusing their appointments.

Towards the end of the century refusals and non-payment of fines were being met by prosecution. In 1668 an assistant, Lionel Emps, was taken before the lord chancellor, the

12. A lord mayor's procession in Cheapside, 1639.

The city livery are ranged in their stands to greet Marie de' Medicis, the mother of Queen Henrietta Maria, and Charles I with his court. On the north side of the street is a fine row of shops, and the church of St. Peter Chepe can be seen at the corner of Wood Street. On the right of the picture are the Cross and the tavern sign of the Nag's Head in Friday Street, beyond which was Goldsmiths' Row.

13. A lord mayor's show on the Thames, 1789.
The water pageant with the companies' barges between Somerset House and the first Blackfriars Bridge.

company having to pay *2s. 6d.* for boat hire to Whitehall. However he produced an order from king and council exempting him both from office and from the customary fine on refusal; he was told not to attend meetings until he had paid up, and by 1672 he was back on the court. In 1691 Robert Lancashire, having served an apprenticeship, refused to take up the freedom or pay his quarterage, claiming that he had already obtained his freedom from the Shipwrights' Company though they had no livery; eventually he agreed to comply with an order of the court of aldermen, who remitted both the livery fine and the freedom fine of £20, ordering him instead to give the company a 'treate', which he agreed to do. Five years later, William Fordham refused the livery saying that he had only been a freeman for two years and needed more time. The court of aldermen ordered him to take it on, giving him two years to pay the fine (then £5), but he, 'shuffling and prevaricating', refused and was committed to Newgate: after a few hours in prison he capitulated. The stewards, whose duty it was to provide dinners for the livery, could also be reluctant: in 1694 they paid the fine and the company provided the dinner, in 1695 they made excuses – one was out of town and the other was sickly – and in 1697, having no excuse, they were prosecuted.

Searchers continued to be appointed for many years though the extended radius of operations must have made trade discipline difficult to enforce. Before the end of the previous century, the closed shop was ceasing to be a feature of every craft, and with its departure went the power to enforce standards of quality; as early as 1600 came a judicial decision, the first of a series, that the power to seize defective goods under a royal charter was contrary to common law. The only Wax Chandlers' search book in existence records their activities continuously from 1574 to 1664, but later books may have been lost. In 1671 an order was made specifying the materials and methods to be used in the manufacture of torches, and references to searches resulting in bad wares being seized and condemned still appear in the court minutes in 1677, when the penalties incurred by a successful search ranged from £1 to *2s.*

A troublesome search leading to action in the courts took place on 11 October 1664, when a party of Wax Chandlers including the master and a warden, searched the houses of Bryan Ayliff, Tallow Chandler, in Old Bailey and Giles Longe, sackman, in Bread Street. Faulty goods – candles made of wax mixed with tallow and other materials – were taken to the Guildhall, tried and condemned to be burned, which was done publicly before the Royal Exchange, at Leadenhall Market, and in Cheapside. Ayliff subsequently indicted the search party for riot, unlawful entry and seizure of candles, but on trial before the lord chief justice in February 1665 they were acquitted 'with abundance of satisfaction unto the Company'. This appears to have been an instance of a Tallow Chandler dealing in wax, and bad wax at that.

The craft apprenticeship system became more difficult to maintain, and under James I a judge ruled against compulsory apprenticeship in favour of common law, in accordance with which a man might exercise any trade whether trained to it or not. Though by no means all who were bound apprentices became freemen of the city, 80% of those admitted to the freedom in the second half of the seventeenth century were ex-apprentices; they came from all parts of the country, and their parentage varied widely – from knights to labourers. The Wax Chandlers continued to take on apprentices as is shown by their registers of bindings and presentments for and admissions to the freedom, and in 1704 it was ordered that a court should be held on the first Friday in each month for binding and making free. The binding fees laid down in the ordinances were 2*s.* 6*d.* to masters and wardens, 2*s.* to the clerk and 1*s.* to the beadle; by the end of the century, as has been seen, the 2*s.* 6*d.* was being passed over to the city orphans' fund.

Dress and behaviour were strictly regulated by the ordinances. At all meetings, 'decent and meet apparel' had to be worn, formal dress (livery gowns) rather than everyday wear (cloaks); working clothes (aprons) were strictly forbidden. The Reformation had brought a change to sober hues for the livery, and in the time of James I it was customary to wear a black gown trimmed with fur, 'foins' (polecat) for the master and wardens and 'budge' (lambs wool) for the rest. Hoods remained parti-coloured like those of university graduates. For a state procession (judging by the engraving in plate 12) a high-crowned hat might be the favoured wear. Physical and verbal abuse were frowned upon, as in the past; it was laid down that not only the livery but anyone who practised the art of a wax chandler should pay quarterage, and when attending at the hall should 'reverently carry himself towards the Master and Wardens'. Earlier, in 1616, an assistant had been dismissed the table and the court 'for scandalous words'.

Accounts were to be carefully kept and audited: in 1610 the renter warden had been dismissed the table and the court and placed lowest in the livery for not passing his accounts or paying his money in time. Later a safeguard against dishonesty was provided by a decision that no money should pass through the renter warden's hands, though the accounts were kept and receipts given in his name. Valuables such as jewels, plate, and ready money were to be kept in a chest with four locks, one key each to be held by the master, wardens, and one assistant. By 1676 similar precautions were in force for the common seals and important documents, and the renter warden had to give £300 security on taking over.

Though the need for a clerk had been recognised in the ordinances of 1514, the first name on record is John Bennett, whose signature is included with those of some liverymen of 22 companies in 1651;[42] the Wax Chandlers' list starts with Grace Hardwin master, Will Graves – warden, Thos. Hage and William Lovell. The first clerk to appear in the minutes was Lancelot Monox, a Fishmonger, who was appointed in 1670 and paid £5 a year. The clerk's salary was much less than the beadle's, which was £8 a year in 1607, and later raised to £10; in 1675 Robert Higginson was allowed an extra 1*s.* a day, but five years later his salary was stabilised at £16. In 1669 the beadle was appointed to the additional post of parish constable, good evidence of his standing in the neighbourhood. There was also some pluralism within the company: William Hitch, who died in 1695, was succeeded as beadle by Edmond Bryant, and as clerk by Robert Hanslapp after an interregnum.

The company's income continued to be derived from the rents of trust property (less the charitable distributions), fines, and quarterage – in descending order of magnitude. The ownership of properties in Aldersgate Street, Coleman Street, Maiden Lane, Old Change, and Queenhithe was confirmed by James I in 1619, the company paying £160 for the letters patent, and in 1649 they bought a further property adjacent to their land in Aldersgate Street for £40. For the year 1649–50, the total income was £242 3*s.* 5*d.*, and expenditure £221. 11*s.* 10½*d.*, leaving a credit balance of £20. 11*s.* 6½*d.* Quarterage was payable at the rate of 8*d.* for a 'housekeeper of the livery' and 6*d.* for a 'freeman of the yeomanry'; in 1669, these payments totalled £11. 6*s.* 8*d.*, including 16*s.* 8*d.* each from many members, who must have been sadly in arrears.

In 1623 there were 48 members on the livery and 100–109 on the yeomanry, in 1650 there were 32 on the livery, the total membership being 85; and in 1699 the livery numbered 79. It seems that increasing the numbers on the livery, if not limited by charter or otherwise, was a common method of recouping a company's fortunes after the Fire. By this time the yeomanry in general had become less effective in protecting the manufacturing masters from the merchants, and the name had come to mean little more than the general body of freemen below the livery. The master-piece had become a usual requirement, and it was often used to keep journeymen in their place as daily wage-earners.

Charitable distributions continued to be made under the various trusts, and the usual pensions were given to retired members together with assistance to those in need and funeral observances at the end. For an upper warden, John Morris, who died in 1651, the company attended the funeral, some going by water and their gowns being carried to the church; 'six torches' (perhaps link-boys), costing 3*s.* 6*d.*, lighted them back to the hall, where they spent £3. 0*s.* 2*d.* on their supper. Education was occasionally supported, as in 1645 when an exhibition of £2 a year was awarded to 'the sonne of a Minister towards his maintenance at Cambridge'. The company also became the trustee for two small charities – Parnell's and Frankwell's – both of which are still in operation. By his will dated 13 July, 1622, the renter warden, William Parnell, gave his messuage and tenement in Puddle Dock[43] in the parish of St. Andrew Wardrobe,[44] to provide £2 a year for poor freemen and widows of freemen of the company. And on 1 November 1658, Nicholas Frankwell, sometime vicar of Bexley where the Wax Chandlers had distributed Kendall's charity gifts for many years, gave two sums totalling £140 and yielding £6 a year for the use of the poor of that village; the court minute states that they received from Frankwell 'by his own hands £40, and more by his appointment (John Coldwell Esq of Bexley) £100 to the use of the Company paying therefrom yearly to the use of the poor of Bexley £6 on 1st November'.[45] Gifts were thus distributed at Bexley from both Kendall's and Frankwell's charities, and it became customary for the whole company to go down there with the money, no doubt a pleasant though expensive outing; sometimes the duty was left to the renter warden and the clerk.

In 1668, as a result of 'the late dreadful Fire', the court of judicature decreed that for the next forty years St. Michael's Queenhithe should receive a half-yearly payment of £13 instead of the coats and gowns that had been distributed under John Thompson's charity.

Church and parish

St John Zachary continued to be the scene of the election service and a small though regular drain on the funds. The church itself was almost completely destroyed in the fire and not rebuilt;[46] the churchyard wall was re-erected, and the site used as a burial ground. The parish was united with its neighbour, St Anne & St Agnes, whose church was also burnt down but was rebuilt by Wren. The accounts were kept separately, and the south side of St Anne's was regarded as the St John's side.

For their election service the Wax Chandlers paid, in 1610, 6*s.* 8*d.* to the parson for the sermon and 1*s.* to the clerk; from 1612, the preacher was paid 10*s.*, and in 1622 an extra shilling to the sexton 'for tolling to the sermon'. In addition the company had regular liabilities for tithes and for contributions to the church staff and the poor of the parish. Tithes were the subject of a new settlement in 1638, when Wax Chandlers' Hall was rated at £30 a year and a tithe of 8*s.* was payable; at this time there were 118 houses in the parish. 'Parish duties' in 1624 amounted to 10*s.* for 'Parson, Clarke, poore, scavenger, and Watchman' and 'more for warding'; by 1641–2 they had risen to £3. 3*s.* 8*d.* The poor rate had risen from 1s. a quarter to 4*d.* a week (for 'the poore of the p'rish of Sachareys') in 1611 and 8*d.* a week in 1625. Payments were also made to the parish lecturer,[47] a class of preacher that had been introduced to the Church of England in 1559; in 1615–6 candles for the lectures cost 13*s.* 1*d.* Casual payments included 5*s.* in 1605 and 10s. in 1609 'towards the bylding of a house for the Parson', and £2 in 1611 towards extensive repairs to the church; also 16*s.* in 1643–4 'for the reliefe of maymed souldiers' of the Civil War. For the first five years after the fire, the city paid £100 a year to the parish poor, but thereafter the company was liable for £2. 12*s.* 0*d.* a year, which was reduced to £1. 14*s.* 8*d.* in the early eighteenth century. The parson was paid £1. 10*s.* 0*d.* 'for his yeare's duties' in the 1670's.

In 1679–80 the Wax Chandlers (with the Goldsmiths) demurred against an assessment of £15. 12*s.* 0*d.* for pews and other ornaments; proceedings against the company at Doctors Commons[48] were successful and resulted in payments of £9 in 1683–4 for pewing the church and £4. 17*s.* 6*d.* for 2½ years' poor rate at 9*d.* a week, and also agreement that the poor rate should go back to 8*d.* a week. The company's expenses are shown as –

Paid Councellors ffees att Doctors Comans, 4*li*
spent there, 1*li* 6*s* 9*d*
with the parson of the parish, 3*s*
and with the workmen, 6*s*
given the Lord Cheife Justice's Clarke, 2*s* 6*d*
expended when the sentence was pronounced, 10*s* 6*d*.

The churchwardens' accounts show that they spent 'at Mr. Fowler's at the Half-moon Tavern with the Master & Wardens of the Wax Chandlers & Committee there of our parish 5*s.* 6*d.*' and that they paid 'at Captain Tucker's on receiving of Wax-chandlers money', £1. 9*s.* 0*d.* Richard Tucker was the renter warden.

There are few records of Wax Chandlers living in the parish but interments included those of James Edmantes (a former beadle) in 1603, William Hitch (clerk and beadle) in 1695, and George Davison, described as 'a Child out of Wax Chandlers' Hall', in 1701.

The hall and the plate

The Tudor hall, which had been redecorated in 1610–1 for £8 as part of local improvements in honour of the Goldsmith's mayor, Sir James Pemberton, whose mansion lay nearby, seems to have remained structurally intact until the middle of the century. There was an abortive attempt to 'enlarge and beautify' it in 1640, and in 1657 a substantial rebuilding scheme was put in hand. The minute of 30 January reads: 'in regard Our hall is to Little for the Companie to meete in itt is this daye ordered that the Cock Ale house now belongeinge unto the said Companie bee pulled downe and that itt bee new built for the inlargeinge the hall and makeinge A new parlor with Other roomes Over itt and shoppes And sellers under itt and alsoe under the hall and alsoe that the shopp in which the haberdaishere noe Liveeth with the parlor now belongeinge to the said hall and the Tresury roome[49] bee made into A Teniment for the best Advantage of the said Companie.' The next meeting ordered a model to be made from drawings supplied by the architect, Samuel Berry; at this stage, the hall door was to be in Gutter Lane, but it was later decided to keep it in 'Maydenlane as itt was in time past.' Two meetings were held to consider alterations in the plans, and £23 was spent with Berry and Peter Mills, the city 'surveyor' or architect on 'priseing (appraising) the old house'. By October it was clear that the new hall would not be ready for lord mayor's day so the steward was told 'not to mak his feast' for the time being; for this release from duty he paid £15 towards the rebuilding.

By the end of 1657 the rebuilding costs totalled £492. 10*s.* 0*d.*, towards which £483 was taken out 'oft the thessary chist':

Samuell Berry £100	Mr. Rogers plumber £20
Mr. Fry[50] £30	Mr. Harding smith £20
Mr. Berry £100	Mr. Bowne glazier £10
Mr. Fry £57. 10*s.* 0*d.*	Mr. Dogood plaisterer £50
Mr. Berry £80	Mr. Evanson joiner £25

There were also miscellaneous expenses such as 48*s.* for black-and-white tiles for the parlour chimney, £3. 2*s.* 0*d.* for 'a dosen of rushy leather chairs and stools', 7*s.* 0*d.* for '1 dosen turky chairs'. Running water was provided, perhaps for the first time, 22*s.* 8*d.* being paid to Sir Hugh Myddelton's New River Company, which had constructed a 40-mile channel from springs in Hertfordshire in 1609–13.[51]

On 25 January 1658, William Russell, who had leased the adjoining house in Maiden Lane, was given leave to make two rooms over the treasury room. The expense of rebuilding must have left the company short of money, for in the following June it was decided to dispose of some plate – '68 silver gilt spoons, 3 old fashion belly pots, one masyure cupp tipt with silver and 1 jugg with a silver cover'; these were sold the same day and brought in £55. 17*s*. 10*d*. A full inventory prepared in January 1659 still includes 82 spoons, which may have been the balance remaining after the sale or may indicate that the spoons sold had been brought in by members and given back to the company; there were many precedents for this. The full plate list was as follows –

A Basson and ane Euer
Seven gilt Salts
Three Beakers parcell (partly) guilt
Three Standing guilt cups with covers
Three great Broad wyne bowles parcell guilt
Sex guilt cupps two bigger the other four smaller
Eight wyne bowles whyte
Three beer boules whyte two bigger the other Smaller
Eighty and two Silver Spoones

There was also a quantity of pewter including a chamber pot,[52] together with kitchen utensils, weapons, and a balloting box. Leather fire buckets were kept in the gallery, and a lead cistern in the yard; in 1618 there had been '2 Sesternes of Lead in the kitchen', but one must have been turned out. There had also been a 'hearse Clothe for Burialles' in the gallery.

The accommodation consisted of a first-floor dining room with closet and kitchen behind, two bed-chambers above, and two garrets; on the ground floor was a shop (perhaps the old Cock?) with a cellar beneath and an entry. The dining room was 'wainscoted around' with faced benches on each side and was furnished with three tables, nine forms and two old chairs. Little is known of the decorations, except for the Tudor stained glass and tapestry hangings. The parlour had the twelve 'Turkey work' chairs and six 'Rushy leather' chairs with six matching stools. One of the chambers was partly wainscoted. In the chamber over the parlour, which may have been used as a store room, were kept twenty-three green feather cushions, two cloth-of-gold cushions, and 'a cushione given by Mr. Bewly with the companyes Armes'; 'four window Cussiones off blue velvett wrought with figures off gold', a 'Blew barge cloth'; 'Severall old streemers for the Barge'; and a 'Great Chist', perhaps the one that came from St. Blaise.

Six years later, in 1666, came the destruction of the buildings with most of their contents in the Great Fire. However, within a fortnight (on 21 September) the court was able to hold an emergency meeting at 'the sign of Redd Cross in Little Britain'. It was found that the company owed £250, which had been borrowed on behalf of the king, but an assistant, Edward Reeve, offered to lend them £200 at 6%, which, with £60 in the treasury chest, enabled the debt to be repaid; they also decided 'to weigh the plate and make a bill of sale of it at 4*s*. 6*d*. per ounce' to Reeve, perhaps as security for the loan. A few days later they handed £12 to William Rutt, the immediate past master, 'for certain goods he lost at the Hall by the Fire in saving the Company's plate writings books and other goods and money etc'. In December, when it was still difficult to assemble a court as 'they were all busy looking after their houses', a committee was appointed with instructions to sell the plate and other goods, get back the £250 lent to the king, and put rebuilding in hand. Three months later, in March 1667, £150 was borrowed on the security of the Aldersgate Street property, which had escaped the fire, and this money was allotted to Rutt, who, following his good work in rescuing chattels from the hall, seems to have been given the main responsibility for the rebuilding; he was told to start with 'the Kitchin and a Roome over it with a convenient little garret'. Though the new kitchen was duly brought into use, money must again have run short, for it was not until November 1668, when a windfall of £310 1*s*. 8*d*. had come in from the king and the scale of fines had been increased, that it was decided to clear the ground and rebuild the outer walls of the hall itself; £350 was allotted to this work.

One of the leading city architects, Edward Jerman, was engaged and was paid an initial fee of £50, and later £38 'for work' and a further £100 'for work already done or to be done'; he also designed the new Royal Exchange (at the same fee) and the halls of many other companies.[53] Also concerned was Peter Mills, the city surveyor, who would have had to pass the plans and may have acted as a consultant. Mills and Jerman with Robert Hooke, the physicist of Hooke's law and a notable inventor, had been appointed by the city to work with three government 'commissioners for rebuilding'.[54]

Some extracts from the accounts are given below:

To June 1667:
Paid to Mr. Mills the Surveyer 10*s*
10 poles and 20 putt loates (padlocks?) £2 10*s*
Boat hier Cartage and Wharfage 3*s* 8*d*
Mr. ffry Per Bill £4 9*s* 6*d*
Mr. Robinson for brickes £4
Mr. ffry 2 Bills £11 1*s* 2*d*
6000 Bricks £3 10*s* 0*d*
the Scrivener £1
3500 bricks £4 7*s* 6*d*
Mr. ffry as per Bill £4 17*s* 8*d*
9500 Bricks £9 10*s*
4C & ½ Boardes at 7*d* per Pi (piece?) £31 10*s*
Cartage & Loading 8 Loades £1
Mr. ffry as per Bill £9 3*s* 6*d*
Mr. Hunt as per Bill £81 5*s*
given the Workmen to drincke 2*s*
Mr. Robinson per Bill £3
Mr. ffry per bill £9 16*s*
the Carpenter as per Bill £45 3*s* 8*d*
in full for 6500 Brickes £2 10*s* 6*d*
Mr. ffry as per bill £6 9*s*
in full for Tyles £8 15*s*
a Cart 1*s*
a peece of Timber 10*s*
Mr. ffry as per Bill £1 14*s* 2*d*
Lathes as per Bill £2 7*s*
3 Boardes for the Table and Cariadge 16*s*
the Ironmongers Bill £3 15*s*
the Carpenters Bill £16 19*s*
a Locke 1*s* 4*d*
a Dresser £1 6*s* 9*d*
the plasterers bill £9 11*s*
the plumbers bill £3 4*s*
the Ironmongers bill £1 3*s*
Also for a Riddle 9*s*

9 Bagges lime 4*s* 6*d*
300 Tyles 7*s* 6*d*
15 Bundles Lathes £1 1*s* 6*d*
15 of Burnt Lead at 8 per Pi £7 17*s*
24 Boardes at 14*d* per peece £1 8*s*

1667-9:

Paid to Mr. Jerman's man 12*d*
pulling downe the pales about the hall ground 6*s*
Mr. Jerman £50
the bricklayer £30
the Plaisterer bill £40
Cookes bill £18 6*s* 6*d*
the Scrivener 20*s*
the measurer for the bricke worke 20*s*

1669-71:

Paid to Mr. Jerman for work £38
Carving work £9 10*s*
Stonecutter £5 7*s*
Plumer £40
Smith 31*s*
2000 Tiles 40*s*
drink and bread when Mr. Fry paid his money 15*d*
putting a stop to the next work 3*s* 6*d*
Candlelight at the hall door 22*d*
a labourer for clearing the yard 18*d*
Davis the joiner in full £43 6*s* 8*d*
Cosford the plasterer £20 13*s*
" " " £15
Mr. Drake upholsterer £9 5*s*
Sanders for painting the Arms 30*s*
Carver for carving the Company's Arms £6
Upholsterers for covers for chairs £1 16*s*

Eventually the new hall was completed, and the first meeting was held there on 29 September 1670. It was almost certainly built of brick with stone dressings, in accordance with the post-fire statutory regulations against timber, and probably in the English classical style as practised by Wren. The accommodation provided was much as before, though a narrow strip of land on the Gutter Lane side was lost for street widening entailed by the replanning of London. There were a 'great roome' and a 'little parlour' with cellar beneath, a 'great Garrett' and a buttery; behind the hall itself was the paved yard and kitchen, and above this two more rooms and a garret. The total cost must have been considerable, certainly more than £500,[55] say £5000 in modern money. Member's contributions ranged from £5 for each of the livery to £1 for a freeman and 10*s*. for an apprentice, and this and other means of raising money were still being employed in 1674.

Running water continued to be supplied by the New River Company, an agreement of 1681 reading (in part) as follows:

> Indenture made 30 March 33 Charles II between the governour and Company of the New River brought from Chadwel and Amwel to London on the one part, and the Worshipful Company of Wax Chandlers on the other part . . .
>
> The said governor and Company in consideration of the sum of thirty shillings in hand paid, in the name of a fine or income . . . have demised and granted to the Company one watercourse, conveniently furnished with water running in and through one small Branch or Pipe of lead containing half an inch of water or thereabouts and in and through five small cocks of Brass souldered and set into the same, and placed in the kitchen and yard . . .
>
> (Seal attached 'Brought from Chadwell and Amwel to London').

No portraits or pictures are mentioned in the inventories of the new hall, but the company's arms were displayed, and also the royal arms when appropriate. As always, the latter had to keep up with the times, and the cost of loyalty was not negligible –

1641–2: Paid for taking out the King's armes out of our Cullors, being comaunded to doe so from above, xxiiij*s* xj*d*.

1651–2: Paid for painting the flag with the States (Commonwealth's) arms 3*li* 5*s*.

1668–9: Paid the Harould Painter for the King's and for the Companye's Armes, vij *li*.

1675–6: Paid for the King's Armes Carved for the Parlour, 3 *li* 10*s*.
for painting and gilding the Armes and to the Smyth for worke about them, 2 *li* 2*s*.

In order to expedite the rebuilding of London, many craft rights were abrogated by the king's orders, and it was laid down by statute that all those who assisted should be allowed to work in the city for seven years thereafter, and then for their lives, becoming equal with freemen. Also the common council ordered that every practising joiner, carpenter or mason should be made free of the companies concerned, even though they were already freemen of another company, and as late as 1699 the Wax Chandlers had to lead a resistance movement to protect their members from poaching.

Though left with a load of debt, all the companies had rebuilt their halls within five years of the fire: despite the loss of their property investments they were on the road to prosperity, and the city was regaining its 'Ancient Shows and Solemnities'. The Wax Chandlers' feasts were usually held on lord mayor's, midsummer, election and quarter days, but they might be omitted when economies were necessary. In 1656, when money was to be spent on the hall, feasting had been confined to one dinner on midsummer day, and nine years later the plague had caused all feasts to be abandoned. Towards the end of the century economies were again the order of the day: in 1690 'a small Collation for the Court of Assistants only' was served on election day, and in 1696 the election feast was cancelled for the next eight years since 'the company's stock was low'. In normal times, musicians were in attendance, and in 1655 the court decided to invite wives regularly on lord mayor's day; this continued for 40 years or so. In 1692 there was a feast for livery and their wives, but no mention of 'damsels', who in some other companies appear to have been recognised as dining companions.

Two lists of expenses for seventeenth-century feasts are given below:

A Midsummer Dinner

	£	*s.*	*d.*
2 Leggs of Lamb and Collyflowers		6	0
2 Gallons of Beans 3*s* 6 lb of Bacon 4*s*		7	0
2 Geese 6*s* 4 Chickens 6*s* Strawberries 6*s*		18	0
	£1	11	0

A Quarter Day Dinner, June 24, 1669

	£	*s.*	*d.*
A Sr Loyne and 4 Ribs of Beefe Weight 7 stone 1½ lb at 2*s* 4*d* per stone		16	10 (*sic*)
4 Legs of Mutton Wt 41 lb at 3¾ [*d*] per lb		12	9
4 Shoulders of Veale...		14	0
10 lb of Bacon		7	6

	£	s	d
9 lb of Butter...		4	10½
Carrets and Collyflowers		3	6
3 Gallons of Beans		3	0
Bread		5	6
Wine	1	8	0
Oranges and Lemons		2	6
Strawberrys		3	8
Sugar		1	0
Tobacco			6
The Cook		5	0
The House Bill	2	2	8
	£7	11	3½

'A Bill of Fare for the Stewards' who provided the dinner on 'Ld Maior's Day', probably towards the end of the seventeenth century, was as follows:

Boyled Pullets & Bacon 3 in a dish wth Oysters
Rost Tong & Udder
Venison Pasty
Rost Gees 2 in a Dish
Minced Pyes
Rost Capons 2 in a Dish
Custard
Warden Pye[56]
Wine
Bread & Beere

On the same page of manuscript is a note of '7 Belts and 15 or 16 knotts of Blew & Yellow Ribbons for Whifflers and bearers,' presumably a reminder to provide these accessories. A further note calls for 'Rost Beefe for Breakfast' and 'A Sr Lyne of Rost Beefe for ye side Tables'.

From time to time the new hall was let, a common practice in many companies and usually for dancing which had become popular in the reaction against Puritanism. In 1678 'all that greate roome, commonly called the Hall, being in the messuage or tenement commonly called Wax Chandlers' Hall' was let for £20 a year. In 1708, when the rent had gone up to £25, the tenant was George Priest,[57] a dancing master from Chelsea; the use of hall, kitchen, and cellars was reserved to the company for public occasions, and a room over the kitchen to the master and wardens eight times a year. A more troublesome tenant of a shop under part of the hall was a blacksmith, who in 1693, having resisted attempts to remove him, proposed to put in a forge; with the co-operation of the landlady of the house next door an accommodation seems to have been reached.

Nearly all the company's plate was rescued from the fire, as were many of its books and documents and also the twelve Turkey-work chairs and other furnishings. However the plate appears to have been sold to help pay for the rebuilding, and the extent of the loss may be gauged from a list drawn up in 1664. It included 97 silver spoons, no doubt livery fines. From this period there survives one spoon (plate 7), 9 ins. long, having a gilt knop forming a seal-top engraved with a bee-hive; the stem is inscribed on one side 'WILLIAM COLEBVRNE 1653' and on the other '1667 Twice presented to the Company for their use & no other ways to be disposed of.' There is also a silver head for the beadle's staff, which is still carried before the master on ceremonial occasions; it is embossed in high relief with the company's arms surmounting a bee-hive, and first appears as one of two in 1664.

Several other pieces of silver go back to the time of Charles II and are still in the company's collection: these include two tankards, a set of six trencher salts, a pair of spoons, and a tall standing cup and cover (plates 7 and 6). The tankards are inscribed 'Samuel Shepheard', probably the name of the donor, and are dated 1673; a matched pair of this period is almost unique. The salts were purchased in 1675 at a cost of £2. 13*s*. 3*d*. The spoons are hall-marked 1681 and were probably gifts of liverymen on admission; they are of the trifid pattern with two notches in the flat end of the stem.

But the greatest treasure is the standing cup, which was acquired in 1683 from Richard Normansell, the company's tenant in Aldersgate Street, and is still known by his name. Normansell, who is said to have been a 'secondary' or deputy-in-charge of the Compter in Poultry, owned property in St. Botolph-without-Aldersgate, and he had become interested in 'two messuages near the church', which were leased to a tenant at £20 a year. They were in such a bad state of repair that he spent £250 in putting them in order, and on 18 October 1683 the Wax Chandlers granted him a repairing lease[58] for 53 years from Christmas 1691 at £10 a year; for this he paid the company £170 and handed them silver plate to the value of £20 – hence the Normansell cup.[59]

The chief feature of this cup, and one that suggests it was made specially for the Wax Chandlers, is that it is engraved with scenes relating to bee-keeping and beeswax candles (fig. 4). On the cover are shown a taper-roller fitted with scissor-snuffers, a melting cauldron on a fire, a man with a ladle and turnspit, a figure lighting a large taper beside a reading-desk, and a woman with a sickle cutting cotton for wicks. On the bowl, besides the arms of Normansell and the company and an inscription recording the gift, are a man 'tingling'[60] or charming a swarm of bees and another hiving bees from the bough of a tree. On the foot are bee-hives on stands and some miscellaneous devices. The cover has a gilt finial depicting a female figure, probably Minerva, with spear and shield.

The Normansell cup is one of those used regularly at the company's banquets for the ceremony of the 'loving cup':[61]

> This custom is believed to have originated in the ninth century when Alfred, king of the West Saxons from 871, had suzerainty over the whole of England, but did not control directly the Danish kingdom of York, so that the country was still divided. Many attempts were made to get Saxons and Danes to live peaceably together, but treachery was common, especially during the act of drinking. So Oslac the cup bearer, who was also a grandfather of Alfred, arranged for the leaders of the two sides to pledge in public their goodwill to maintain the king's peace. To make sure that the dagger hands of their unruly followers

were visible and occupied, every drinking cup was fitted with a cover, which had to be held by the man facing the drinker. However his back was still unprotected, and in about 978 Edward the Martyr[62] is said to have been stabbed from behind while drinking. As a result it became the custom for a second man to stand back to back with the drinker, thus giving the additional protection required.

In the London loving cup ceremony as used by the Wax Chandlers, the master, as host, and the principal guest drink first, each from his own cup, the covers being held aloft by the cupbearer and his assistant. To the music of *Gaudeamus*[63] the covers are replaced and the host and the principal guest turn to their neighbours, who are now standing. All bow, and the neighbours remove the covers; the host and the principal guest drink a second time, and their neighbours replace the covers and turn to the next guests. The ceremony is repeated by everyone in turn, and so the cup passes round the table. While anyone is drinking his neighbour stands back to back with him in order to prevent an attack from behind.

Hope, like the gleaming taper's light,
Adorns and cheers our way . . .
GOLDSMITH

4. Chinoiserie engraving on the Normansell cup.

Among many scenes associated with bees and candles, the two larger designs above show a man first tingling and then hiving a swarm.

Notes on Chapter III

[1]'Begun to burn wax candles in my closet at the office . . . to see whether the smoke offends like that of tallow candles' – an experimental approach that was worthy of a president of the Royal Society; the Admiralty had always specified the best London tallow.

[2]Under 9 Anne *c* 6. A further act in 1784 did not apply to candles of wax or spermaceti.

[3]Excise duties, which were levied on home-produced consumer goods, brought indirect taxation into the fiscal system. First enacted by the Long Parliament in 1643 to pay for the Civil War, they were a more efficient substitute for the sale of monopolies.

[4]A tax of 1*s*. 6*d*. to 3*s*. on each tun of wine or liquor and 6*d*. to 1*s*. on each pound of dry goods imported or exported. It was first levied in 1371 and finally abolished in 1787; James I asserted his right to vary the rates, and the widespread discontent expressed by Hampden contributed to the outbreak of the Civil War.

[5]The prospectus was entitled 'Motives and Reasons to induce the Cittie of London to understake Plantation in the North of Ireland'; incidentally it pointed out that 'The countrie is very fitt for honnye & waxe'.

[6]The difficulties in raising the money led to some wardens being sent to prison.

[7]The Haberdashers sold their land, also to the Beresford family, in 1741.

[8]The whole enterprise was dogged by misfortune, the returns were negligible, and in 1624 the crown took over the colony, revoking the Virginia Company's charter.

[9]In 1634–5 £2 was paid through the parish for the 'Pallatinate briefe'.

[10]The city had to provide a total of ten ships, the last of which was paid for by the twelve great companies. The tax was abolished in 1641.

[11]The Irish Society was re-established under Charles II in 1662.

[12]Under 16 Charles I, *c* 9.

[13]*A perfect Diurnall of some Passages in Parliament* (Thomason Tracts, British Museum).

[14]The hearth (or chimney) tax was most unpopular and was abolished in 1689.

[15]The large amount of £1,200,000 was raised privately and lent to the government at 8% interest, the birth of the National Debt, and the subscribers were incorporated as The Governor and Company of the Bank of England.

[16]So important was 'the Greenwax' that it became the usual term for the money collected thereby.

[17]The king's faithful financial adviser, and the initiator, rather than Nell Gwynn, of Chelsea Hospital; his influential position in the royal household and government was retained under Anne, and his many places brought him enormous wealth, at one time amounting to £200,000.

[18]From the Holland House Papers (British Museum).

[19]The cathedral spire had been struck by lightning in 1561, and not replaced, and by the time of Charles I the whole building had deteriorated almost to a ruin through neglect and ill-usage; though some restoration was carried out by Inigo Jones, it was the complete destruction wrought by the Great Fire that allowed Wren to build his great classical monument. In the years before the fire, the company had been paying 2*s*. 6*d*. a year 'for the pews at St. Paul's Church', perhaps to reserve sittings for special occasions.

[20]They had previously decided to buy a barge, the members contributing towards the cost, but nothing came of it.

[21]Built by Humphrey, Duke of Gloucester, in the reign of Henry VI and used extensively by Plantagenet and Tudor monarchs; it was destroyed in the Great Fire.

[22]Link: a crude type of torch; Shakespeare makes Falstaff declare to the red-nosed Bardolph: 'Thou hast saved me a thousand marks in links and torches, walking with thee in the night betwixt tavern and tavern.' (*King Henry IV*, part 1, III, iii). Links were still used in the nineteenth century for lighting doorways and, carried by link boys, for escorting sedan chairs.

[23]A force raised by the companies in 1572 for service in Holland was taken into the army in 1665 and long known as The Buffs; in recent amalgamations they were brought into The Queen's Own Buffs The Royal West Kent Regiment.

[24]'An Act for the Rehabilitation of Orphans and other Creditors of the City of London' (5 & 6 Wm. & Mary *c* 10); a framed extract can be seen in the hall.

[25]The former importance of such duties is recalled by the present Coal and Corn and Rates Finance Committee, which controls the city's cash.

[26]The orphan's debt was gradually redeemed, coal being the most important element, and by 1820 it had been extinguished.

[27]This was the last appearance in England of bubonic plague, the 'black death' of the fourteenth century, which had become endemic and had originated earlier Stuart outbreaks, causing 31,000 deaths in 1603 and 43,000 in 1625.

[28]They covered the city, the out-parishes and Westminster.

[29]A chaldron is stated to have equalled 36 bushels, perhaps 1 or 2 tons of coal.

[30]A noble was a gold coin, usually worth 6*s.* 8*d.*

[31]The custom that royal patents expired with the sovereign and had to be confirmed (with fees) ceased in 1660, when feudal dues were abolished in return for the promise of a fixed regular income.

[32]In this century the name Grace was sometimes given to boys.

[33]The original document was lost, probably by James II (see page 76); the extracts are from a contemporary transcript (*MS 9498*) with some added punctuation.

[34]In years to come – otherwise it would contradict the references to elections 'every second year' and holding office for 'the ensuing two years' in the ordinances.

[35]*Quo warranto*, the Statute of Gloucester (1278), authorised the justices to inquire into the private courts held by the great feudal lords.

[36]He was formerly the city's recorder.

[37]Clarendon, born Edward Hyde, was Charles' faithful chancellor and architect of the Restoration; the two judges who signed were Robert Hyde and Orlando Bridgeman.

[38]Penalties in ordinances 18, 19, 20, 27 and 30 were subject to a *caveat*: 'or such less sum as master, wardens, and assistants shall decide'.

[39]Book candles: for use in spring-loaded sockets to keep the flame at reading height.

[40]Cering candles: for waxing cerecloths or winding sheets. In 1603 Sophia, the infant daughter of James I, when she was embalmed, was cered by the wax chandler, laid in lead by the plumber, and entombed in a cradle monument.

[41]Of the right consistency??

[42]*Harleian MS 4778*, printed in J. C. & W. Whitebrook, *London Citizens in 1651*, 1909.

[43]Puddle Dock, near Blackfriars, was originally the wharf of a Norman fortress, the first Baynard's Castle; it is now only a street-name alongside the modern Mermaid Theatre.

[44]St. Andrew (by the) Wardrobe took its name from the royal Wardrobe, the office that kept the Sovereign's ceremonial clothing up to 1709.

[45]The records of Frankwell's gifts are confused, but his piety is clear enough: he is also stated to have given in 1621 £10 'to pay £10 a year to twenty Poor Inhabitants of Bexley attending in the church'.

[46]The lead and the bell metal were sold for £77, and the stones and rubble for £37.

[47]Lecturers proliferated owing to the Puritan demand for a preaching clergy independent of the hierarchy. They were usually chosen by the parish and supported by voluntary contribution; their duties were not ministerial but were mainly to deliver afternoon or evening 'lectures' or sermons.

[48]The building in Knightrider Street where ecclesiastical courts were held and doctors of civil law dined together at a common table.

[49]Perhaps the 'chamber' where the charter and title-deeds were kept.

[50]This was Robert Fry, Bricklayer and Tyler, to whom the Queenhithe property was leased in 1660; his premium or 'fine' provided the £30 contributed by the company towards welcoming Charles II at the Restoration.

[51]The Metropolitan Water Board still has its headquarters at New River Head in Clerkenwell.

[52]This was specified as for use in the hall itself, but there was an old-fashioned privy in the 'vault' or cellar.

[53]E.g., the Drapers, Fishmongers, and Mercers.

[54]As there were few professional architects, it was necessary to choose experienced amateurs, both for the city representatives and for the royal commissioners; each of them designed many notable buildings, though one of the commissioners, Christopher Wren, was a professor of astronomy and mathematics and at that time the least qualified in architecture.

[55]There was no fire insurance until the Phenix opened in 1680, but by 1699 the hall was being insured 'for £500 as formerly'.

[56]Made from the Warden pear, a good keeping variety.

[57]Priest (Preist) was a member of the Turners', whose own hall was also let for dancing.

[58]*MS 9512*, item 17.

[59]*MS 9507*, item 20. The wording on the cup reads 'The Gift of Richard Normansell Gent. Tenant to ye Companie'.

[60]The tinkling sound from two pieces of metal was thought to attract the bees of an air-borne swarm and induce them to settle.

[61]A tall standing cup was invariably used until the eighteenth century, when the large two-handled cup was introduced as an alternative. An inventory of 1856 uses another name, 'grace' cup, which derives from a ceremony instituted in the eleventh century by Margaret, the saintly queen of Malcolm Canmore; she had a cup filled with the choicest wine and circulated after the meal to induce the Scots to stay for grace.

[62]Edward the Martyr, the young king of England, was murdered in 978 by his stepmother while drinking mead at Corfe Castle; he was long venerated as a saint in the Roman martyrology, and 18 March is still a black-letter day in the English Prayer Book.

[63]The very ancient student's song beginning '*Gaudeamus igitur, juvenes dum sumus*' (let us therefore rejoice while we are young); the tune was used by Brahms in his Academic Festival overture.

14. Wax Chandlers' Hall, 1793.

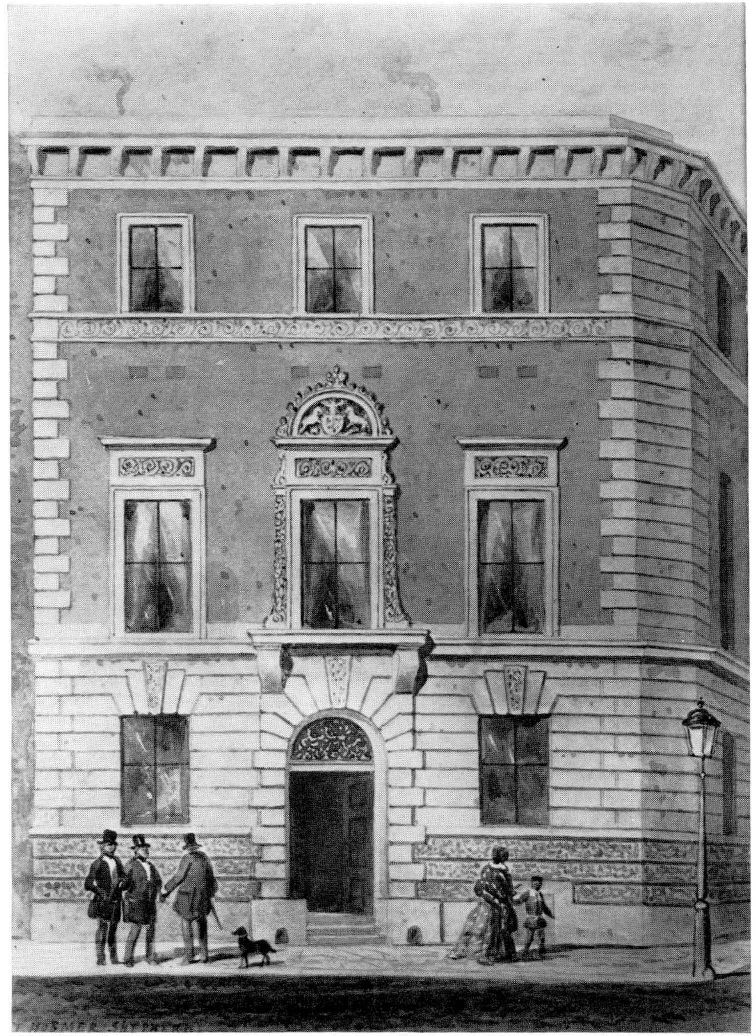

15. Wax Chandlers' Hall, 1854.

16. Wax Chandlers' Hall: the rebuilding of 1958.

On the right is part of Goldsmiths' Hall and the site of St. John Zachary church (immediate foreground).

CHAPTER IV

Industrial Revolution : 1714 - 1899

AS WITH many other livery companies the most memorable period of Wax Chandlers' history ends with the seventeenth century, though there is still much that is interesting to record. However, most companies had ceased to carry out searches, and those that continued became rare exceptions. Where some control of the trade survived it was eventually broken by the Industrial Revolution; manufacturers would not submit to searches by competitors or supervision by an independent body like a gild. The triumph of free trade spelled the end not only of protection but also of the powers of protected crafts.

In spite of the decline of their original functions the companies rose to a peak of prosperity owing to the rise in the value of property, and many of them accumulated considerable wealth. It was therefore no surprise that in the mid-nineteenth century there arose a hostile element, which considered that they had ceased to fulfil any useful functions and that their money could be more usefully employed. In 1880 a movement to investigate the companies' operations led to the appointment of a Royal Commission, which produced two largely contradictory reports: the majority were highly critical, but the minority put up a strong defence. It was pointed out that on average more than a third of the corporate income was given to charitable purposes and less than a third went on hospitality and entertainment, and that land purchased under the charters was inalienable: any excuse for confiscation could be applied equally to any friendly society. No action was taken, but inasmuch as the extent of the companies' benefactions received general recognition, the investigation served a useful purpose, and it seems to have stirred up many of them to play a more useful part in the life of the nation.[1] An earlier commission set up to enquire into municipal corporations had also dealt with the city and the livery companies in its second report of 25 April 1837, but again no action was taken. However, the 1837 and the 1884 reports together provide a wealth of useful information, though not always accurate or complete.

For the Wax Chandlers, with the general reduction in the use of candles and the replacement of beeswax by other materials, the original craft lost much of its importance, and the company's activities became centred more and more on its domestic affairs. However the years were not without their highlights, for instance a personal contribution to the government of the city, besides common councilmen, aldermen, and a city chamberlain, the company provided five sheriffs, and three of these proceeded to lord mayor –

though it must be admitted that one was a lapsed Wax Chandler as he had previously transferred to another company. The hall was rebuilt twice, once because the old building could no longer be repaired and once because of compulsory acquisition for street widening. The company survived an attack on its major charity, that of William Kendall, though not without considerable financial loss (owing to long and expensive litigation) and a permanent reduction in its scope for benevolence. Apart from these events the court minutes deal mainly with the welfare of members, the management of trust and other property – they were always 'taking views' – and various charitable and educational projects, together with the formal business and ceremonial.

The wax trade

No doubt the traditions of craftmanship inspired the technical skill and ingenuity of the first industrialists, but the rise of the factories meant the disappearance of the craft companies as organising bodies in industry. Workmen had ceased to market their own products, and their interests lay more in wages than in prices. Having only their labour to sell they tended to turn away from the gilds, an essential feature of which was that masters and men had a common interest in maintaining standards and restricting output, and sought for other organisations that could fight for better pay and conditions. In the second half of the eighteenth century came the great mechanical inventions and the factory system with its higher efficiency but less personal freedom. The master capitalist was concerned to increase output rather than limit it, and to erect factories employing as many as possible, not as few. The putting-out system in its turn was doomed to decay.

Candle-making however remained a craft, employing the old methods with relatively few workers in any one establishment.[2] Though candles were gradually disappearing for general lighting purposes owing to the improvements in oil lamps (followed at the beginning of the nineteenth century by the introduction of gas and electricity), they retained their decorative value; used in large quantities in the right surroundings they could make a great impression, as for instance, the 3,000 wax candles in Westminster Hall for the coronation banquet of George III and the '28 lustres, each holding 60 wax lights' for that of George IV. Their lavish use in the royal household was so much abused that a grace-and-favour resident could write in 1812 that 'ye pages charged ten thousand pounds a year for wax candles and sold the half of them for their own profit' to 'all the people of Windsor'.[3] The candle tax was repealed in 1831, but by that time both beeswax and tallow were being superseded by new materials – spermaceti followed by stearine[4] and finally paraffin wax, still the most important of all.

For church candles on the other hand, beeswax continued to be prescribed, though increasing sales were accompanied by a relaxation of the 100% purity originally required. By the time of James II Roman Catholic rites had been openly celebrated despite the penal laws, and toleration was extended by the Catholic Emancipation Act of 1829 followed by the re-establishment of the English hierarchy in 1850. Henceforward beeswax had to form only 'a notable part' (65%) of candles lighted during mass;[5] it still had to be white, except at masses for the dead, funerals, and Holy Week services when yellow unbleached wax was permitted. In the Church of England the Anglo-Catholics of the mid-nineteenth century brought back lighted candles for the altar, and they were officially recognised in 1890; though candles came into general use, it was without the original liturgical significance or indeed the necessity for an inclusion of beeswax.

Another major product lost by the trade was sealing wax.[6] There had been an extensive business in seals in London, where the chief courts of law lay within the ten-mile radius of the company's monopoly, but during the nineteenth century beeswax, which had long been the main component, was generally abandoned in favour of shellac and resin. A paper substitute is now in common use.

The status of the Wax Chandler, his working conditions and wage rates can be gathered from two publications of 1747.[7] One, a recruiting pamphlet addressed to parents, guardians, and trustees states that though 'the number of this trade . . . is not near so great as that of the other' (the Tallow Chandlers), it is 'esteemed a very reputable as well as a gainful business, to transact which in they have also handsome Shops. As to the work it is full as heavy, dirty, and noisome, though not so much in the Night; yet they expect with an Apprentice 50*l.* a journeyman can earn at it 15*s.* a Week or 16*l.* a Year and Diet; but it will take 500*l.* to set him up'. The second book avers that the business 'is still more than that of the Tallow Chandler and reckoned the more genteel trade. Journeymen earn the common Wages from Twelve to Fifteen Shillings. A Youth may be bound about Fourteen years of Age, without any particular Genius or Education.'

Though the company's control had become less effective, it was not entirely cut off from the trade. For instance, around the 1770s two Wax Chandlers, Isaac Barrett who was master in 1762 and his son Bryant, carried on a wax bleaching business said to be the finest in England or perhaps in Europe; the son became a partner in Vauxhall Gardens, having married the manager's daughter and thus secured a local outlet for his wares. Isaac had a shop at the Three Kings in the Strand but the bleaching was done at Stockwell.[8] Many eighteenth-century Wax Chandlers figure in the trade cards and bill heads at the British Museum, and a trade card of 1795 was probably issued by the Barrett son –

J. B. Barrett Wax-Chandler

To their MAJESTIES
PRINCE OF WALES, & ROYAL FAMILY,

at his Manufactory
No.4 Haymarket, London

The finest Wax and Spermaceti Candles, Flambeaux,
Sealing Wax and Wafers, Wholesale, Retail, and for
Exportation on the lowest terms.

Fine Spermaceti and Chamber Oil.

In the same year he sold '144 lbs Wax Lights & Box' for £20. 14*s*. 6*d*., say 2*s*. 10*d*. a pound.

There are two bill-heads relating to women Wax Chandlers. One, dated 1758, reads –

> Eliza Bick and Company at the Golden Beehive, opposite the Mansion House, London, who Make and Sell white and yellow Wax Candles of all sizes, Branch Lights, Winding and Searing Candle, Superfine & all inferior sorts of Sealing Wax, Wafers of all Sizes, Flambeaux, yellow & black Links . . .'

No doubt she inherited the business from Edmond Bick, who was master in 1724. Later, as Bick & Cowan, it was associated with the family of the future master and lord mayor of 1837; his own bill-head reads 'John Cowan, Manufacturer of every article of Wax Chandlery. Importer of and dealer in Genuine Spermaceti Oil.'

Another woman Wax Chandler was Hannah Jones, probably the widow of Thomas Jones who flourished in 1748. Two bills show that she supplied 48 lb. of white wax lights every month to the Duke of Bedford, and in 1778 she sold 42 white wax lights for £6. 16*s*. 6*d*. to Magdalen College, Cambridge. She must have specialised in sealing wax, for her trade card was headed –

Superfine Sealing-Wax made by
Hannah Jones Wax Chandler
LONDON
at the Star & Garter in the Poultry.

By this time it was not uncommon to find the same man dealing in both wax and tallow, for instance in 1815 the firm of Penney at 418 Strand were describing themselves as 'Wax Chandlers and Tallow Chandlers to their Majesties'.

One trade card of the nineteenth century is of particular interest as it relates to a Wax Chandler whose family has been associated with the company for upwards of 450 years and is still represented on the court:

John & Charles Field
Wax Chandlers
To His Royal Highness the Prince Regent
No.12 Wigmore Street, Cavendish Square
(and at their Manufactory Upper Lambeth Marsh)

Thomas Field started the family business of wax bleachers at Lambeth in 1508 – in the reign of Henry VII. On retirement in 1581 he or a second Thomas claimed a pension of 10*s*. a quarter from the company as did another Thomas in 1655, and an Abraham in 1670. For more than 350 years and nearly a score of reigns the Fields are recorded continuously as apprentices and freemen. At least five were admitted to the livery, and three have been elected to the court, John Field of the trade card becoming master in 1830.

New halls for old

Twice in a period of 60 years it became necessary to rebuild the hall in spite of frequent and extensive repairs. The building erected after the Great Fire was put in order in 1717 following a complaint from the tenant (still Priest, the dancing master) that the 'hall and houses were very much out of repair', and 50 years later there were further repairs for which the proceeds from the sale of £500 South Sea Annuities were used; however in 1791 a surveyor, Richard Wooding, reported that the hall was 'in so decayed and ruinous a state that expenses of repair would be very great and he recommended taking down and erecting a new building on part of the ground.' It is somewhat surprising that the work of a good architect, some of whose buildings are still standing, was falling down, but there seems to have been a good deal of jerry-building in the aftermath of the fire.

Eventually it was decided to put up a new hall provided that the cost was not more than £1,000. In order to raise the money, part of the property was let on ground lease, annuities were granted from the company's income on the lives of the annuitants (this produced £600), and an advance of £200 at 5% was received from the clerk, Barnard Gregory;[9] a further £240 was to be raised by loans from members of the court, and £350 by the sale of 3% Consolidated Bank Annuities. A debt of £100 to a past master, William Caldwall, was discharged by his will made in 1789. All these contributions enabled the court to accept an estimate of £1,242 for 'erecting the Company's new Hall and the extra expenses attending the same', but late changes such as the addition of double doors and a musicians' gallery brought the cost to £1,430. The new building (plate 14), which was completed in 1793, had the hall itself on the first floor (as before) and a court room on the ground floor;[10] there were also two kitchens with iron ranges and some ancillary accommodation.

This hall was repaired and modernised in 1834 at a further cost of £1,308, and the court congratulated themselves on securing 'superior accommodation, comfort and respectability . . . not only for themselves and successors, but also for the resident officer of the company'. But in 1847 their contentment was dispelled by the introduction of a parliamentary bill authorising the widening of Gresham Street;[11] this would have sacrificed part of the northern end of the hall.[12] The Wax Chandlers had their premises struck out of the schedule, but with a further bill introduced two years later they were not so successful. However they demanded £6,000 as compensation for cost of rebuilding and reduction in site area, and, after fruitless discussions with the city surveyor, an umpire awarded £4,014.

The design of the new hall was put out to competition and awarded to Charles Fowler,[13] who was not only a member of the livery and a future master but also an architect whose sense of structure and planning has been compared with that of Rennie and Telford. The lowest estimate for the building was £3,493, and the foundation stone was laid by the master, Joseph Pulley, using a silver trowel on 20 July 1852. Beneath it were buried a glass bottle, hermetically sealed, containing a document with particulars and a set of current coins,[14] presumably still there. In October 1853 the architect reported completion at a final cost of £4,417, about three times that of its predecessor, and after refurnishing, for which £1,200 was allocated to the renter warden, the new hall (plate 15) was declared open on 20 April 1854.

Constructed in Aberdeen granite up to the first floor and in dressed brick for the upper floors, the building was said to be 'of the most substantial and durable character, being for the most part fireproof' – which did not save it from being practically burnt out in 1940. It was described in a trade journal[15] as 'a dignified and simple composition, well raised on a rusticated basement, but the internal treatment is plain and utilitarian in character' – a verdict that few who remember it would dispute. The 'livery hall' was on the first floor with robing room and service room. and on the ground floor a committee room, clerk's office, and cloakroom.[16] The upper floor provided living accommodation for the clerk or his assistant. A later addition was a stained glass window on the staircase. This was put up in about 1888 and shows the names, dates, and personal arms of six worthies – Barnard Gregory, the eighteenth-century clerk, and Charles John Todd,[17] Plaxton Samuel Carless, Francis Tullie Wollaston, Thomas Allt, and John Ives Vaughan, all of whom were past masters. In the centre was the coat-of-arms of the Wax Chandlers for which the company paid.[18]

The old tradition of feasting was maintained throughout the eighteenth and nineteenth centuries, though the frequency and location of dinners varied with the state of the funds; the time also varied, 2 or 3 o'clock being fashionable at the start of the eighteenth century and 5 or later towards the end. As well as on their quarterly meeting days, the court dined together on the biennial election day, when wives were invited; the election dinner in 1720 was to cost not more than £12 for forty places. The livery, who appear to have been excluded from the election feast after the seventeenth century, were accustomed to attend the lord mayor's day dinner, which was held with music 'as usual' up to 1858 or so, and also the summer dinner,[19] which was instituted as an 'entertainment for the livery' in 1828. Both these functions, involving larger numbers, were usually held at taverns, the City of London being popular at one period, and the West India Dock, the Artichoke at Blackwall, and the Crown & Sceptre, the Trafalgar, and the Ship at Greenwich being other favourite rendezvous. Stewards and whifflers disappeared with the lord mayor's day dinner, many stewards having paid their fines to avoid this duty. When money was short (for instance at the time of the law-suit in connection with Kendall's charity) court dinners might be reduced to one a year, and livery dinners either merged into court dinners at the hall or omitted. However by the 1880's the livery were dining with the court twice a year. In 1862 it was decided that at any meeting when a meal was served a box of sweetmeats to the value of 7*s*. was to be supplied for each member of the court and guests to take home, a custom that continued until about 1939; the sweets had come to be regarded as a sop to the diner's wife, ladies being then excluded from the company's functions.

Among the gifts of plate from members of the court were four tapersticks from John Lancashire and James Thomasson, still our most charming pieces of silver (plate 7). Other gifts have not survived the passage of time. There is no trace of 'two Branches (candelabra) to be hung in the Hall' for which Lancashire, Thomasson, Isaac Barrett and others subscribed 45 guineas in 1751, nor of a pair of ormolu candelabra offered by Boughey Burgess in 1834: his hope that they would be both useful and ornamental to the table and certainly a more permanent service than many haunches of venison (the customary gift of the senior liveryman not past the chair) was only partly fulfilled. Many years later, when old and infirm, he was awarded a pension of £50 a year.[20]

In 1864 the plate inventory listed the Commonwealth and Charles II items previously described – a 'grace' cup (Normansell's), two tankards, six salts, and three spoons – together with the George II tapersticks mentioned above; there were also two rose-water dishes (plate 8), described as 'plated' in an inventory of 1856 and having no hall mark. In 1897, to commemorate Queen Victoria's 'sixty glorious years', a past master and common councilman, Charles John Todd the elder presented the company with a Diamond Jubilee cup (plate 9) a companion for the Normansell cup of 1683; on the same occasion the company gave each member of the livery a silver-gilt spoon of ornate design, the handle being embossed with the arms, a bee-hive and the date of the first charter.[21]

London and the companies

During the eighteenth and nineteenth centuries London continued its expansion outside the boundaries and beyond the control of the city. The figures tell their own story: from nearly 250,000 at the beginning of the eighteenth century, the city population had fallen to 144,000 by 1750, and by 1801 it accounted for only 134,300 out of a total of 900,000 for 'greater London'.[22] By 1891 the number of city residents had fallen to a mere 37,694, but the daytime population had increased to 301,384. With manufacturing towns arising all over England the City of London was ceasing to be the main centre of trade and was becoming instead the financial centre of the world. The companies had ceased to be valuable as a source of money for the government, and with the gradual shedding of craft functions, accompanied by an increase in admissions by patrimony or redemption compared with apprenticeship, fewer and fewer members were connected with a trade.

At the same time the city's organisation and ceremonial were becoming antiquated, and the citizens' powers were diminishing. The freemen lost the parliamentary vote under Walpole's statute of 1725, and their other privileges were whittled away; by the nineteenth century the exclusive right to practise a craft or trade in the city had fallen into abeyance, and it was formally rescinded by the common council in 1856. As ward voters they were replaced by householders in 1867. The livery lost their exclusive right to the parliamentary vote under Peel in the great electoral reforms of 1832 when the franchise was extended to include inhabitant householders and occupiers; thenceforward they needed to possess both a residential qualification and a freedom (or a father's freedom) by servitude. They retained only their right to elect the chief officers of the city.[23]

Ex-apprentices accounted for more than half of those admitted to the city freedom during the eighteenth century, and apprenticeship was still almost universal in 1750. The sharp decline in the following years and the corresponding increase in the number of redemptioners suggest that the freedom was becoming attractive in terms of politics or status rather than of economics.[24] The legal basis of the apprenticeship system disappeared in 1814 when the relevant clauses of the Statute of Artificers were repealed,[25] throwing open all trades and handicrafts to non-apprentices, but the wording of the London indenture and its seven-year term remained unchanged. In 1889, though merely a formal entry to the freedom of the company and city,[26] the terms of the indenture were modified to allow apprentices to marry, receive wages instead of food and lodging, and complete their apprenticeship in as little as four years. A premium was still ruled out, but some 'consideration' appears to have been customary at certain periods.

The companies continued to take part in royal and civic events, and in 1747 it was stated that the Wax Chandlers had 'a Stand, near King's-street in Cheapside, in which they sit, to attend the Lord-Mayor, on the Day of his Installation'. The water pageant (plate 13) was held up to 1857 when the city lost its exclusive control of the Thames to the new Conservancy Board.[27] The train-bands, which had been embodied when the Pretender reached Derby in 1745, were reorganised in 1794 and absorbed into the militia, eventually becoming the 7th Royal Fusiliers (City of London Regiment). For many years the companies maintained their armouries, if only in token form: in 1752 the Wax Chandlers kept a bayonet, cartouche (cartridge) box, belt, buff coat and musket at the hall.

Personalities in the city

Not since the fourteenth century had the Wax Chandlers provided candidates for high office in the city, but in 1718 their re-emergence began with the appointment of George Ludlam, a past master, as chamberlain; the principal duties of this office were (and are) those of city treasurer[28] and keeper of the roll of freemen. Though a salter by trade, Ludlam had been on the Wax Chandlers livery since 1691 and served as common councilman for Bread Street. He was knighted in 1719.

In 1722 Humphrey Parsons, a Wax Chandler and alderman of Portsoken, was elected sheriff; he became lord mayor in 1730 and was re-elected ten years later. Parsons had joined the company late in life, having been made free in 1720 when he was 50 years old, and when subsequently elected as master he asked to be excused. In 1725, with prospects of the mayoralty ahead, he was translated to the Grocers, a move that was customary at that time in order to make the resources of a great company available to an expensive office. As a successful brewer, a duty-free monopoly of beer imports into France rewarded his gift of a horse to Louis XV at a hunting party. Parsons was a popular lord mayor, and in 1740 he put on an unusually splendid pageant, in which the state coach was drawn for the first time by six horses with gay trappings. A broadside entitled 'Whittington Revived' was sadly premature as he died during his second term.

William Smith and Nathaniel Thomas were two more Wax Chandlers to attain the shrievalty. Smith was elected in 1741, knighted in 1744, and later became alderman of Aldgate ward; a precise man and also very rich, he ordered that a fine oak on his estate be cut down for his coffin, which was to be fastened with screws 9 ins. long. Thomas was elected sheriff in 1776; he was alderman of Walbrook and had been master of the company, though a drysalter by trade. Both were colonels in the train-bands, Smith of the Green Regiment and Thomas of the Blue.

During the nineteenth century two Wax Chandlers attained the supreme position in the city. In 1837, the year of Queen Victoria's accession, the master, John Cowan, was elected lord mayor and made a baronet, and in 1862 a member of the court, William Anderson Rose, M.P., became lord mayor and was subsequently knighted. Cowan was alderman of Bread Street ward and had been sheriff in 1831. He was a practising wax chandler in Mansion House Street, dealing in wax candles and sealing wax and also in sperm candles and sperm oil. Rose, who at 42 was believed to be the youngest to reach the chair, was alderman of Queenhithe, where he had a white lead, colour, and varnish business, and had been sheriff in 1855; knighted in 1867, he was elected master of the Wax Chandlers in 1872, having been previously master of the Spectacle Makers and the Loriners. For ten years he was Governor of the Irish Society, and they presented him with a silver-gilt rose water dish and ewer (plate 10), which were later passed on to the company by his family.

Now that translation to a major company was no longer necessary, it was up to the Wax Chandlers to support their eminent members, and they went to a good deal of trouble and expense. When Cowan became sheriff, he was accompanied on ceremonial journeys by 16 Wax Chandlers, with clerk and beadle, and on great occasions the company's banners. Four new ones were ordered from a herald-painter – the Royal Standard, the company's banner with coat-of-arms, the banner of the sheriff-elect, and the banner of the city; all were to be of the richest silk with silk fringes, and the cost was not to exceed 60 guineas. These banners must have been suitably impressive for in the following year the lord mayor asked if he could borrow them for use on Easter Monday.

On Cowan's election as mayor the company made even more elaborate arrangements. On lord mayor's day they sent sixteen members in four carriages with the procession as far as London Bridge, where the mayor embarked, and thence via the South Bank to join the river party at Westminster and attend the swearing-in at Westminster Hall.[29] Later in the day the queen came to the city to be entertained; she was welcomed at Temple Bar by the lord mayor, who then headed her procession to the Guildhall mounted on his charger (plate 17).[30] The instructions for the Wax Chandlers party read –

Marshalmen and City Officers in front to clear the way.
The Beadle of the Company, Mr. Bishop, and four Assistants
bearing the following Banners: The Royal Standard, The Arms of the
Company, The Arms of the Lord Mayor; and The Arms of the City.
The Band of the Grenadier Guards,
The Clerk[31] in his Chariot.

The banquet, which lasted from 3.30 to 8.30, was held in high Georgian fashion with the queen and the royal family at the top table, and the mayor and the other great officials in a lower place. Meanwhile the Wax Chandlers, who had greeted the queen from their booth in St. Paul's Churchyard, were feasting in their own hall with the upper warden, Thomas Brandram, in the chair.

When Rose was lord mayor he had the duty of receiving Princess Alexandra of Denmark at her entry into the city before marrying the Prince of Wales in 1863. The Wax Chandlers arranged to have 150 seats in St. Paul's Churchyard for the livery and their ladies. Back at the hall there was a cold collation, which cost the considerable sum of £216, and the wine bill was said to be particularly heavy,[32] the consumption averaging half a bottle a head.

A political rather than a civic honour came to a Wax Chandler in 1893, when a baronetcy was conferred on Joseph Pulley, Liberal M.P. for the City of Hereford; he was a member of the court and the son of a master of the same name.

Organisation and finance

The ordinances of 1664 continued in force, and in 1839 a committee concluded that no changes were desirable except for the replacement of oaths by declarations, as permitted by a recent statute.[33] However the quarter-day assembly of the whole company and the monthly court were often neglected, and from 1815 they were replaced by a quarterly court to be held on the second Thursday after each quarter-day. Attendances too had been irregular, and from 1795 40*s* was to be shared equally among the first 12 arrivals; from 1801 those coming late had to pay 2*s*. 6*d*. In 1829 penalties again gave place to rewards, £6 being distributed among those present on time; from 1856 late-comers had to forfeit their fees. By 1881 the attendance fee had been stabilised at £3. Fines, which produced irregular amounts, were increased from time to time. Those payable by officers on election were unchanged, but by 1714 new assistants were paying £2. 10*s*. instead of £1, and liverymen £5 instead of £1. 10*s*. Later a much higher fine was charged for admission by redemption: by 1837 a redemptioner was paying £15 compared with £10 for patrimony or servitude, and in 1882 there was a payment of £150 for the privilege.

Membership of the company over a 20-year period at the beginning of the eighteenth century is recorded in a contemporary book of clerk's remembrances. In 1714 there were 97 on the livery and 60 yeomen or freemen – a total of 157, of whom only 35 were wax chandlers by trade: in this year it was decided to pay the hall keeper at the Guildhall a guinea for each new member he introduced to the company. In 1832 there were 93 livery and 59 freemen, and admissions were running at the rate of three or four a year. Later there was a steady fall in numbers, to 60 liverymen in 1865 and 41 in 1882 (with 25 freemen); the average rate of admission fell to less than one a year, and by 1892 there were only 27 on the livery. The yeomanry had disappeared as a separate class by 1837, and probably long before.[34]

Promotion to the cloth was not always welcomed. In 1715 seven out of eleven who were called upon were excused, one being William Colbourne, perhaps a descendant of the earlier Coleburne whose silver spoon we still possess. In 1737 William Budd and others were summoned 'to take on them the Livery'; during the next two years Budd received further warnings to bring his livery fine or be taken before the mayor, and a copy of the mayor's order to all constables to produce his body to answer our complaint is to be seen at the hall. In 1741 he had reformed sufficiently to offer to pay his arrears of quarterage, but the court was slow to respond.

Among the members in 1714 were half-a-dozen women, who appear to have been widows and were often in receipt of pensions, but during the eighteenth century several became freewomen in their own right. Eight were admitted either by patrimony or redemption, though only one, Ann Lokes in 1796, practised as a wax chandler. Three women took male apprentices; one of these, the son of an Oxford gardener, was the William Budd who ran into trouble in later life. Between 1686 and 1748 12 women, one a city 'Orphan', were apprenticed to members of the company, but none seems to have proceeded to the freedom. In the next 50 years there were three more female apprentices. Rebeckah Relph was bound to Richard Cooke, Wax Chandler, in 1758 'to learn that trade and to board and lodge with the master', the standard way of providing accommodation and care; Margaret Couchman and Ann Dodson were apprenticed to Thomas Brown of Ludgate Hill, a haberdasher, which by then may have been a more promising career for a woman. In 1799 Elizabeth Applegarth, probably a member of a Wax Chandlers family, was admitted to the freedom by redemption, and by 1834 she was the only woman left in the company.

From the early days the companies had been no misogynists, having had wives, widows, and other female companions in addition to women members at their feasts. The Wax Chandlers appear to have invited wives to dine on election day in the seventeenth and eighteenth centuries, but not thereafter; attempts to include them at the summer dinner in the 1840's were rejected. But in 1748 the court had decided that women and children should be admitted to the company's stand on lord mayor's day.

The company's normal sources of income were unchanged and were supplemented by savings, occasional donations from members and other windfalls. In 1738 the money from two £100 East India bonds was laid out in 3% Lottery Annuities, but apparently without success. The receipts from quarterage cannot have been more than a few pounds a year: 'Quarteridge Recd' in 1729 totalled £8 12*s.* 0*d.* and included arrears ranging up to 5*s.* 4*d.* The rates remained at 8*d.* for the livery and 6*d.* for the yeomanry, but by 1834 the yeomen's contribution had been remitted. In 1837 quarterage was suspended and never restored.[35] Searches seem to have been few and far between, and in 1798 when the company considered the possibility of more effective trade regulation no action seems to have been taken. At this time beeswax was being rapidly superseded in most of its original applications, and by 1837 control had fallen into disuse 'for want of sufficient powers to enforce the regulations'; the city authorities were no longer prepared to support out-dated rules in a dying trade.

The income for 1750 was £372. 15*s*. 3½*d*., and expenditure was £342. 1*s*. 7*d*., made up as follows:

Income	£	*s.*	*d.*	*Expenditure*	£	*s.*	*d.*
Rents	223	15	0	Salaries	25	10	0
Bindings	3	13	4	Food and drink*	72	0	4
Freedoms	6	12	0	Allowed to tenants†	67	14	8
Fines	29	5	0	Charities	49	9	0
Quarterage	10	4	4	Casual payments	127	7	7
Casual receipts	99	5	7½				
	£372	15	3½		£342	1	7

*Cook's bill and money spent at taverns.

†Refunds of tax paid by them

For 1833–4 the gross income was about £845, which included rents amounting to £668 from real property and also the interest on a capital sum of £3,300 in 3% Consols, accumulated by savings since 1820. In 1790 the company had bought a property at 20 Old Change, adjoining Kendall's bequest, for £350; this appears to have included part of the King's Head public house (No. 18). Over the years the rents increased with the value of land in the city, rising from £847 in 1856 to £1117 in 1881 – £350 from 20 Old Change, £312 from Queenhithe, £275 from Coleman Street and £180 from Aldersgate Street. The total income in 1881 was £1,605, which included interest on stock valued at £750 and held in trust for various charities; there was also the company's share in the Royal Fisheries – the remnant of the Irish estates held under the Haberdashers – which in 1837 produced about £38 every ten years but seems to have disappeared before the end of the century.[36]

Payments out of income covered the normal housekeeping expenses – taxes, rates, salaries and maintenance – pensions and grants to needy members or dependants, distributions under charitable trusts, and the cost of company dinners and other functions. Pensions paid in 1833–4 amounted to £80 of which £20 went to widows of deceased masters. Occasionally there was also the additional expense of taking part in state ceremonies: for instance, at the official entry of George I in 1714, stands were set up for the companies, and the Wax Chandlers ordered 'that there be new banners and a standard provided, i.e. the King's Banner, the City Banner, and the Company's Banner, two yards square each, and the Company's Standard, five yards long, and that Mr. Charles Wiseman do prepare and paint the same, the price whereof is left to him, but not to exceed £23.' When the young Queen Victoria came to St. Paul's for a thanksgiving service after her accession the company had an illuminated booth, lighted one hopes by wax candles but more probably by the modern gas burners.

In 1870–1 the total expenditure of £965 was made up of £159 for rates and taxes, £210 for salaries, and £142 for charities, leaving £454 for internal expenses such as court fees, maintenance and entertaining. The rateable value of the hall was £173 in

1840 (compared with £1,000 for the Goldsmiths') and £417 in 1881; in 1804 the fire insurance was raised to £4000.

A poor rate continued to be payable to St. John Zachary, though the amount was often in dispute; in 1715 the master and wardens brought the churchwardens before the mayor to press the necessity of keeping to the agreed figure, and in 1731 the company refused to pay. At this time there were 88 houses in the parish, and during the eighteenth century the sums required increased from 13*s.* a quarter in 1725 to £1. 15*s.* 0*d.* in 1750 and £3. 15*s.* 0*d.* in 1775; after a reduction in 1801 to £12 a year, there was a further increase to £4. 6*s.* 6*d.* quarterly (6*d.* in the pound on the rateable value of the hall) in 1840. In 1751 £10. 2*s.* was paid towards a fire engine for the parish. There was also a rate for church expenses and repairs;[37] this amounted to £1. 13*s.* 4*d.* a year in 1750, £3 in 1775, and £8. 4*s.* 0*d.* in 1801, when the company gave the rector an additional 'subscription' of £5 towards church repairs. In the following year the lecturer of St. John's was paid 5 guineas for his past services, and it was decided to contribute £2 a year in future. Unlike some other companies, the Wax Chandlers do not appear to have had a regular chaplain of their own. In 1836, however, a parson and liveryman, Gilbert Gilbert, was appointed honorary chaplain, presumably in order to act as lord mayor's chaplain on Cowan's election in the following year.[38]

The clerk's salary in 1834 was £100 a year, and the beadle's £40 (it had been £20 since 1794); by 1884 the clerk's pay had been raised but only to £120. In both cases there were small fees for attendance on ceremonial occasions. Attendance fees for each member of the court averaged £8 a year in the 1880's.

'Money well spent'

Individual members continued to give money for the company to hold in trust for charitable purposes. For example in 1740 John Lancashire, a future master, gave £100 of South Sea Annuity Stock (the respectable successor to the South Sea Bubble) on condition that they distributed 'the yearly summe of Five Pounds to the Poor of the Company on St. Thomas's Day in every year for ever', but no trace remains. In 1789 a past master, William Caldwall, discharged a debt of £100 due to him from the company by leaving it £100 2½% Consols, from which £2. 10*s.* a year was to be distributed on St. Thomas's day to poor freemen and widows of freemen.

The older charitable distributions continued as directed by the terms of the trusts, and, for a time at least, they were accompanied by the customary eating and drinking. The responsibility for the potation may have been shared, for according to a court minute of 1715 'the parish (St Mary Magdalene, Old Fish Street) treated this time with Two bottles of Wine, 1 of Claret the other of Sack, and 4 Rolls'; as Prince Hal said to Falstaff, 'O monstrous! but one half-pennyworth of bread to this intolerable deal of sack.'[39]

The John Thompson charity property at Queenhithe brought in a gross income of £267 in 1865 and £312 in 1881. In the latter year 60 qrs. of coal and four gowns were handed out on Good Friday, and five coats on St. Thomas's day; the coal cost £18. 19*s.* 6*d.*, the gowns £3. 2*s.*, the coats £7. 10*s.* The Parnell property at Puddle Dock was taken down by the Metropolitan Water Board under an improvement Act of 1863, and the sum of £75 received in compensation provided a small income for charity.

Under Kendall's charity (and Frankwell's) the long-standing connection with the parish of Bexley was kept up, and by 1844 about £50 was being distributed from the profits. However, the gross receipts from the property amounted to £310 a year, and in 1864 when the income had risen to £330, there was an official inquiry. The Wax Chandlers contended that they were absolutely entitled to the net residue for their own use, since letters patent of James I in 1619 had released the land and premises to the company and its successors, but the inspector's conclusion was that they had no beneficial interest in the property, 'the residuary bequest being for the reparation thereof', and that the whole of the net income must be spent 'in accordance with the will'. In 1867, at the instance of the Charity Commissioners, an information was filed against the company in the Court of Chancery. The Wax Chandlers argued that surplus funds, after fulfilling the conditions of Kendall's bequest, should be used for the benefit of the company of which he had been master, and in 1869 the Master of the Rolls gave a very clear judgement in their favour. An appeal by the Attorney-General was rejected by the Lord Chancellor, but in 1873 the final appeal to the House of Lords was upheld by a majority.

A further five years' negotiation with the Charity Commissioners produced a 'scheme' for the future management of the charity, and this was approved by the Master of the Rolls in July 1878. After the continuance of various minor bequests, half the net income was to be paid to the Parochial Charities of the City of London,[40] and a quarter to the parish of Bexley for charitable purposes. Only the remaining quarter was left for the Wax Chandlers to distribute to poor people of the company or to others: the master and wardens were permitted to retain 1/8 of this, i.e. 1/32 of the whole, for their own use. In 1880 the total income from Kendall's was £509 and the net income £461, which was allocated in accordance with the scheme: after deducting £48 for expenses and specific bequests, £231 was distributed among forty-four London hospitals and institutions, £115 to Bexley charities, £101 to the poor of the Wax Chandlers, and £14 to the master and wardens for company use.

In the educational field the companies sponsored an important development in 1876, when they anticipated the growth of technology by initiating the foundation of the City and Guilds of London Institute. This was established in 1884 as a joint undertaking with the city authorities for the promotion of technical education and research, and it included the City and Guilds College, now part of the Imperial College of Science and Technology in the University of London. In the field of technological examinations 'City and Guilds' has become a household word. Since the inception of the Institute the companies as a whole have subscribed more than £1,500,000, and the Wax Chandlers', as one of the foundation donors, has recently renewed its support.

Donations to good causes were made from the company's general funds, their frequency and amount depending on the current financial position. Examples of nineteenth-century gifts are £10 towards the Cripplegate Volunteer Corps, the hall being situated in that ward; 20 guineas to the City of London School, of which the master, George Watts, was appointed a governor; £25, via the curate of St. John Zachary, to relieve 'the suffering Irish clergy', £10 towards the building of National Schools at Bexley[41] and an Episcopal Chapel at Bexley Heath, where an organ was required 'capable of being played by hand, or by barrel to save the salary of an organist'; £25 towards the relief of suffering from 'the late mutiny in India'; and 50 guineas to an Indian famine relief fund. In 1881 the company made a donation of ten guineas to the Tallow Chandlers' Benevolent Society at the request of its treasurer. Such gifts would be worth very considerable sums today.[42]

How far that little candle throws his beams!
So shines a good deed in a naughty world.

SHAKESPEARE

Notes on Chapter IV

[1]An impressive example is provided by the Drapers', who between 1884 and 1917 gave £958,973 from their corporate funds to universities, hospitals and objects of benefit to the public and whose subsequent benefactions total many millions of pounds.

[2]The rough account and commonplace book of a Wax Chandler, Lambert Wilson, for 1640–5 can be seen at the Guildhall Library (*MS7429*); he was perhaps the son of Lambrecht Wilsen, who was married in the Dutch church, Austin Friars, in 1596.

[3]Olwen Hedley, *Royal Palaces*, 1972

[4]In 1835–40 stearine was 1*s.* 0*d.* a lb, only 1*d.* or 2*d.* less than beeswax; tallow was about half this price.

[5]Votive candles for burning before images or shrines as personal offerings do not contain beeswax.

[6]Two eighteenth-century sealing-wax accessories are still known and treasured by those who possess them: 'wax-jacks' or 'taper-boxes', usually in brass or silver, for holding coils of taper, and 'tapersticks' or miniature candlesticks (page 100).

[7]Anon., *A General Description of All Trades* (London); R. Campbell, *The London Tradesman.*

[8]A drawing by Sandby, in the possession of the Greater London Council, shows bleaching in progress at the Barrett house.

[9]Four members of the Gregory family starting with Barnard in 1765 became clerks of the company, and also vestry clerks of St. John Zachary where they were buried in the family vault. Three descendants were elected master, either twice or three times; over 200 years of the connection were celebrated in 1966 by the re-election of C. B. Gregory, the court giving him a special dispensation from a recent decision to avoid second terms of office as tending to hold up progress for the livery.

[10]The court had been meeting at the New London Tavern.

[11]The name given in 1845 to commemorate Sir Thomas Gresham, the Elizabethan merchant who founded the Royal Exchange and Gresham College (from which sprang the Royal Society) and was the originator of Gresham's Law.

[12]Some ground had already been lost from the original site, perhaps by sale as well as by statutory widening, and the yard was to be built on to compensate.

[13]Fowler was responsible for Covent Garden and Hungerford Markets and in 1822 was first prizeman for a new London Bridge, though his design was rejected by the Corporation in favour of Rennie's.

[14]They included a sovereign, half-sovereign, crown, half-crown, florin, shilling, fourpence, threepence and penny together with two half-pennies and a farthing.

[15]*The Builder*, 29 June 1917.

[16]The seventeenth-century lead cistern was installed then or later as a show-piece in the entrance hall, where it remained until it was melted in the fire of 1940; the style was early Jacobean and the ornamentation represented the four seasons.

[17]The Todd family have a remarkable record of service and benefaction. Charles John, admitted by servitude in 1843, was a member of the court for over 50 years and was common councilman for Queenhithe for a similar period; he was also one of the city commissioners of lieutenancy, an office that was instituted in 1662 to levy and maintain the train bands and is still responsible for the upkeep of Finsbury Barracks. Twice

17. Lord mayor and master of the Wax Chandlers, Sir John Cowan, Bt., rides at the head of Queen Victoria's procession on 9 November, 1837.

The Wax Chandlers' coat-of-arms: a present-day realisation of the original blazon

master himself, his four sons all occupied the chair, some of them twice or thrice. A grandson, C. G. Todd, a past master, served as clerk from 1952 to 1970 and did much to re-establish the company on a firm footing after the war; he also gave it many pieces of furniture and plate (see page 119 and appendix 16). The Todd family business originally included the importation of honey, and later the manufacture of sealing wax.

[18]The window was re-erected, one floor higher, when the hall was rebuilt in 1958.

[19]The first summer dinner was held at the sixteenth-century Canonbury House, which had had many distinguished occupants such as Bacon and Goldsmith and part of which still stands in Islington.

[20]In 1841 he was re-elected master for eight months when Samuel Clay died in harness, a procedure that followed a precedent of 1711 and was repeated in 1892. His candelabra were still in the company's possession in 1856, but not in 1864.

[21]The year of the charter was given as 1483, in accordance with the legal and ecclesiastical calendars of that time.

[22]In 1888 an Administrative County of London was created, covering 117 sq. miles with 4,227,954 inhabitants (1891 census) and governed by the L.C.C.: by 1901 it was approaching its peak population of some 4,540,000.

[23]Since 1888 the city has elected two sheriffs of its own, Middlesex being excluded from their jurisdiction.

[24]In 1835 the fee for the freedom was reduced from £25 to £5.

[25]54 George III, *c* 96.

[26]Since 1835 the freedom has been obtainable without the intervention of a company.

[27]The mayor was represented both on the Thames Conservancy and on the Port of London Authority, which in 1909 took over the river from Teddington to the Nore.

[28]In previous centuries the city chamberlain had had an extremely lucrative post: the cash balances of the chamber's accounts were at his disposal.

[29]From 1882 the mayor was presented to the lord chancellor at the law courts, instead of at Westminster. The date was changed from 29 October to 9 November in 1751, when eleven days were to be omitted from the calendar.

[30]The queen's entry is one of the scenes depicted on the memorial that replaced Wren's Temple Bar when it was removed to Theobald's Park, near Waltham Cross, in 1878.

[31]The clerk, Mark Henry Gregory, was presented with a silver tray, inscribed with an acknowledgement of his services on this royal and civic occasion.

				£.	s.	d.
[32]	Champagne	34 bottles @ 5/6	.. ..	9	7	0
	Sherry	30 bottles @ 4/6	.. ..	6	15	0
	Port	9 bottles @ 5/-	.. ..	2	5	0
	Moselle	9 bottles @ 5/6	.. ..	2	9	6
	Brandy	1 pint @ 3/6	.. ..		3	6
			Total	21	0	0

[33]5 & 6 William IV, *c* 62.

[34]A yeomanry is still maintained by the Ironmongers, Clothworkers, Apothecaries and perhaps other companies. The Ironmongers are exceptional in that their court of assistants consists of the whole livery.

[35]In some companies quarterage payments are still kept up.

[36]When asked in 1911 to provide a stained glass window for the Guildhall at Londonderry, the Wax Chandlers felt unable to oblige.

[37]In 1807 there were the remains of a stone wall at the east end and a monument to Sir James Drax and his lady, but in 1838 only a small fragment remained; in 1845 they spent £5 on preserving the relics of the church and the church wall.

[38]From this period up to the present day there have been several clergymen on the court, including three masters – Charles John Todd II, John Roberts Dummelow, and Herbert Frederick Robins. W. M. Atkins, R. Simpson, A. J. Watts, and J. Robinson are clergy now on the livery.

[39]Shakespeare, *King Henry IV*, Part I, II, iv.

[40]The money for London charities is now administered by the City Parochial Foundation.

[41]The company had long supported the national schools at Bexley in view of its connections with that parish.

[42]Perhaps 7 times as much.

CHAPTER V

The Twentieth Century

THOUGH the company's work as a trade association was over and its part in the government of London might be acknowledged a formality, the twentieth-century Wax Chandlers did not forget their origin and history. They formed a connection with the British bee-keepers – heirs to the original suppliers of beeswax – and they maintained some contact with the city. The decline in membership was arrested, the numbers rising to 52 in 1910 and 106 in 1972, of whom 72 are on the livery. On Midsummer and Michaelmas days liverymen meet at a common hall for the city elections, and near Lady day they attend a United Guilds Service at St. Paul's, where the company's candles light the high altar. In recent years successive lord mayors have accepted an invitation to lunch informally at Wax Chandlers' Hall in the January following their election; there is also a personal connection with the city in that two members of our livery, one a past master, are deputies and common councilmen.[1] On official occasions the master, wardens and clerks are arrayed in gowns of contemporary design, yet preserving links with the past in their use of the company's colours combined with emblems of the honeycomb.

While maintaining the traditions of ceremony and hospitality, the company has not neglected its third duty – that of charity. Trust property and investments have been carefully managed, and the grants supplemented from corporate funds; some new trusts have been inaugurated. Regular donations, often under seven-year covenants, have been made to selected organisations for helping the sick and needy, and for medical research. Education has been promoted by personal contact with and contributions to Christ's Hospital, the City and Guilds Institute, and the new City University.

But the most considerable undertaking of the century has been the rebuilding of the hall, which with other Wax Chandlers' properties was severely damaged in the war of 1939–45. What with inadequate compensation and rising prices the company had to sell much of its other property, but the new hall provides a useful income from the letting of office accommodation and is a worthy successor to earlier buildings on its historic site.

The city and the companies

The square mile of the city remains a compact island of independence in the vast metropolis of 610 sq. miles and 7,379,014 people (in 1971), which is now governed by the Greater London Council.[2] The population of the city itself, once entirely residential, is now largely commuter, rising to 400,000 by day from 5,000 or less by night. Nevertheless, there remains much of the old independence and character and there is still no charter of incorporation, the term 'corporation of London' being comparatively modern; 'the mayor and commonalty and citizens of the City of London' is the legal name.

The freemen of the city and the livery of the companies retain some of their former status and privileges, and, though in all but a very few companies apprenticeship is a formality, the old procedures of binding, enrolment and admission to the freedom are maintained. The form of indenture contains many of the original prohibitions, and an unruly apprentice could still be committed to Bridewell, though the former palace and prison have gone and underground cells are no longer available for his reception.

Though most of the freemen's privileges disappeared during the eighteenth and nineteenth centuries, the freedom is still necessary for admission to the livery and for the holding of high civic office such as lord mayor and alderman. It is also a qualification for benefit under a number of city charities. Distressed freemen and their widows and daughters may be eligible for admission to the Freemen's Houses and Rogers's Almshouses, both at Brixton, and widows may receive small money gifts at Christmas. The children of freemen or freewomen are given preference for admission to one of the corporation schools, and orphan children may be considered for free maintenance and grammar-school education at the City of London Freemen's School at Ashtead in Surrey; the fees on admission to the freedom go towards the upkeep of this school.

There is still a regular flow of applicants for the freedom as a mark of identification with the city, and it has also been conferred *honoris causa* on some distinguished persons. As far back as 1674 Charles II had been made an honorary freeman, and in 1971 his namesake, the present Prince of Wales, followed his grandfather and great-grandfather in claiming the freedom by patrimony, the ceremony being shown on television.

The livery lost the last vestige of their exclusive parliamentary franchise in 1918, though the vote was retained until 1948[3] for a special list of liverymen qualified by the possession of business premises in the city. They still form the sole electorate[4] for candidates for the mayoralty, shrievalty and other offices, and each year, at Midsummer and Michaelmas, they are summoned to assemble at a common hall held in the Guildhall.[5] Here, where posies are carried and fragrant herbs strew the floor to ward off infection and sweeten the air, the livery elect the sheriffs, chamberlain and other officers and make two nominations for mayor. From these the court of aldermen choose one, who is presented to the Lord Chancellor for royal approval and, after admission and swearing-in at the Guildhall, to the Lord Chief Justice to make his final declaration of office, replacing the former oaths. The procession to the Law Courts is the occasion of the Lord Mayor's Show (now always held on a Saturday for the benefit of traffic and spectators), which is the last survivor of the elaborate pageants known to early Wax Chandlers. The modern tendency is to stress by *tableaux vivants* the needs, ideals, and aspirations of the moment, though these may be spiced with a background of historical development; in 1971 for instance the theme was the place of the City of London in international finance, and the show was called 'The City serves the nation – today and tomorrow'.

In the city the mayor is still directly responsible to the sovereign, who, for a state entry, is ceremonially admitted at Temple Bar, the civic sword being offered and returned. The city also restricts the entrance of armed forces, seven units only[6] being privileged to march through the streets with bayonets fixed, colours flying, and bands playing. A reminder of the train-bands came at the beginning of the century when the Wax Chandlers with other companies received medals commemorating the raising and equipping of the City of London Imperial Volunteers; the C.I.V. had given distinguished service in the South African War of 1899–1902, their dash and spirit impressing the young Winston Churchill. The old custom by which the companies accompanied the mayor 'on his going to St. Paul's' was revived in 1943 when a United Guilds Service was held in the cathedral on Lady day, the first day of the year according to the old calendar; now an important annual event, this service is attended by the mayor – the chief liveryman – with his state retinue and a fanfare of trumpets, and it has attracted many eminent preachers. Another function at which all the companies are represented is the annual banquet for masters or prime wardens and their wives at the Mansion House, where in the Egyptian Hall the tables are laid with the famous gold plate and the food is laced with wine, music and speeches.

Wars and properties

The Wax Chandlers embarked on some substantial property transactions in 1913, when they bought the freehold of 53 Fleet Street for £12,000, of which £10,450 came from the sale of 20 Old Change; the adjacent property (17, 18, 19) was sold on behalf of Kendall's charity for £31,000, and £25,000 of this was used to buy 3 Lloyds Avenue, the balance being invested. The 1914–18 war left the company's property intact; the hall was open to the public – at its own risk – as a shelter from Zeppelin bombs, and from 1919 to 1925 it was let to the Ironmongers, whose own hall was the only one to be demolished. In the 1939–45 war however, Wax Chandlers Hall was largely destroyed by enemy action,[7] and other valuable buildings were lost – the company's corporate property in Aldersgate Street with the adjacent Albion Buildings (purchased in 1932 for £6,500) and the Thompson trust property in Upper Thames Street and Sugar Loaf Court. In January 1948 the company was asked to provide estimates of the cost of rebuilding, ostensibly as a basis for compensation under the War Damage Act, but comparative figures suggest that though the claim may have been pitched too high the compensation awarded was too low:

Property	Estimated cost	Compensation awarded
	£	£
196–7 Upper Thames St. & 1–6 Sugar Loaf Court	50,000	3,550
186 (formerly 165) Aldersgate St.	50,000	4,500
15, 16, 17 Albion Buildings	20,000	6,860

The Upper Thames Street properties were sold to the Hudson's Bay Company in 1951 for £20,000, and the Aldersgate Street and Albion Buildings sites, being involved in street improvements, to the city corporation in 1956 for £11,000. The perpetual rent charge of £20 p.a. on Upper Thames Street was released by making over £800 of 2½% Consols to the Official Trustee of Charitable Funds.

The destruction at the hall occurred on 29 December 1940 when the German Luftwaffe set much of the city ablaze (fig. 5). Some 60 fires were started by incendiary bombs, and in the three days' conflagration much of the Guildhall, many churches, and most of Paternoster Row were burnt out. A land mine had already exploded close by, doing a great deal of damage, when fire spread to our hall from adjoining buildings. Only the basement and ground floor survived, thanks to the fireproof floor above, but fortunately the clerk and his family who lived at the top of the building were able to escape and save many of the company's belongings, particularly the best silver and many of the pictures. Most of the furnishings, many portraits, the engraved table-silver, and the silk banners displayed on dinner nights were destroyed or seriously damaged, and the lead cistern that had survived from the seventeenth century was melted by the heat. The ancient documents had been deposited with the company's bankers.

Within a few days the wardens held an emergency meeting in the cellars, and a court meeting on 29 January 1941 was to be the last held on the old ground for some 17 years. Activities were much reduced, but the court continued to meet regularly elsewhere in the city; the hospitality of other companies – for example, the Armourers and Brasiers and the Dyers – was gladly accepted for major functions, the former company's hall being used in 1953 for a coronation banquet[8] attended by distinguished guests. The silver was moved to underground vaults at Bath. It was decided that the fines paid on joining the court should go to a plate fund for use when the hall was rebuilt; since 1901 each new assistant had had to present a piece of silver as part of his fine. After the war the ancient documents and records, going back to the thirteenth century or earlier, were deposited in the Guildhall Library for safe keeping; a complete list with the manuscript reference numbers is given in appendix 17. Several boxes of documents were first examined and calendared by a member of the court, A. R. B. Fuller.[9]

In 1947 the clerk, Albert James Wood, who had played a large part in keeping the company going during and after the war, was presented with an antique clock commemorating 60 years' service during which he had never failed to attend a meeting. Wood had been elected an assistant in 1942, and on retiring from the clerkship seven years later he became renter warden. In 1952 he was elected master, a fitting crown to his career: he was a staunch upholder of the traditions and a great Wax Chandler. In 1970 a son, T. J. Wood, then renter warden, was appointed clerk and was re-elected to the court.

Among the churches totally destroyed in December 1940 was St. Vedast-alias-Foster, whose parish incorporates that of St. John Zachary[10] and preserves some monuments and plate from our pre-Fire church. During the war the St. John's site was made into a pleasant garden by fire-watchers of the Goldsmiths' staff. St. Vedast's was rebuilt and re-hallowed

5. The ruined hall and its surroundings after the 'blitz' of 1940.

The granite-faced ground floor (incorporated in the present building) is in the centre of the picture next to Goldsmiths' Hall, which with the spire and tower of St. Mary-le-Bow had escaped destruction.

in 1962 by the Bishop of London, when the master reported that the altar candles provided by the Wax Chandlers burned clear and bright; the company has recently decided to supply all the liturgical candles required by the church. The organ, a fine baroque specimen built by Harris and Byfield in 1731, has been restored by a Wax Chandler, N. P. Mander, who is one of the churchwardens.

At St. Paul's Cathedral, where the high altar was destroyed by a bomb in October, 1940, a new altar was consecrated in 1958 as the British Commonwealth war memorial, and the Wax Chandlers renewed one of their oldest associations by undertaking to supply it with candles in perpetuity. It will be remembered that nearly 600 years earlier a few members of the craft had bound themselves to supply wax for a candelabrum in Old St. Paul's. The company also subscribes to the St. Paul's Cathedral Trust.

The present hall

After the war the court was faced with a major problem, the future of the hall. With faith and courage they decided to rebuild on the old site, and when the war-damage claim had been settled, Seely & Paget were chosen as architects, the late Lord Mottistone being the partner responsible for the design. Owing to the financial position they were to retain the outward character of the building with the existing ground floor walls, but to design the interior so that two floors could be let as offices. Modifications to the original proposals, including the substitution of a concrete staircase with iron balustrade for the old marble and mahogany, and the omission of a passenger lift for the time being reduced the estimate by some £11,000, and plans were finally approved in 1954. After two years of negotiations, the contracts were let to Ashby and Horner, and in 1958 the building was completed – at a total cost of £57,900, of which £21,600 came from company funds.

The new hall (plate 16) may be thought to combine the virtues of tradition and modernity. This applies particularly to 'the great chamber called the Hall' – to quote the medieval documents – which is the scene of the company's principal functions and is illustrated in the frontispiece. Some 60 diners can be accommodated. The walls are lined with cork tiles, which reduce noise during the service of meals and give good acoustics for after-dinner speeches and occasional music. The curtains are lime-green, and the red-and-gold patterned carpet is after a design made for Holyrood House. An uncovenanted addition by the clerk of the works was the gilded bee-hive on the railings of the minstrels' gallery.

A show-case for plate incorporates some fine wood-carving, which came from earlier halls and has been attributed, perhaps optimistically, to Grinling Gibbons;[11] it is the survivor of two overmantels removed from the company's premises in Aldersgate Street. Of the oak doors, the main pair were the gift of J. C. Field, an assistant whose family has the unrivalled record of membership noted on page 98. The chandeliers are magnificent specimens of Victorian crystal and also a remarkable example of repair and re-assembly by experts. A central unit of graceful design is flanked on either side by two more imposing units, probably of later date; all three, with their glass lustres, were found in thousands of pieces in the ruins of the hall.

Other survivals from the previous hall include a master's chair (pre-1840), 36 chairs (probably purchased in 1853), and a bronze dinner-gong on mahogany frame. There are also two glass-lustre candelabra, from a set of four presented by Herbert Frederick Robins, two having been destroyed in 1940. Two Chippendale wall brackets and a stick barometer were given by C. G. Todd. A full-size bee-hive or 'skep' in the traditional wickerwork was recently presented by a liveryman, W. J. Sturdy, who was formerly a commercial bee-keeper and whose cousin and brother-liveryman, H. A. Sturdy, is head of a firm of wax bleachers and refiners.

Of the five oil paintings on the walls, four are portraits of former masters. The two oldest show William Caldwall and Joseph Pulley and were acquired in 1840; the former was presented by the master, Thomas Brandram, Caldwall having been one of the original members of his firm. The portrait of Sir William Anderson Rose was painted by S. Rosenthal in 1863 when Rose was lord mayor, and was presented by his son, James, in 1882. That of Charles John Todd I was painted by J. C. Michie in 1902 and commemorated his fifty years' service on the court. The fifth painting is a copy of the van Dyck portrait of Jean Grusset Richardot in the Louvre.[12] A painting by Miss Hibbert of Sir John Cowan, the lord mayor of 1837, is represented by a photograph: the original was exhibited at the Royal Academy in 1839 but appears to have been lost. Also on the walls are some miscellaneous original documents[13] of the period 1694–1741, mounted and framed, and copies of the charter of 1484 and the grants-of-arms of 1485/1530 and 1536.

Adjacent to the main hall, which occupies most of the second and third floors of the building, are an ante-room and a servery, and above these a clerk's office and wine pantry. On the fourth floor is a two-bedroom flat for the caretaker, who also acts as the beadle[14] at civic ceremonies and company functions. The kitchen is in the basement, with a lift to the servery. The ground and first floors are let as office accommodation.

The ante-room contains two pieces that pre-date the Great Fire of 1666. One is a wooden ballot box acquired in the mid-seventeenth century and still in use at elections. The other is a framed panel of embroidery, which has been put together from pieces of varying periods and bears the date 1650. The ground is of white satin on which have been embroidered in silk the coat-of-arms and two bee-hives in eighteenth-century style; around these are stitched small embroidered pieces of 1650–70 work, mostly showing animals and flowers.

Also in the ante-room is some fine marquetry furniture, which was given to the company in 1959 by C. G. Todd:[15] it includes a long-case clock made by Richard Baker in about 1685,[16] a Dutch china cabinet, a card table and six chairs. Among the bric-a-brac in the cabinet are Roman iron and pottery remains, which were found during excavations for the rebuilding – a small coarse-ware cooking pot (A.D. 50–75), a pottery flask with the handle and neck missing (A.D. 60–100), and an iron hammer head; artificial flowers and other decorations show that there are still expert wax modellers, one of the very oldest professions.[17]

On the walls of the anteroom and the clerk's office are views of the two previous halls: the building of 1793 (plate 14) is shown in a water-colour drawing by George Shepherd dated 1811 and also in a photograph of a pencil drawing dated 1810, while that of 1854 (plate 15) is a photograph of a water-colour drawing by T. Hosmer Shepherd.[18] An original drawing in line and colour-wash by Dennis Flanders showing the present hall and surroundings in 1966 (plate 16) was presented by C. G. Todd, whose portrait in oils by Reginald Lewis hangs nearby. There is also the original of a *Punch* sketch by George Morrow showing 'the Wax Chandlers burning the candle at both ends' (fig. 6), but the members defy identification.

Less closely connected with the company's history but of real antiquarian interest is an engraving dated 1646 by William Marshall, a famous book-illustrator whose portraits are valued for their scarcity and historical interest. The subject is a 70-year-old Hungarian alchemist, John Banfi-Hunijadis Rivuliensis,[19] who is shown holding a retort. He was believed to have owned a silver-gilt tankard (plate 10), dated 1650 and made in Hamburg, which was presented to the company together with the engraving by Charles Edward Hartley, master in 1900 and 1924.

The exterior of the ground floor, which was the only part to survive the blitz, needed only slight repair; the entrance doors had their decoration of bees and candles restored in gold leaf. Above the doorway the carved stone roundel depicting a bee-skep is one of two from the 1793 hall. The walls of the upper floors were completely rebuilt in brick with 'stone' dressings and a copper-clad roof.

The court met at the new hall for the first time on 7 October 1958, and in the following April the master (A. R. B. Fuller) and wardens (J. Dummelow and T. H. Winterborn) were able to invite the livery and ladies to dine there. Two dinners were held so as to accommodate all who wished to attend, and the menu indicates a notable change from Edwardian banquets in that the number of courses had been halved:[20]

Old Custom House Sercial	Consomme julienne
Liebfraumilch 1953 Hans Christof Wein	Filet sole veronique
Volnay 1952 Lejay Legoute	Caneton rôti bigarrade
	Pommes persillées
	Petits pois à la menthe
Port Tenor Messis	Corbeille de roses friandises
Cognac Bisquit Dubuché	Scotch woodcock

The hall was later visited by the Princess Royal in connection with the centenary of the British Red Cross Society, and it has been used for corporation and other city functions.

Court and livery dinners continued to be held with the traditional ceremonies and the tables laid with silver from the company's collection. The list of plate (appendix 16) has been considerably extended during the present century by gifts and bequests from mem-

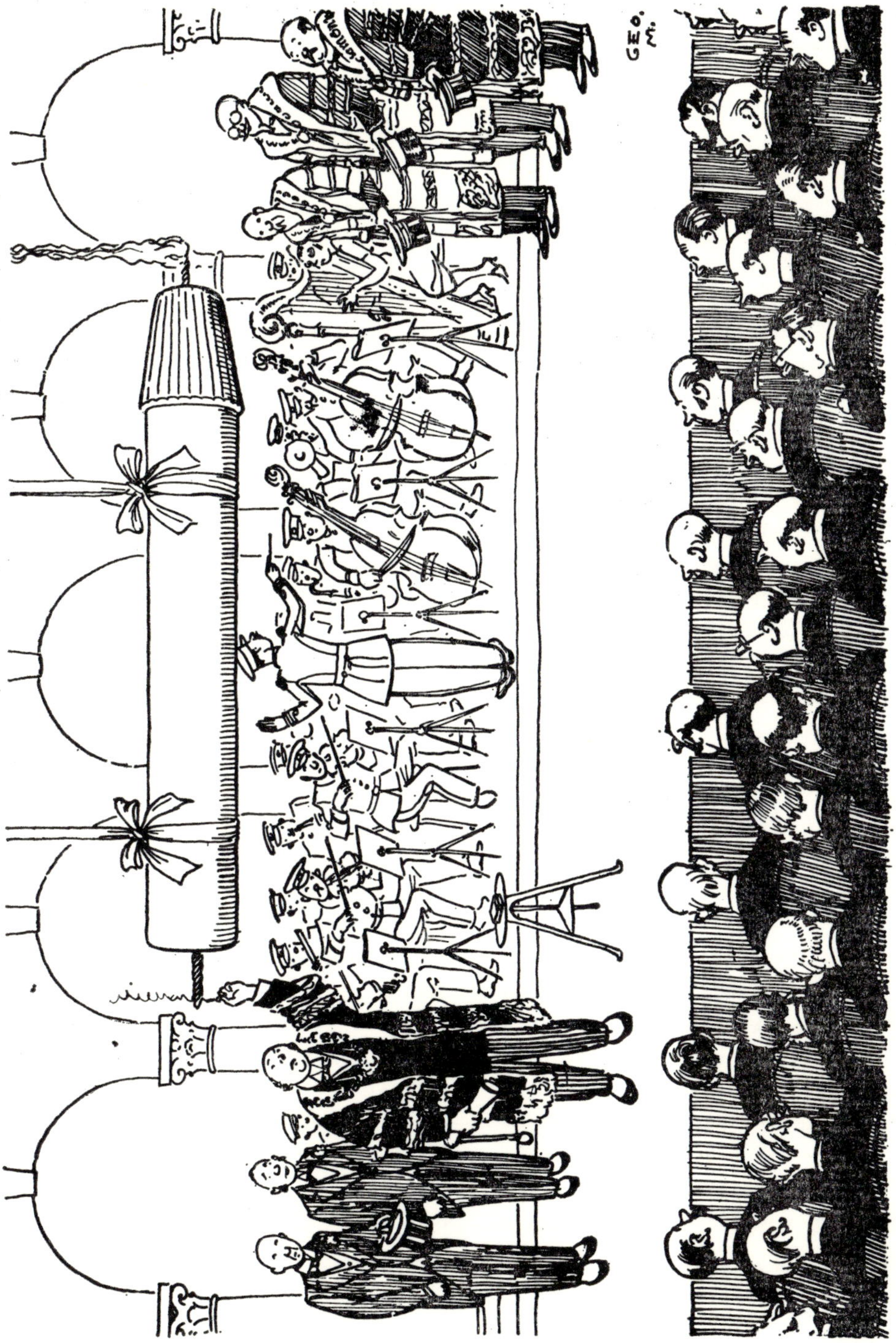

ENTERTAINMENTS AT WHICH WE HAVE NEVER ASSISTED.
The WAX CHANDLERS COMPANY perform the Ceremony of "Burning the Candle at Both Ends."

6. A fine piece of waxchandlery—as imagined by a *Punch* artist in 1926.

bers and friends. Those elected to the court are required to present a piece of plate in addition to paying the usual fine.[21] Recently a notable addition was received when a Mrs. E. E. Morgan left the Wax Chandlers most of her Georgian silver in the hope that it would find a permanent place among the company's treasures.

Bee-keeping, education and charities

Beeswax, once so important to the Wax Chandlers, is still a valuable commodity,[22] though candles and sealing-wax have ceased to be its principal applications. In the Roman Catholic church it is still an essential constituent of candles for liturgical use: paschal candles and the altar candles for mass need only contain 51% beeswax, and other altar candles 25%. Elsewhere, beeswax is used for making polishes, effigies,[23] models and artists' moulds for casting; in varnishes and cosmetics; and for medical purposes, being non-irritant and the best emulsifier for creams and ointments. The waxworks at Madame Tussaud's are made of three parts beeswax and one part Japan wax.

It was appropriate that in 1906, on the death of Baroness Burdett-Coutts, the Victorian philanthropist and the first woman to be made an honorary freeman of the city, the council of the British Bee Keepers Association should have named the master of the company as its new president; at the formal election, he was represented by the renter warden, John Roberts Dummelow, whose family had extensive Wax Chandlers connections.[24] In 1945 the B.B.K.A. was re-organised, and the private members formed the Central Association of Bee-keepers, which inherited the master as its patron, a position to which he had been elevated in 1922. In 1960 the Wax Chandlers invited the Association to hold an annual lecture meeting in the hall, the subject to be, if possible, related to beeswax, and in the following year the hall was used by the Bee Research Association to launch an international appeal, which enabled them *inter alia* to build a new research headquarters. The company subscribes regularly to both of these bodies.

In 1965 a liveryman and bee-keeper, A. G. Horton, became chairman of the Central Association, and at his suggestion the Wax Chandlers offered an annual award of £50 for the most successful candidate in the B.B.K.A's senior written examination; the prize, together with a diploma bearing the company's arms, is presented at a ceremony in the hall.

The Wax Chandlers' continuing interest in education was shown by further donations to the City and Guilds of London Institute, and by support for two other institutions connected with the city. One is Christ's Hospital, of which the company became a 'donor governor' in 1962. Now removed from Newgate Street to Horsham in Sussex, this most famous of Bluecoat schools was founded by Edward VI in 1553 for the accommodation and education of poor fatherless children. At the moment the company has two presentations, each of which provides full expenses for a boy or girl for seven years, the starting age being from 10¾ to 12¾, and it also supports the school's current development appeal.

There is also a link with the City University, which was inaugurated in 1966 with a charter naming the lord mayor as chancellor *ex officio* and the Wax Chandlers, among other companies, for representation on the court of governors. Founded in 1891 as the Northampton Polytechnic and designated a College of Advanced Technology in 1956, the new university has embarked on a programme of rapid expansion not only in engineering, mathematics and science but also in social science and humanities – and, very important for the city, in business and management studies. The students have already established a tradition of participation, in the Lord Mayor's Show as well as in social work. The company is subscribing to a fund launched in 1968 to support the university's £3½m. development plan.

The quarterly court meetings have long been supplemented by an audit court for passing the year's accounts and a bounty court for considering grants of money and charitable purposes generally. In recent years it has been the policy to allocate a third of the company's disposable income to charity. Much of the money goes to various benevolent, medical and educational instititutions, but a substantial sum is devoted to increasing the grants made to individuals under the various charitable trusts. It will be remembered that the bulk of the income from Kendall's, the only trust of any size, is allocated in accordance with the judicial decision of 1873. Part goes to the Parochial Charities of the City of London and part to the Bexley United Charities, where it helps to maintain a terrace of 12 almshouses for poor persons of good character who have been resident in the area; only the balance – at present of the order of £300 a year – is available for distribution by the Wax Chandlers to deserving cases. The gifts from Kendall's are supplemented by the small sums available from other trusts, including the ancient charities of Parnell, Frankwell and Caldwall. In 1961 one of Parnell's direct descendants, a widow, enquired if the Wax Chandlers could help in the education of her sons; the court was happy to honour the old connection by arranging for the second boy to follow the elder into Christ's Hospital and to be apprenticed to a past master.

In 1945 a small charity was inaugurated under the will of a past master, Havard Noel Bridgwater, and in 1963 a liveryman, H. R. Aldridge, set up a Lilian Fanny Rendell Aldridge fund in memory of his wife, a descendant of William Allt[25] who was apprenticed to a Wax Chandler in 1791; the proceeds contribute to the supply of the St. Paul's candles and to charitable purposes generally.

The Wax Chandlers' connection with its oldest charity, John Thompson's, was broken when the property was sold after the last war, and the company's obligations were redeemed by a single cash payment. However, it was felt that our earliest known benefactor should not be forgotten, and the company continues to honour his memory by gifts of overcoats to poor men of good character, and preferably of the city of London; there is a ceremonious presentation at the hall on St. Thomas's day each year.

Envoi

So far the fortunes of the London wax chandlers have been followed from the earliest days, when the self-employed craftsmen combined in a trade-association-*cum*-friendly-society, on to the time when a changing pattern in industry made the trade function redundant and the benevolence, once confined to the company's own members, could be extended to good causes generally.

Today, with the new hall as base and nerve-centre, the Wax Chandlers continue to follow the old pattern of ceremony, hospitality and charity and have added some touches of their own. Most recently, in 1969, they commissioned a set of gowns of entirely new design (plate 11). Blue and gold being the company's colours, the new gowns are made of blue cloth (black for the clerk) with multicoloured honeycomb enrichments on a gold background. The basic design is used for a livery gown to be worn by each liveryman at his admission ceremony when the master charges him with certain obligations (appendix 12), and more elaborate versions are worn by master, wardens and clerk on formal occasions.

Another innovation that is on the way to becoming a tradition is the 'clerk's toast'. This dates from 1959 when the company purchased some furniture and silver from the clerk, past-master C. G. Todd; at his request the money was paid into a Todd Memorial Fund, and it was agreed that once a year at some livery function the clerk should read out the names of the company's benefactors, giving details of their gifts and asking the livery to drink to their memory.

In 1966 the company inaugurated an annual but informal lunch at which the court entertains the lord mayor of the day; these functions afford him an opportunity of meeting members of the livery, and appropriately enough they take place shortly before Candlemas, the day when wax candles were consecrated for the service of the church.

And in case the Wax Chandlers at table might feel too far removed from the trade of their forbears, they remind themselves of the source of their raw material by burning beeswax candles, by serving mead in the loving cup, and by giving thanks in a grace written by a member of the livery:[26]

For thy creature the Bee,
The Wax and the Honey
We thank thee, O Lord.

By the light of all men,
Christ Jesus our King,
May this food now be blessed.
Amen.

Notes on Chapter V

[1]H. T. Pike (Cornhill) and E. T. Floyd Ewin (Castle Baynard). An alderman's deputy is *ex officio* H.M. Lieutenant for the City of London.

[2]In 1965 the G.L.C. and the 32 London Borough Councils in its area replaced the London and Middlesex County Councils, the County Borough Councils of Croydon and East and West Ham and eighty-two metropolitan borough, non-county borough, and urban district councils.

[3]The constituency was united with that of Westminster by the Representation of the People Act 1948.

[4]There are about 16,300 on the livery today.

[5]Now one of a large group of municipal buildings, which is often called 'Guildhall' without the definite article.

[6]Including The Honourable Artillery Company and also The Queen's Regiment and The Royal Regiment of Fusiliers, both descended from forces raised in the city.

[7]Of the 34 halls in existence at the beginning of the war 16 were destroyed, and only three saw the war through without severe damage; among them was the Ironmongers' to whom the Wax Chandlers had given refuge in the 1914–18 war. One disaster of 1666 was repeated when fire swept through the premises of some 30 publishers in Paternoster Row and consumed over 4m. books.

[8]The coronation of George VI in 1937 had been commemorated by the presentation of a case of silver-gilt coffee spoons, miniature replicas of the anointing spoon, to each member of the livery.

[9]*MS 9506–9* and *9511–2*: a copy of his notes can be seen on application to the clerk.

[10]St. Anne and St. Agnes, with which St. John Zachary had been united after the Great Fire, was damaged in the war of 1939–45 but is again in use, serving a Lutheran congregation.

[11]Other possible attributions are Edward Pearce the younger, who worked at St. Paul's under Wren, and William Kent (1720–50); the style is perhaps more like the eighteenth century.

[12]It was painted by P. A. Labouchère; his grand-daughter married Horace Mark Gregory, whose ancestors, when clerks of the company, had lived at the hall. Several companion works given to the company by the family were lost in the fire of 1940.

[13]They include copies of the Oath of a Freeman of the City of London (of Georgian date); an Act for the Rehabilitation of Orphans . . . (1694); an order that 'no negroes or other blacks' should be bound apprentices (1731); a notice to produce the body of William Budd, a reluctant liveryman (1739); and an order – reason unknown – to produce the certificate of apprenticeship of Ellis Juxon, Citizen and Merchant Taylor (1741).

[14]In 1901 the full-time office was put in abeyance, apparently for financial reasons. The present incumbent, J. Barker, and his wife are also responsible for the catering at the hall.

[15]It came from the home of his grandfather, Charles John Todd I, as did other furniture including a desk and a firescreen.

[16]This type of clock is described in F. J. Britten's *Former Clock and Watch Makers and their Work*, 1894.

[17]The cabinet also contains a miniature of Charles John Todd II, which was presented by his wife together with a miniature of her father, George Winch (an assistant in 1907); she also presented the painting of her son, C. G. Todd, now hanging in the ante-room.

[18]The originals of the photographs are in the Crace Collection at the British Museum. Both the Shepherds were well-known in the early nineteenth century as topographical artists specialising in London buildings.

[19]Probably a Protestant refugee from Transylvania, he is said to have worked in Gresham College and to have taught chemistry to John Webster, the parliamentary surgeon-chaplain and metallurgist.

[20]The menu for a dinner held in 1910 – not a special occasion – was as follows:

Punch	Hors d'oeuvres
Madeira Old Black Seal	Clear turtle
Hock Steinberg Cabinet 1893	Trout, verte sauce
	Whitebait
Moselle Berncastler Doctor 1904	Terrines de foie gras
	Miroton of duck and peas
Champagne Pol Roger 1900	Saddle of mutton
	Quails
Port 1870	
Dow's 1887	Ham salade mariette
Claret Dueni Beaucaillon St. Julien	Orange jelly
	Meringues
	Fruit salads
Sherry Choice Old (Wollaston)	Devilled lobster
	Ices

[21]This was £21. Other fines were as follows:

	servitude			*patrimony*			*redemption*		
	£	*s.*	*d.*	£	*s.*	*d.*	£	*s.*	*d.*
Freedom	2	8	6	3	5	0	10	8	6
Livery	26	5	0	26	5	0	52	10	0

[22]It is mainly imported from Africa, America or Australia.

[23]Some old examples of waxwork can be seen in the museum at Westminster Abbey: among them are contemporary effigies of Charles II, William and Mary, and Anne.

[24]James Dummelow was apprenticed to Samuel Brandram on Lady day 1800 and became master in 1846; three of his sons were admitted as freemen, and his grandson and great-grandson became masters in their turn. In the early part of the nineteenth century Dummelow was a partner in the firm of Brandram Bros., manufacturers of saltpetre, vitriol, and white lead at Rotherhithe with offices in Size Lane in the city. Seven members of this firm and its associates became masters of the company, starting in 1770 with William Caldwall, who founded a minor charity and whose portrait hangs in the hall, and continuing with Thomas Templeman, Thomas Brandram, Samuel Brandram, James Dummelow, Samuel Carless, and Plaxton Samuel Carless.

[25]He was connected with the Brandrams and the Dummelows, and his son and grandson also became masters of the company.

[26]Rennie Simpson, sometime a Minor Canon of St. Paul's and now Precentor of Westminster Abbey.

List of Appendices

APPENDIX I

ORDINANCES OF 1358[1]

This Ordinance was made in the time of John de Stodeye,[2] Mayor, at the Feast of the Nativity of St. John the Baptist in the 32nd year [Ed III].

For redress of many grievances and damages that divers folks have in many cases suffered in the City of London, as to the which remedy has not been ordained heretofore; the Mayor, Aldermen, and Sheriffs, with the assent of good folks[3] of the Commonalty, have ordained the Articles underwritten, for the profit of the common people.

In the first place it is ordained that all the Waxchandlers who are dwelling within the said city, and in the suburb, as well freemen as foreigners, who shall make torches, cierges,[4] torchettes,[5] priketz, great candles, or any other manner of wax chandlery, for sale, shall make such torches cierges, torchyz, priketz, and all other things which pertain unto their trade, of as good wax within as without, making the whole thereof of the same wax; and that they shall not put into their wykes any fat, code,[6] rosin, or other manner of refuse; nor shall they use old wax and worse within, and new wax without. And that they shall not make their wykes, which they put into such manner of work, of excessive weight, so as to be selling wyke for wax, to the damage, and in deceit, of the common people; but let their wyke be in accordance with the quantity of the wax, as it reasonably ought to be. And if any waxchandler shall from henceforth do to the contrary of the Ordinance, and of the same be duly convicted, the first time, all the torches, cierges, torchyz, priketz, and other waxchandlery, that shall be found in his possession made, shall be burnt before the door of him who shall have made the same, at the place where he dwells, and his body shall be committed to prison; until he shall have made fine to the Commonalty, at the discretion of the Mayor and Aldermen, for such manner of deceits and falsities committed, to the damage of the common people and the scandal of the said city. And on a second default, let the torches and other works be burnt as is before ordained, and his body be put upon the pillory. And the third time, he is to forswear the City, and all torches and such work.

And that this Ordinance may be the more surely kept and maintained, let there be forthwith chosen two or four of the most lawful folks of the said trade; who shall be sworn before the Mayor and Aldermen, lawfully to present all the defaults that they find in their trade, from one day to another. But in case any reputable man shall come to the aforesaid waxchandlers, and shall wish them to make torches, torchettis, prykes, cirgez for mortuaries,[7] or other large candles, of old and new wax, mixed together for his own use, the waxchandlers may have the same made at the will of the owner, without hindrance thereof, so that he make no sale thereof, on the pain aforesaid.

[1]Translated from the original Latin and Norman French of Letter Book G and printed in Riley's *Memorials*, p. 300; see also *MS9495*, fol 10r–10v.
[2]A notable Vintner who left his company the land surrounding their first hall.
[3]*Les bons gentz*: the better sort or most discreet, not the whole commonalty.
[4]Cierge: wax taper or candle (F). [5]Torchette: small torch. [6]Code: cobbler's wax.
[7]Mortuaries: funeral or memorial rites.

APPENDIX 2

ORDINANCES OF 1371[1]

To the honorable menne, the Maire ande Aldremen of the Citee of London, shewen the goode folkes of the Waxchaundelers of the saide Citee, howe their crafte hath been evill ruled and governed afore this tyme, and yet is gretely slaundered of all the good folke of the saide crafte and of the Citee, for that they have not Maisters chosen of the saide crafte and sworne afore you Maire and Aldremen as other crafts have, to overse the defaultes which ben in their said craftes and theym to the Maire and Aldremen present of the said Cite: and for that, honorable Sirs besechen the saide goode folkes your gracious lordshippes, that it please youe to graunt to the said good folkes that they may chuse among theym iiij goode people of the said folke, and that they be sworn afore youre honorable lordshippe to overse all the defaults in theyr saide crafte, ande theym present afore the Mayre and Aldremen for tyme beying, so that the trespasours may be punnyshed after theyr defect, and that the poyntes undrewriten may be graunted unto theym and enrolled in the Chamber afore you, for the comon profite of the said Citee.

First, that no Waxchandler of the saide crafte make any torches, tapers, pryketts, nor non other manr of chaundelerie of wax mixed with rosyn and code, but of goode wax and wyke. And if any Waxchaundelere of the saide crafte make in tyme to come torches, tapers, pryketts, or other chaundelerie of wax to selle, that is mixed as is aforesaide, that may be founde and pved by the Maisters of the said crafte afore the Maire and Aldremen not convenable wax or wyke, that he that shal be so atteynt pay to the Chamber[2] at the first time vi*s* viij*d*, and at the ijde tyme to the Chamber xiij*s* iiij*d*, and at the iijde tyme to the said Chamber xx*s*, and at the iiijth time forswere the crafte for evermore.

Itm. That every chandeler of the said crafte within the franchises of London, take for hire of Pound tapers for entiermentes[3] for every lb. wax 9*d*, paying to the chandelere for the wast of the said tapers, and for the hire of the herses[4] and chaundelers to bere the said tapers reasonably.

Itm. For square tapers within the said fraunchises of London, take for the hyre of pounde tapers for every pounde 9*d*, paying to the chaundeler for the wast.

Itm. For the hire of torches for every lb. 9*d*, paying to the chaundeler for the wast.

Itm. If any manne bryng wax to the chaundeler thereof to do or make torches, torchetts,[5] prykettes or perchers,[6] chaundell or tapers for women ayenst Candelmas, that the chandeler take for every lb. wax *ob*[7] for the making, and he that shall do it to be made bryng wyke, or pay for wyke.

Itm. If any man bryng wax to make of the same waxe round tapers or square, that the chaundeler take for every lb. wax *ob* for his travaile.

Also prayn the saide goode folkes that evy chaundeler of the said crafte in the said Cite have a marke, and it sett to torches, torchetts and tapers whiche he makith, so that if any defaut be founde in the said torches, torchetts and tapers, that he may be knowen in whom the default is, and be punnyshed after his trespas uppon ordnance; and that such torches, torchets & tapers, not marked in manr aforsaide, be forfait to the Chambre aforsaid; and afterward the Fryday next folowyng avisement theruppon hadd between the Mayre and Aldremen it is accorded and by theym graunted, that th articles aforesaide should be kept, &c. and the trespasours punnyshed in forne aforsaid. And theruppen Waulter Rede and John Pope were chosen and sworn, the Friday next after the Feste of Seynt Martyn the Byshop, xlv yere of the reign of Kyng Edward the iijde, that they well and treuly shuld overse the saide craftes ande the defaultes that they found from tyme to tyme to the Mayre and Aldremen present, &c.

[1]Translated from the original Latin and Norman French and printed in the Royal Commission Report 1837, p. 104; see also *MS9495*, fol 8r–8v.
[2]The city's bank.
[3]Interments.
[4]Herse: iron candlestand.
[5]Torchetts: small torches.
[6]Perchers: tall candles, often placed on a high shelf.
[7]*ob*: halfpenny.

APPENDIX 3

CHARTER OF 1484[1]

RICHARD, by the grace of God Kynge of England and of France and Lorde of Ireland, to all people to whome these present letters shalle come: Gretyng. Knowe ye that of our speciall grace we have graunted and gyven licence and by these presents we graunte and gyve licence for us and our heires as moche as in us is to our welbelovid faithfull and liege men, the free menne of the mistiere or crafte of Wexe Chaundelers of our Citie of London, that they and all their successours, free men of the saide mistier, that is to sey the citizeins of the saide Citie and in the Citie aforesaide and in the suburbs of the same dwellyng and to dwelle from hensforth mutte be in dede, thyng and name one body and one comonaltie for evermore. And that the same commonaltie, that is to sey the free men of the said mistere every yere mutte chose and make of theymselfs after their custume amounge theym aforeused, or better by th'advice and ordinaunes of the same comonaltie herafter thereof to be made, one maister and two kepers or Wardeyns to supporte the nedes of the same and to oversee, rule and governe the mistiere and comonalite aforesaide, and all the men and occupiers, servants, stuffe and werks whatsoever they be of the same mistere in the Citie and suburbs aforesaide forever, and the defawts of the same duely to correcte and doo to be corrected: and that the saide maister and kepers and the comonaltie aforesaide mutte have perpetuell succession and a comon seale for the nedes of the mistere and comonaltie aforesaide for evermore to serve; and that the same maister and kepers and comonaltie and successours forevermore mutte be hable persones and capax in the lawe for to purchace have and possede to theym and to their successours forevermore in fee and perpetuitie or otherwise, londes tenements rents and other possessions whatsoever they be, as wele in our saide Citie and the suburbs as ellswhere, of eny maner persones and that the same maister, kepers and commonaltie and their successours by the name of the maister, keper and comonaltie of the mistere of Wexchaundelers of the Citie of London mutte pleade and be impleaded before al maner Juges and in all maner courts and accions whatsoever they be; and by that the same name they mutte be called and named for evermore.

AND MOREOVER, that the same maister and kepers of the saide mistere and their successours mutte have fulle power and auctoritie for evermore to serche and attempte, and to make and exercice a dewe serche moreover and of all maner weights mesures and stuffe, by whatsover persones and occupiers of the same mistere in the City and suburbs aforesaide hadde used and occupied, and of all stuffe of wexe in whosoever handes it shalle happen to be withyn the said Citie and suburbs of the same, so that dewe, juste and trewe weights of mesures and stuffe in the same mistere and by all other there, mutte be occupied and used; and of all synguler other goodes and marchaundizes of the foresaide mistere by suche men and occupiers of the same mistere, solde and to be solde and to sale putte or to be putte that they mutte be hable, good and laufull withoute disceyte or frawde in enywise; and duely to correcte the defaulte and disceyte whiche in that behalfe they shall fynde, and all maner persones in that behalfe doyng contrarye accordyng to their demerits and delicts, duely to punyssh or doo to be punysshed, by the oversight of the Mayer of our saide Citie of London for the tyme beyng at suche tymes onely what the saide Mayer by the foresaid maister and wardeyns duely shalbe requyred.

AND MOREOVER of our more plentevous grace we have graunted and by these presents graunte for us and our heires that the same maister, wardeyns and comonaltie or their successours mutte purchace of eny maner persones or persone, landes tenements and rents as wele in demeane as in reversion withyn the Citie of London and the suburbs of the same or ellswhere, whiche of us mediatly or immediately or of eny other persones by whatsoever service they be holden, to the valure of fyve marks[2] by yere. To have and to holde to the same maister wardeyns and commonaltie and to their successours for evermore, to the ayde and supportacion of the nedes and poure men of the commonaltie of the crafte aforesaide, to pray for the good state of us while we lyve and for our soule whan we shalle departe from this lyfe, and for the soules of all our progenitours, and for the benefactours of the said mistere and the soules of theym whan they shall departe from this worlde, accordyng to the ordinaunce and disposicion of the saide maister, wardeyns and commonaltie and their successours in that partie to be made. And also by the tenour of these presents we gyve speciall licence to eny persone or persones that he or they mutte gyve bequethe or assigne londes tenements and rents to the yerely valewe aforesaide, to the saide maister, wardeyns and comonaltie and to their successours for evermore withoute impechement, lette, trouble or greve of us or of our heires or the Justices, Eschetours, Shiriffs, Crowners or other Bailyffs or ministres of us or of our heires in eny wyse, and withoute eny Inquisition by vertue of eny our writte of ad quod dampnum[3] or of eny other our commanndement in that behalfe to be taken or pursued: and withoute eny other our licence or other our letters patents to theym in that behalfe to be graunted or made the Statute of Londes and Tenements notte to be putte to mortmayn or eny other statute, acte, ordinaunce or provision thereof in to the contrary made or ordeyned notwithstondyng.

IN WITNESSE whereof these our letters we have doon to be made patent.

TESTIE myself at Westmynster the xvith day of February the firste yere of our reigne. Gunthorp.[4]

By wrytte of the Pryve Seale and of the date aforesaid by auctoritie of Parliament for xxv marks[5] paide in the Hampere.[6]

It is enrolled in the memories of th'Eschequer of the firste yere of Kynge Richard the Thirde, that is to say among the receyts of the terme of Sainte Hillary, the sixte rolle on the parte of the Remembraunces of the Tresorie.

It is enrolled in the courte of our Lord the Kynge in the Chambre of the Yeldehalle of the Citie of London in the book marked with letter L, the clxxxxiiiith leaf of the same booke of the tyme of Robert Billesden,[7] Mayer of the Citie aforesaid the firste yere of the reigne of Kynge Richard the Thirde. Dunthorn.[8]

[1]Translated from the Latin of the original exemplification *MS9517* for *MS9495* fol 76r–77r. [2]*66s. 8d.*

[3]*Ad quod dam(p)num:* L to what loss. This ruled out any enquiry into the loss of feudal or other dues resulting from the grant of a licence in mortmain.

[4]John Gunthorpe, Dean of Wells, was appointed Keeper of the Privy Seal, the third officer of state after the Chancellor and Treasurer, in 1483 at a salary of 20*s.* a day. The privy seal was used for legalising the private expenditure of the sovereign and was also a warrant for letters patent before they passed the great seal.

[5]*£16 13s. 4d.*

[6]The king's Hamper was the department of state in the Court of Chancery to which fees were paid for sealing and enrolling charters and other documents, these being kept in a wicker basket.

[7]Billesden, when mayor in 1483, resolved a disputed order of precedence between the Skinners and the Merchant Taylors by making them change places every other year.

[8]William Dunthorn, town clerk 1461–90, was the first to sign himself by surname only, still an occasional practice in this office. He compiled *Liber Dunthorn*, a book of London customs much cherished in the city archives.

APPENDIX 4

ORDINANCES OF 1488[1]

To the Right honourable Lorde the Mayre of the Citee of London, ande his Worshipfulle Brethrene th Aldremen of the same,

Humbly besechen unto youre good Lordshippe and wise discrecions, Maister, Wardeyns, and hole Felaushippe of the crafte of Waxchaundellers of this honourable & famous Citee of London,

That whereas they, for the reformacion of certain inconveniences in ther crafte, and goode ordre and rule to be hadd and kept within the same from henceforth, not only to the pleasure and weel of the Kyng ouref Sovaryn Lord and profite of his liege people, but also to thonor and worshippe of the saide Citee and crafte, have drawen and devised certen articules hereafter ensuying, whom it may please your said Lordshippe and wise discrecions to overse and under youre correccion to be admitted and enrolled of recorde, so as by th authorite thereof they may be the more fermely kept and obeyde, and this atte reverance of Godde, to whom they shalle pray for your prosperous perseverennce:

First, that alle persones of the saide crafte and Feloushippe, and every of theym, geve ther due and fytting obeysance uppon the Maister and Wardeyns of the same crafte for the tyme beyng, so that noon of theym rebelle ayenst the said Mayster and Wardeyns, nor disobeye theym, but honestly and meanly behave theym self ayenst they, & either of theym, in worde and deede, as right reason and the good ordres and rule of every honest & welledisposed Feloushippe or Commonaltie require uppon payn of forfaitinge of vj*s* viij*d* for every tyme that they or eny of theym offende and be found gilty in the same, the oon half thereof to be paied to the Chambre of the Cite of London, and the other halfe to the said crafte; and that undre lyke payn so to be devided, no persone nor persones of the said crafte and Felaushippe take uppon hym or theym to mayntene, favour or support eny suche rebellion or dissobessance to the saide Maister and Wardeyns; but if any such be attempted, to geve theyr lawfulle assistens to the withstandyng, subduyng and punnyshyng of the same, as the case shalle require.

Also, if eny persone or persones of the said crafte of Waxchaundellers be duely warned and sommoned to come and appere before the Maister and Wardeyns of the saide crafte, be it for attendance uppon the Mayre of the saide Cite, or other thyng concernyng his commandement, or for eny matter or cause touchyng the same crafte, if he faile thereof, and come not to the place to hym appoynted within thour lymyted at his said sommons, without a lawfull and a reasonable excuse, to pay at every suche tyme that he so faileth vj*d*, the oon halfe thereof to the said Chambre, and the other half to the forsaid crafte.

Also, that no manr of person nor persons, occupying the crafte of Waxchaundlers within the Cite of London and the fraunchise of the same, make no do to be made any torches, quarerres,[2] priketts, sises,[3] chamber morters, tapers, candelles, nor ymagery, but of goode and able wax and sufficient weke, that is to say, not puttyng thereto any rosyn, code, turpentyn nor tallough, whereby the Kyng's liege people may be deceyved and the crafte of Waxchaundellers forsaid dishonored; and who so be taken & found gilty in this, to paye for his fyne, the first tyme, xiij*s* *4d*; the ijde tyme, xxvj*s* viij*d*; and the iijde tyme, four marks;[4] the oon halfe of whiche fynes to be paid to the said Chambre, and the other half to the forsaid crafte; and he that offendeth the iiijth time, to be disabled, and never after to occupye the saide crafte within the said Citie nor the franchise thereof, but uttly to be excluded and put therfrom for ever.

Also, that no persone ne persones occupiyng the crafte of Waxchaundellers within the Cite of London and the fraunchise thereof, occupye any prynt, marke or seale to marke their ware with, but oonly suche as the Maister and Wardeyns of the said crafte have imprynted in waxe before theym, and put both it and the name of the owner in th endentuyr therfore ordeigned and made; and who so occupy eny other prynt, marke or seale to marke with his ware, ande therof duely convyct, to pay at eny time that he is so founden xx*s*; the oon halfe therof to the said Chambre, and the other halfe to the forsaid crafte; and if any of the said crafte hang, leye or sett to sale eny torches, torchetts or other wexe wrought that ought to be marked, and is not prynted with his due marke, to pay at every tyme that he is founde in that default ij*s*, to be devided as abovesaide.

Also, if any persone or persones within the Cite of London or the fraunchise therof, sette any wax wrouhgt or unwrought to be sold whiche is not goode and clene waxe, but medled wh other unleufull stuff, to the hurt and disceyt of the Kynges liege people and the grete dishonor and disclaunder of the saide Citee and crafte, that then the Maister and Wardeyns of the same crafte for the tyme beyng have authorite and power from tyme to tyme to sease waxe so medled, and to bryng it to the Chambre of London, ther to be presented.

Also, for asmuche as diverse persones dwelling within the Cite of London and the fraunchise therof, as well of the saide crafte of Waxchandellers as other sette foreyne and aliantes awerke in the same crafte, wherby the fewer prentises ben taken into the saide craft, and suche as have served theyr prntishode the lesse set aworke, not only agenst the profyte and availl of the Chambre of London, but also to the grete hurt and hynderance of the said crafte of Waxchandellers. It is therefore ordeigned & establesshed that no manr persone nor persones occupying the said crafte within the Cite & fraunchise aforsaide, take any foreyn or aliant into his service to worke in the said crafte, nor eny poynt thereof uppon peyn of forfeiture of xiij*s* iiij*d* for every foreyn or aliannt so taken and sett aworke as often as he or they be found gilty in the same, to be devided as is abovesaid.

Also where as diverse and many young men of the said crafte gevyng theym selfe to idelenesse and unlawfulle games, wandryng as vagabunds within the said Cite and the fraunchise throf, and will not applye theym selfe to worke in the saide crafte for reasonable wages, that if eny suche persone or persones so wandryng be desired & required to worke within his crafte for reasonable hire or wages, and it refuse and wille not wyrke, that then the Mayster and Wardeyns of the same crafte for the tyme beyng take and bryng theym afore the Maire of the said Cite or th Aldremen, to be punnyshed as a vagabunde tille he bee reconsiled and offre hym selfe to worke.

Which bill or supplication being read, and by the said Mayre and Aldremen fullie understood, and forasmuch as it seemed to theym the said Mayre and Aldremen that the articles in the said bill or supplication conteined were goode and honest, and agreeable to reason, therfore they, beyng of one minde, assent and will, ordained and decreed that the said articles bee here entred of record, in manner and forme as to theym is desired and firmelie to bee kept and observed in tyme to come.

The Ordinances before written were graunted and inrolled in the tyme of the Maioraltie of Sr William Horne,[5] knight, in the third yeare of the raigne of King Henry the Seaventh.

[1]Translated from the original Latin and Norman French and printed in the Royal Commission Report 1837, p. 104; see also *MS9495*, fol. 12r-13v. [2]Quarerre: large square candle for funerals.
[3]Sise: small round candle used at court and in churches. [4]26*s.* 8*d.*
[5]Sir William Littlesberry, alias Horne, was so named by Edward IV for his skill as a horn-blower; a Salter, he was knighted on the field by Henry VII.

APPENDIX 5

ORDINANCES OF 1514[1]

1. In primis for election of the Wardens: be it ordeyned and established that every ij yeres ones the sayd Maister Wardens and Feliship after their wount maner and laudable custume shall assemble at their common hall, that is to say in the day of the fest of the Transfiguracion of oure Lord God, and then and there to electe and chose oon Maister Warden and two other Wardens associatt unto hym to rule order and governe the same Feliship for ij yeres then next and immediatly ensuyng, whiche sayd Maister and Wardens shalbe elected and chosen of the most wyse sadd discrete and substanciall persons of the same Feliship: and every such persone as hath byn Maister and Warden or oon of them shall not be elected eftsones to the same office of Maister or Warden of ij yeres next ensuyng the tyme of hys office expired onlesse he woll be agreable hym self therunto: and if eny person named and elected to the same office of Maister and woll denye or refuse to occupie the same shall forfett to thuse of the same Feliship xl*s*, and what person being named to be Warden or eny of them and woll denye or refuse same office shall forfett to the same use xx*s*.

2. Item for the generall obett: be it ordeyned that the next day after the sayd feast of Transfiguracion of our Lorde God yerely from yere to yere the sayd Maister Wardens and Felliship do kepe an anniversarie and obett solempnely in their place accustumed, for the soulles of the bredren and sustres of the same crafte passyd oute of this transitory lyffe; and what person beyng warned and comyth nott if he hath byn Maister or Warden shall forfett at every tyme xij*d*, and if he be of the lyverey and have not ben Maister nor Warden shall forfett every tyme viij*d*, and all others makyng lyke defaute apon the sayd warnyng to forfett iiij*d* to the sayd craft, resonable excuse all way reserved and excepted, and the same excuse to be examyned and allowed by the Maister and Wardens.

3. Item for election of the vj viewers and assistencs of the sayd occupacion: be it ordeyned that the sayd Maister Wardens and Felleship every ii yeres shall chose and name vj honest persons to be viewers thorough the same occupacion within the citie and liberties of the same and they to contynewe in the same fully ij yeres; and if eny of them them fortune to decesse then an other to be chosen in the place of hym or them so decessyng; and the same vj persons every quarter oons at the lest or oftener as the case shall require, to viewe aswell the weights of the same occupacion as also almaner of stuff wrought and to be wrought within the same occupacion accordyng to the graunte or grauntes by the Kyng's grace or eny hys progenitors to the same Maister and Wardens and their successors made and graunted in that behalf, so that the Kyng's subiects be not disceyved by corrupte and unlaufull stuff: and if eny stuffe beyng unlaufull and forfeittable and founde to be sold in any man's hands within the same citie liberties or franchies of the same, then apon relacion made by the same viewers the Maister and Wardens shall take oon officer with them and to sease the same stuff being forfetable to the use, that it to say oon half therof to the Chamber of London and thoder half to thuse of the same Feliship; and the same person or persons which made the same unlaufull stuff if he be takyn within the same citie to be therfor punyshed accordyng to the qualitie or quantite of his offence, so that the same stuff shall never afterwardes come to eny person's hands to be sold in deceipte of eny of the Kyng's subiects. And moreover if any person usyng the same occupacion with the sayd citie or suburbs of the same doo worke eny maner prikettes tapers torches torchetts or eny other maner of stuff or thyngs belongyng

to the same occupacion nott beyng clene and convenient stuff, ther for the sayd Maister and Wardens for the first and second defaultes to assesse apon hym soo affendyng such fyne resonable as the Master Wardens and the vj viewers woll assesse, and the third tyme his stuff being forfettable to be seased and ordered as is aforsayd and the same person to be expelled for ever from the same Felloship onelesse he can fynde good and sufficient sureties to be bounden to thuse of the same Felloship that he shall not worke eny maner of stuff of the same occupacion being corrupte but good clene and laufull stuff accordyng to the good order of the same occupacion, so that the Kyng's subiects and the commen people of this Roialme be nott disceyved by eny person or persons of the sayd Feliship.

4. Item for obedience of the occupacion: be it ordeyned that all such persons as be of the same Feliship of what estate degree or condicion he be, in all laufull and honest maters concernyng the same occupacion shalbe at altymes obedyent and conformable to such laufull and resonable rules and divises as from tyme to tyme shalbe ordred divised and made by the sayd Maister and Wardens and assistents consernyng the sayd occupacion, aswell for the fest of Corpus Christi lights midsomer lyghts and burialls, as also for all other thyngs and causes as shall incidently happe and chaunce emong the personnes of the same occupacion from tyme to tyme. And the same Maister Wardens and assistents to putt and sett such reasonable penalities and other fynes apon the offenders and disobedient personnes for their corrections as shalbe by them from tyme to tyme thought metely and convenient for the same.

5. Item for workyng within their houses: be it ordeyned that no maner of person or personnes of the same occupacion use exercise or make nother doo to be made or wrought eny maner candells tapers lynks or torches or eny other maner of thyng concernyng the same occupacion of Chaundrie within the citie or liberties therof but it be within hys or their dwellyng houses or shopps or within a house or shope of a Freman of the same occupacion, so that serche and viewe of the workers and workmanship may be seen taken and had, onelesse it be with grete Lords and estates and other honorable persons and men of worshop which have there stuff wrought within ther houses for their propre uses and expenses and not to be sold and putto sale. And what person or personnes offendeth or disobeyth the ordenaunce shall forfett and pay at eny tyme of his or their offence and brekyng, the same suche reasonable fyne as shalbe assessed apon hym by the sayd Maister Wardens and assistents for the tyme beyng.

6. Item for payng of quarterages: be it ordeyned that all and every person of the sayd Feliship pay or doo to be payd from tyme to tyme all and every suche reasonable somme or sommes of money as they shalbe assessed to doo by the sayd Maister Wardens and assistents, aswell for their quarterages the common charges and other nedes of the same occupacion as also such other imposicions and neccesarie charges as from tyme to tyme shall hap and fall: and every persone and personnes being in this behalf disobedient shall forfett at every tyme such reasonable somme or sommes of money as the sayd Maister and Wardens shall truely without malice assesse apon hym or them so disobeying.

7. Item that every man have a marke: be it ordeyned that every person of the same Felloship kepyng shop or workhouse shalhave a marke to be sett apon his workmanship wrought by him or eny his servaunts so that every man's worke of the same occupacion may be knowen and viewed by the sayd viewers, that it be good and laufull as is above specified.

8. Item that no man use that occupacion but Chaundelers: be it ordeyned that noo man use exercise or practise the sayd occupacion of Wexchaundelers within the sayd citie or liberties therof, but that he in all thyngs concernyng the same craft be obedient to pay and to be contributorie in every behalf as the other bretherne of the same occupacion.

9. Item for obedience: be it ordeyned that all and every person and persons of the same Felliship be at all laufull tymes and in all laufull and honest matters concernyng the same occupacion obedient unto the sayd

Maister and Wardens for the tyme beyng, to come to obetts processions and other neccesarie comaundements and not to absent or withdrawe hym self onelesse he have a good and reasonable excuse; apon payne every person offendyng this ordenaunce to forfett to the use of the same occupacion suche reasonable somme or sommes of money as shalbe assessed apon hym for his offence by the sayd Maister and Wardens.

10. ITEM for entysyng of another man's servaunte: be it ordeyned that no maner person of the sayd occupacion counseill procure intyse nor stirre eny other man's servaunt of the same occupacion oute of service of hys Maister duryng the tyme of his reteindre or as long as the Maister and servaunte be in covenaunt; apon payn of every person offendyng this ordenaunce to forfett at every tyme to the use of the same Felliship xl*s* or more or lesse after the discrescion of the Maister and Wardens, excepte it be laufull and reasonable grounds and causes ordered by the same Maister and Wardens, that the same servaunt shalbe at his libertie from the service of his Maister.

11. ITEM for oone person rebukyng another: be it ordeyned that noo person of the sayd occupacion in eny open audience revile an other person of the same occupacion being both of the clothyng of the sayd occupacion, nether eny person of the same occupacion nott being of the clothyng, in open presence or audience revile any person beyng of the clothyng; apon payn to every person offendyng this ordenaunce to forfett at every tyme to the use of the sayd occupacion vj*s* viij*d* or more or lesse as shalbe thought metely and convenient for the same offence by the same Maister and Wardens.

12. ITEM for the accompts of the same Maister and Wardens and other officers havyng charge: be it ordeyned that within xxx dayes next after the newe Maister and Wardens have takyn their othes and charges, aswell the old Maister and Wardens as also suche persones of the same Felliship as bere office wherby he shall eny thyng medell with receipts or payments or with the goods of the same Felliship, he or they in the common hall of the same Felliship in the presence of the newe Maister and Wardens, callyng to them the assistents and sadd personnes of the same occupacion suche as have ben Maister and Wardens, shall present exhibitt and make a due true perfitt and playn accompte, nott onely of all his receipts and redy money be moynes of forfettures or giftes to the Felliship of joells plate or other thyngs whatsoever they be that hath come to ther hands or to thands of eny of them to thuse of the same Felliship or to thands of eny other to ther knowelegge or consents, butt as well also of almaner of payments reperacions and charges with the names and specialties of such personnes as have nott payd their quarterages forfettures and penalities apon them assessed if emy such be: and then and there in the sayd presence they shall delyver the sayd bokes of accomptes or the true copie of them with the sayd redy money juells plate and other thyngs to the sayd new Maister and Wardens: and if eny redy money juells plate or other thyngs afore specified by reason of the sayd accomptes be founde or appere to remayn in the hands or charge of the sayd old Maister and Wardens or in thands of eny other their officers or in the hands of eny other to their use or to the uses of eny of them, then the same persons so being chargeable therwith shall immediately without delayes with sufficient sureties with hym bynde hym in a sufficient and convenient somme of money by his dede obligatorie at a certeyn and reasonable day to be lymetted by the same new Maister and Wardens, to bring the same redy money juuells plate or other thyngs wherin he is founde in arrerage or the very true value therof; that ys to say within ii monethes then next ensuyng: and the same goods or jowells to be valued by the othes taken apon a boke by such ii persons as have ben Maister and Wardens to be named by the new Maister and Wardens for the tyme beyng, so that by noo colorable moynes or crafty demeanour the goods of the same Felliship in eny maner of wyse be abused myspended or conveid: and as often as eny maner of person in maner and forme aforsayd woll refuse or denye to fynde suche suretie to be bounde as is abovesayd shall forfett at every tyme to the use of the sayd Fellisphip such reasonable fyne as shalbe assessed by the sayd Maister and Wardens for the tyme beyng.

13. MOREOVER to distreyne for penalties: be it ordeyned that if eny person or persons of the sayd Felliship, of what degree or condicion he be, that offendith in eny article or ordenaunce in this boke expressed and will denye or nott pay the same penaltie that apon hym or them is assessid for the same, that then it be laufull to the sayd Maister and Wardens for the tyme being at every laufull tyme to entre into the house or shope of hym or them so denying or refusyng to pay, and there to take a distresse or distresses convenient for the same, and the sayd distresse or distresses so takyn to lede dryve cariaway and kepe to the use of the same Felliship assignyng to the partie a day convenient and reasonable to content and pay the sayd penalties and forfettures, that ys to say within xx dayes next after the takyng of the sayd distresse or distresses and if the same partie at the sayd day to hym assigned wolnott content and pay the sayd forfettures and other premysses afore expressed, then the same Maister and Wardens have auctoritie by theis presents, after the use and custume of the citie of London, to prayse and make sale of the sayd distresse or distresses to the full contentacion of the sayd forfettures penalties arrerrages and other the premisses and every parcell therof. And if eny surplusage or rest of money of the sayd distresse or distresses praysed doo remayn, the same to be immediatly restored to the partie or parties of whome the same distresse or distresses were takyn and this to be don immediatly by the sayd Maister and Wardens for the tyme beinge.

14. ITEM for redyng the ordenaunces: be it ordeyned that every quarter oones the Maister and Wardens shall cause to assemble the hole occupacion and Felliship of Waxchaundelers or as many as they may at their common hall therfore accustumed, and ther openly in the same presence the Clerke of the sayd Felliship shall openly and distinctly declare and rede all the ordenaunces and othes in thys boke expressid and mensioned, or elles such articles and othes as by the Maister and Wardens for the tyme beyng shalbe thought most mete and convenient to be redd and declared, and neverthelesse the same Clerke every yere twyse without eny manner of excepcion shall rede and declare openly in the sayd presence every ordenaunce article and othes in this boke expressed, whereby no person or persons of the same Felliship shall pretende ignorans in the same ordenaunce and othes or eny of them. And what person being warned to come therto and if he have ben Maister or Warden and come nott shall forfett at every tyme xx*d*, and he be absent that is of the lyverey and have nott ben Maister nor Warden shall forfett at every tyme xij*d*, and every person nott beyng of the lyverey nother hath ben Maister nor Warden and come nott apon due warnyng therunto shall forfett and pay to the sayd use iiij*d*, reasonable and laufull excuse alweys reserved and excepte; and the same to be decerned by the Maister and Wardens of the sayd Felliship for th tyme beyng.

15. THE OTHE of the Maister and Wardens: ye shall swere ye shalbe true to oure souverayne lorde the Kyng and to his heires Kyngs and obedient and conformable in all laufull maters of this craft of Wexchaundelers as the Maister and Wardens of the same craft have ben accustumed: ye shall indevour you and every of you shall indevour hym self to the best he can iustly and indefferently to execute and do to be executed all the good and laufull ordenaunces herin expressid and hereafter to be laufully made orderyng the same Felliship, without sparyng of eny person or persons for affection reward mede drede or promyse of reward: duryng the tyme ye shalbe in the same office of Maister and Warden, of all and every such goods jowells plate somme or sommes of money as by reason of the same offices of Maister or Wardens shall come to any of your hands accordyng to your ordenaunces here expressed, ye shall make a good true and playn accompte or elles pay suche fynes as ye be ordered to pay by your ordenaunces for your noone so doyng. Ye shall nott for malice nether for love nor affection amercie any person or persons in a gretter or a lesse somme then after the qualitie or quantitie of his offence after your discressions and accordyng with your sayd ordenaunces. Ye shall nott utter to any straunger nott beyng of that Fellisship the good and laufull secretts and privities of the same craft nott beyng to the Kyng subietts or a commonweall of the Realme preiudiciall, but att

all tymes to your pere ye shall procure and as muche as in you is cause and help to encrease and welfare of the sayd craft. Ye shall nott chaunge your copy of that craft and goo to another craft for malice or evull wyll of eny person without the consent and agrement of the Maister and Wardens for the tyme beyng. Ye shall not colour no foreyns goods or workmanships by whiche the sayd craft shalbe hurt or hyndred and the Kyng's leages and his common people disceyved. Ye shall worke with no man in the sayd craft within the citie of London or the liberties therof but with oone of the sayd occupacion, onelesse it be with greatt lords spirituall or temporall or knyghts and other grett men, nott usyng the same to eny sale but to their propre and neccesarie uses. Ye shall sett noo foreyner to worke in the same occupacion as long as ye may have eny Freman to work your work for reasonable wages and hire, onelesse it be by the licence and concent of the other Maister and Wardens or assistents for the tyme beyng or elles ye to pay such fyne as is reasonable assessed apon you for your disobedience, so helpe you God and his saintes.

16. THE OTHE of all persons now made or herafter to be made free. Ye shalbe true to our souverayne lorde the Kyng and to his heires Kyngs in all maters lauful and convenient. Ye shalbe obedient to the Master and Wardens for the tyme beyng in that office and obedient and redy to come to there laufull somons excepte ye have good and laufull excuses, or elles ye to pay such penalties as ye shall forfett for your disobedience accordyng to the laufull ordenaunces of your craft, whiche ordenaunce and every of them to your power ye shall observe and kepe or elles as is aforsayd pay such penalties as ye shall forfett by reason of your noon observyng the same, all the good and laufull statutes of the sayd Felliship and all such thyngs as at eny tyme of assemble shalbe lefully in communicacion emong the Felliship at ther comon hall nott beyng to the Kyng's subiectts or a comonweall of the Reialme preiudiciall. Ye shall kepe secrett and nott disclose the same to eny of the Felliship and specially to eny suche person whom the same matter in eny parte doth concerne or toche, nother to eny other person what so ever he be to thentente it shuld be disclosed, so help you God and hys saints.

17. THE OTHE of the Clerke. Ye shall be true to our souverayne lorde the Kyng and to his heires Kyngs. Ye shalbe laufully obedient unto the Maister and Wardens of the same Felliship for the tyme beyng, and so from tyme to tyme ye shall rede or do to be redd all the ordenaunces in this boke expressid and make due and true entres as the Wardens shall truely comaund you, without sparyng of eny person for affection or for mede or for malice or for drede to hurt eny person by reason of eny entre. Ye shall not delyver the copies of any books conernyng the same Felliship nor eny articles wherby the Felliship may take any hurte, nother shewe the same books or make eny copies of them to eny person, withoute the comaundement assent or agreament of the sayd Maister and Wardens for the tyme beyng, so help you God and his saints.

18. AL WHICHE acts ordenaunces and othes in maner and forme afore specified at the request of the sayd Maister and Wardens and Felliship by auctoritie of the same acte of parliament, we the sayd Chaunceller Tresourer and Cheif Justices of ether benche aforsayd for good laufull and laudable ordenaunces Estatutes and othes doo accepte admitt and by theis presents asmuche as in us is ratifye laude and approve. PROVIDED alweys and forseen that these ordenaunces within this boke expressed or any of them in no wise extende or be preiudiciall or hurtfull to the Kynge's prerogatyfe, nother to the hurte of any graunte or grauntes by the Kyng or his noble progenitours before tyme made to the citie of London, or any other or any laudable custumes nowe used in the same citie. And in caas any article or articles in this booke expressed be preiudiciall or hurtfull to the Kyng's prerogatyve or to any graunte by the Kyng and his noble progenitoures made to the sayd citie of London or any other or to any laudable custumes above expressid, then the same article and articles and every of them so beyng preiudiciall and hurtfull as is abovesayd, to be voyde cassate and of noon effecte, any thyng by us the sayd Chauncellour Tresourer and two Chief Justices in this behalf doon or made

to the contrary notwithstondyng. IN WITTNES whereof to this present booke we have sett our signe manuels the xxiiij daye of Maye in the sixte yere of the reigne of our soveraigne lorde Kyng Henry the viijth.

[1]Transcribed from the original exemplification *MS9504* for *MS9495*, fol 15v-20r.

APPENDIX 6

ACCOUNTS FOR 1530–2[1]

Thys ys the Accompte of Thomas Lane Master William Hull and John Shepard Wardens of the Crafte & Mystery of the Waxchaundelers Countyng from the ffeast of seynt Michell tharchaungell in the xxijth yere of the Reigne of Kyng Henry the viijth Unto the same ffeast of seynt Michell tharchaungell in the xxiiijth yere of the sayd kyng that ys to say by the space of towe hole yeres complet

Mony Remaynyng in the Box

ffyrst Resceyvid of William Rogers late Master Edward Byllyng & John Skampion late Wardens of the Crafte of Waxchaundelers for the ffote of ther Accompte made for ij yeres endyng at Mihilmas in the xxijth yere of the sayd kyng . . . . iiij*Li* iiij*s* viij*d*

Summa iiij*Li* iiij*s* viij*d*

Resceyttes of Rentes the ffrst yere

ffyrst Rec of Mr Chamley ffor the fferme[2] of the Tenement[3] next the Trinitie hall in Aldersgate strete that ys to say for iij quarter of a yere endyng at the ffeast of Seynt John Baptist in the xxiijth yere of the reigne of kyng henry the viijth after xl*s* by yere And the first quarter that was Mihilmas quarter stode voyd . . . . xxx*s*

Also Rec of Roger Yong for the fferme of the tenement in the parishe of Seynt John zachary next vnto our hall for one hole yere endyng at the ffeast of Seynt John Baptist in the sayd xxiijth yere of the reigne of kyng henry the viijth . . . . xl*s*

Also Rec of John Stacy for the fferme of our Tenement in Colman Strete callyd Buns Aley that ys to say ffor iij quarter of a yere endyng at the ffeast of Seynt John Baptist in the sayd xxiijth yere after xxvj*s* viij*d* and the first quarter that was Mihilmas quarter stode voyd . . . xx*s*

Summa iiij*li* x*s*

Resceyttes of the Renttes

Also Resc of John fflege for the fferme of the tenemente in Colmanstret at xxiij*s* iiij*d* by yere that ys to say for iij quarter of a yere endyng at the ffeast of Seynt John Baptist in the xxiijth yere . . . xvij*s* vi*d*

Also Resc of John hynde for the fferme of our tenement in Colman strete at [ ] by yere that is to say for [ ] ayere endyng at the sayd ffeast of Seynt John Baptist in the xxiijth yere . . . . ij*s* vj*d*

Summa xx*s*

Resceyttes of the Renttes in the second yere

Also Rec of Mr Chamley for the fferme of the tenement in Aldersgate stret for one hole yere endyng at the ffeast of Seynt John Baptist in the xxiiijth yere of the Reigne of kyng henry the viijth . . . xl*s*

Also Resc of Roger Yong for the fferme of the Tenement in the parishe of Seynt John zachary for one hole yere endyng at the ffeast of Seynt John Baptist in the sayd xxiiijth yere . . . xl*s*

Also Rec of John Stacy for the fferme of the Tenement in Colman stret callyd Buns Aley for one hole yeres Rent endyng at the sayd ffeast of Seynt John Baptest in the sayd xxiiijth yere . . . . xxvj*s* viij*d*

Also Resc of John fflege for the fferme of the tenement in Colmanstret for one hole yere endyng at the ffeast of Seynt John Baptist in the xxiiijth [yere] . . . . xxiij*s* iiij*d*

Also Resc of John hynde for the fferme of another tenement in Colmanstrete for one hole yere endyng at the ffeast of Seynt John Baptist in the xxiiijth yere . . . . x*s*

Summa vij*li*

Summa of all the Renttes for two yere xij*li* x*s*

Resceyttes of Quarterages for ij [yeres]

ffyrst Rec of Master Lane	viij*s*	William Kendall	viij*s*
Resceyvid of Mr Hull	,,	William Symmys	,,
Mistress Shepard	,,	John Yerle	,,
Mr Lynd	,,	John Kechyn	,,
Mr Byllyng	,,	George Blancherd	,,
Mr Rogers	,,	Thomas Cressy	,,
Mr Skampyon	,,	Renold Ashe	,,
John Vawse	,,	John ffrankelyn	,,
Thomas Dersey	,,	Roberd Graye	,,
William Ormond	,,	Roberd Nashe	,,
John Davell	,,	Roberd Ward	,,
William Perse	,,	William Hyllyard	,,
William Russell	,,	Thomas Pykeman	,,
William Baynard	,,	Edward Lowman	,,
Thomas Lawles	,,	Roberd Phillipson	,,
Thomas Day	,,	Alysaunder Cotyng	,,
Thomas Grenell	,,	Alyn Creswell	,,
Thomas Sawkyns	,,	Thomas Vawse	v*s* iiij*d*
Water Sawkyns	,,	John Blythe	vij*s*
Roberd Bollmer	,,	John Roberdes	vj*s*
Nicholas Burton	,,	Symond Burton	vj*s*
Mistress Shorte	,,	Thomas Kempe	iij*s*
Mr Colte	,,	Thomas Wolpytt	ij*s* viij*d*
Mr Overton monk (*sic*)	,,	John Knyll	iiij*s*
Mr Nashe	,,	Thomas Johnson	iiij*s*
Mistress Gybson	,,	William Southwell	xij*d*
Richard fford	,,	William Wakefield	ij*s*

Summa of the quarterages for ij hole yeres xix*Li* xiij*s*

Rescyettes of ffynes[4] *in the Spase of thys ij yeres*

ffyrst Rec of Mistress Nashe for a ffyne of iiij Torchis vj*d*
Rec of her for overholyng of vj di lb[5] tapers iij*d*
Rec of her for a ffyne of x Torchis iiij*s*

Rec of Thomas Grenell for a ffyne of xx Torchis ij*s*
Rec of hym at Candelmas for di lb tapers to lyght viij*d*
for viij quarter[6] tapers & xxx penny tapers overholyd xvj*d*
for a ffyne of iiij Torchis viij*d*
for late commyng to poulles[7] on Jesus day iiij*d*
for topyng[8] of a lyght at seynt Tolys[9] And for topyng of a lyght at sent Thomas of Acres & for a fyne of xij torchis ix*s* viij*d*

Rec of Thomas Cresse for a ffyne of viij Torchis xvj*d*
the same tyme for a ffyne of xij Torchis ij*s*
at Candelmas for xvj quarter tapers overholyd viij*d*
A ffyne of xij Torchis ij*s*
for Amyttyng of Richard hys Prentys ij*s* vj*d*
for A ffyne of iiij Torchis Croppyd[10] xij*d*
ij pesys of pullen wax[11] weyng vij lb quarter di for A strese[12] for brekyng the pryse at Seynt Mary Mawdelyns in South Warke agenst Ester the same strese sold to Mr Davell for iij*s*

Rec of Misterys Rogers for Mr Rogers dynner and for ffynes xxij*s* vj*d*

Rec of John ffrankelyn for a ffyne of ix Torchis xvj*d*
for a ffyne of iij Torchis viij*d*
for brekyng of his owre iiij*d*

Rec of William Symys for a ffyne of vi Torchis xij*d*
for a ffyne of vj Torchis more xij*d*
at Candelmas for ij di lb tapers overholyd & x peny tapers to lyght iij*d*
for a ffyne of iiij Torchis Croppyd xvj*d*
for A ffyne of Midsomer Images[13] iiij*s* viij*d*

Rec of Reynold Ashe for a ffyne of viij Torchis xx*d*
for a ffyne of viij Torchis more xvj*d*
for brekyng hys ower iiij*d*

Rec of Robert Warde for A fyne of viij torchis xvj*d*
at Candelmas for a fyne of xx peny tapers to lyght iiij*d*
for a fyne of iiij di lbes tapers overholyd ij*d*
for a fyne of his Midsomer Imagis vij*d*
for brekyng of hys ower iiij*d*
for a fyne for lynyng of a lyght with gold ffoyn[14] xij*d*

Rec of Richard fford for a ffyne of viij torchis viij*d*
for a fyne of ij peny tapers to lyght ij*d*
for a fyne of viij torchis & tapers to lyght xij*d*
for brekyng of his ower iiij*d*
for a fyne of holy Candell over chargid vj*d*
for Revylyng of the Master & Wardens iij*s* iiij*d*
for Amyttyng of Mannyng his prentys ij*s* vj*d*
for a fyne of vj torchis & Gomyd[15] quaryers vij*s* viij*d*
for Rebewkyng of William Ormond ij*s* vj*d*

Rec of Mr Russell for a fyne of xxiiij torchis ij*s*
for a fyne of xl di lbes tapers to lyght iiij*d*
for amyttyng hym his prynte[16] ij*s* iiij*d*
for amyttyng of William Welles his prentys ij*s* vj*d*

Rec of Thomas Day for afyne of di lbes tapers to lyght viij*d*
for overholyng of iiij quarter tapers ij*d*
for afyne of iij dossen & ix torchis vj*s* viij*d*
for a Weyght to lyght iiij*d*
for a fyne of Midsomer Images iij*s* iiij*d*
for none commyng to prosession xij*d*
for his disobedyens on Johns day iij*s* iiij*d*

Rec of George Blanchard for a fyne of di lbes tapers to lyght iiij*d*
for overholyng of xviij quarter tapers & vj d tapers vj*d*

Rec of William Baynard for a fyne of iiij staf[17] torchis iiij*d*
for iij tapers Vnpryntyd iiij*d*
for commyng late to powlys to the generall Obet viij*d*
for xxiiij staf torchis & vj dossen quaryers Vnprynted ij*s* viij*d*
for none commyng to powlys vj*d*
for a fyne of Midsomer Images ij*s* iiij*d*
for a fyne of x torchis ij*s* iiij*d*
for his prentys more then the good order of the crafte wold suffer xl*s*

Rec of Thomas Darsy for a fyne of ij tapers Vnpryntyd j*d*
for a fyne of vij torchis xij*d*

Rec of Robert phyllipson for xliiij di lbes tapers Vnpryntyd xx*d*
that was dew before vj*s* viij*d*
for iiij quarter tapers Vnpryntyd viij*d*
for amyttyng of Hary Wadyngton his prentys bounde to Mr Devell ij*s* vj*d*

Rec of Mr Shorte for a fyne of xvj torchis vj*s*

Rec of Thomas pykeman for a fyne of vij quarter Roulles[18] beyng to sore chargid xvj*d*
for a fyne of Midsomer Images xij*d*
for ij bondelles of obit candelles to lyght iiij*d*
for lynkes nastely made xij*d*
for a fyne of Midsomer Images iij*s*

Rec of Robert Graye for overholyng of ij di lbes & ij quarter tapers ij*d*
for a fyne of vij torchis iiij*s* ij*d*
for toppyng of seynt Tolys lyght iij*s* iiij*d*

Rec of Robert Boulmer for xj d tapers to lyght iiij*d*
for a fyne of Midsomer Images ij*s*
for dressyng of atorche with Rachementes[19] xij*d*
for a fyne of Midsomer Images xvj*d*

Rec of John Blythe for j d tapers over weked[20] vj*d*
for mittyng hys prynt ij*s* vj*d*
for a fyne of ij torchis viii*d*

Rec of Mr Davell for obit candelles over weked ij*d*
for a fyne of xij torchis ij*s*
for xx quarter tapers over holyd iiij*d*
for a fyne of Midsomer Images xij*d*

Rec of John Vawse for iij quarter tapers over holyd ij*d*
for late commyng to powlles viij*d*
for a fyne of xij torchis for the sent xij*d*
for a fyne of Midsomer Images xx*d*

Rec of John Knyll for vj d tapers & ij quarter tapers over holyd iij*d*

Rec of Mistress Gybson for x quarter tapers gommyd vj*d*
for xxx quarter tapers & xxxj d tapers to lyght xx*d*

Rec of John Robertes for amyttyng of his prynt ij*s* iiij*d*
for hawkyng abought wth grene wax viij*d*
for a fyne of Midsomer Images xij*d*

Rec of Robert Nasshe for iiij di lb tapers overholyd ij*d*
for a fyne of viij torchis xx*d*

Rec of Nicolas Burton for viij quarter tapers to lyght vj*d*
for a fyne of viij torchis iij*s*

Rec of John Kechyn for a fyne of vj torchis xviij*d*
for brekyng of hys ower iiij*d*
for xl d tapers overholyd viij*d*
for A fyne of x torchis xx*d*

Rec of Thomas Sawkyns for Images ffyned xvj*d*
for another fyne for Images iiij*s* x*d*
for a fyne of xxviij torchis v*s*
for Amyttyng hys prentys Olyver Oker ij*s* vj*d*

Rec of Symond Burton for dressyng of a torche with rachementes xij*d*
for amyttyng of his prentys Thomas Rokelyf ij*s* vj*d*
for amyttyng of his prynte ij*s* vj*d*

Rec of Alyn Creswell for Rebewkyng of Water Sawkyns vj*s* viij*d*
for goyng away when the ordenances was Red at the quarter day vj*d*
for makyng of Charles Copers lyght with Collers v*s*
for that he cam not to the Courte at the Courte day viij*d*
for goyng away at a Courte day vj*d*

Rec of John Erle for brekyng of his ower iiij*d*
for a fyne of v torchis viij*d*
for a fyne of Midsomer Images xij*d*

Rec of Thomas kempe for amyttyng his prynte ij*s* vj*d*
for a fyne of Tenebris[21] candell gommyd xvj*d*
for brekyng of hys ower iiij*d*
for nawghty makyng of staf torchis xij*d*

Rec of William Kendall for afyne of ij dossen & di of torchis v*s*
for a fyne of Midsomer Images ij*s*

Rec of Mr Skampyon for afyne of Midsomer Images xij*d*

Rec of William Southwell for a fyne of Midsomer Images viij*d*
for amyttyng of his prynte ij*s* vj*d*

Rec of Edward Lowman for a fyne of Midsomer Images iiij*d*

Rec of Water Sawkyns for Rebukyng of Alyn Creswell at sent Mary Mawdelyns vj*s* viij*d*
for Edme for takyng the strese and for havyng hym before my lord mayer ij*s*
a strese A pese of pollen wax weyng lix lb di presyd at v*d* the j lb Summa xxiiij*s* ix*d ob*
more A pese of bole wax[22] weyng liiij lb presyd at iij*d ob* the j lb Summa xv*s* ix*d*

Rec of Mr Cotte for a fyne of obit Candelles to light xvj*d*
for a fyne of Midsomer Images viij*d*
for over wekyng of obit Candelles vj*d*
for a fyne of xviij torchis iij*s* iiij*d*
for a fyne of xxvij Croppis v*s*
for a fyne of Midsomer Images xij*d*

Rec for gommyd wax forfeyt in temys stret weyng lj lb at ij*d ob quarter* xj*s* viij*d quarter*
for nawty torchis endes weyng l lb at j*d ob* vj*s* ij*d*
for iiij staf torchis weyng xj lb di at iiij*d* iij*s* x*d* for iij lb of old wax xij*d*
Summa of the ffynes for ij hole yeres xviij*li* ij*s* xj*d ob quarter*

Resceyttes for Lyveres this ij yeres

ffyrst Rec of Richard fford	A spone & in mony	vj*s* viij*d*
William Kendall	,, ,,	vj*s* viij*d*
	The Second yere	
John Yerle	A spone & in mony	vj*s* viij*d*
George Blanchard	,, ,,	vj*s* viij*d*
William Hyllyard	,, ,,	xx*d*
William Symys	,, ,,	vj*s* viij*d*
Thomas Pykeman	,, ,,	vj*s* viij*d*
Thomas Wolpytt	,, ,,	[ ]
	Summa xlj*s* viij*d*	

Rec of Misteris Bateman for her husbondes bequest[23] A standyng Cupe gylt with A cover gravyn abought with Scripture.

Rec for the Dyners of ij hole yeres

ffyrst Rec of Master Lane	xl*s*	William Baynard	iiij*s* viij*d*
Mr Hull	xxvj*s* viij*d*	Thomas Day	,,
Mr Shepard	xxvj*s* viij*d*	Mistress Gybson	,,
Mr Rogers	iiij*s* viij*d*	Thomas Grenell	,,
Mr Lynde	,,	Thomas Sawkyns	,,
Mr Byllyng	,,	Robert Bolmer	,,
Mr Skampion	,,	Nicolas Burton	,,
Mistress Nasshe	,,	Richard fford	,,
Mr Shorte	,,	William Kendall	,,
Mr Colte	,,	Reynold Ashe	iiij*s* [ ]
John Vawse	,,	John Yerle	iiij*s* iiij*d*
Thomas Darse	,,	George Blanchard	ij*s* iiij*d*
William Ormond	,,	William Hyllyard	ij*s* iiij*d*
John Davell	,,	William Symys	iiij*s* iiij*d*
William Russell	,,	Thomas Pykeman	iiij*s* iiij*d*
Thomas Lawles	,,	Thomas Wolpyt	ij*s* iiij*d*
William Perse	,,	Alysander Cotyng	[ ]

Water Sawkyng	ijs iiij*d*	Robert Ward	ij*s*
John ffrankelyn	ij*s*	John Kechyn	,,
Robert Nasshe	iiij*s*	William Southwell	,,
Alyn Creswell	,,	John Robertes	,,
Robert Gray	,,	Thomas Cresse	ij*s* iiij*d*
Symond Burton	,,	John Blome	[ ]

Summa of the Dynners for bothe the yeres xij*Li* xv*s*

Summa of all the Resceyttes for the space of ij yeres lxix*Li* vij*s* iij*d* *ob quarter*

Here after folowith yerely paymentes for ij yeres as Quyte Rentes & Wagis with other yerely paymentes

ffyrst payde to my Lorde of Seynt Johns for the Quyete Rente goyng out of the tenement callyd the Cokk in the parishe of Seynt John zacharies for ij hole yeres endyd at the ffeast of seynt John Baptist in the xxiiijth yere xl*s*

Item payd to the Mastere of Jesus in the Crowdys at poulles for ij yeres xl*s*
to the parson of Seynt John zacharies for his tythes for ij yeres xiij*s* iiij*d*
to the Churche Wardens ther for the Clerkys wages for ij yeres iiij*s*
to the Skavengers for ij yeres endyng at Midsomer ij*s* viij*d*
for the lantorne lyght for ij yeres ij*s*

Item payd to John Alman our Officer for his wagis for ij hole yeres endyd at the ffeast of saynt John Baptist in the xxiiijth yere at xl*s* by yere iiij *Li*
to the Good Wyf Alman for her wagis for ij yere iiij*s*

Item payd for the hire of the Barge to Westminster when my lorde Maire takyth his othe for ij yeres at x*s* by yere xx*s*
for Russhes for bothe the yere viij*d*
to the Watermen to drinke for bothe the yeres xvj*d*

Item payd for xviij yeardes of White Cotton to make Cottes for iiij harnest men at Midsomer in the first yere at vj*d* the yeard ix*s*
for xviij yeardes of White Cotton for to make other iiij lyke Cottes At Midsomer in the second yere at vj*d* the yeard ix*s*
for the makyng of the same viij Cottes at viij*d* the pese v*s* iiij*d*
for Redd Clothe for the same Cottes for Crossis xij*d*
on Midsomer evyn & seynt Peters evyn for bred & drinke for the wachemen xij*d*
for iiij Scochyns with the Armes of the Crafte to sett on the same Cottes xiiij*d*
for iiij wachemen for my lord mayer for both yeres vj*s* viij*d*

Item payd to Thomas holmys on Jesus day for both the yeres ij*s* viij*d*
to the iiij poremen for both the yeres at xvj*d* by yere ij*s* viij*d*

for ther dynners for both the yeres iij*s*
for kepyng of the Cusshynges for both the yeres iiij*d*
to holmys wyf for Jesus lyght xij*d*
to the Bell Ryngers for bothe the yeres ij*s*
for iiij dossyn of Skochyns for both the yeres xiiij*d*
to the wayttes for bothe yeres iiij*s*
for Russhes at powles for both the yeres viij*d*
to the Joyner for makyng of the fframe for Jesus light xiij*s* iiij*d*
for Gold & Collers for payntyng & Gildyng of the same ix*s* vij*d*
for xvij lb of wax for Jesus lyght more then was rec of the craft vij*s* j*d*
for ij Obbettes At powles for both the yeres for tapers & Caustykes ij*s*

Item payd for the Obbett of Lawrence Stokwod to the parishe prest x*d*
for Dirige[24] & Masse vi*d* & for the bede Rowle[25] iiij*d*
to ij prestes more viij*d*
to ij Conductes[26] viij*d*
to the Clerke for dirige & mase iiij*d*
to hym for Ryngyng xij*d*
to the Sexton ij*d*
to the prestes & Clerkes to drynke when dirige was don viij*d*
to iiij Children synging in the quyer iiij*d*
gevyn in Almes to pore ffolke viij*d*
for ij gilte Caustykes & ij tapers xij*d*
for bred Ale & wyne for the Company when dirige was don ij*s* ij*d*
for the same Obbett in the second yere viij*s* vj*d*

Item payd to Misteris Spyser for her Annuite for half a yere endyng at our lady day in lent in the xxijth yere xxiiij*s* iiij*d*
to Mistress Spyser for her Annuite for half a yere endyd at Mihilmas in the xxiijth yere xxiij*s* iiij*d*
to the sayd Misteris Spy[s]er for her Annuite for half a yere endyd at our lady day in lent xxiijth yere xxiij*s* iiij*d*
to Misteris Sargeaunt for her Annuite for lxvij wekes at vj*d* the weke xxxiij*s* vj*d*
to Mistress Capast for xvij wekys from the xx day of May vnto the xvi day of September at vj*d* the weke viij*s* vj*d*

Item payd to John Almon for his Gowne when we gave newe lyvere xx*s*
for iij yeardes & a half of Cloth for Thomas Stones Gowne x*s* vj*d*
for A doblet & a Jerken of ffrees[27] for Thomas Stone ij*s* viij*d*
to Wolpytt for makyng of Thomas Stones Gowne xx*d*
for xj yeardes of Canvas to make Cottes hoddes & vyssers to the same for the Correccion of lewede (obstreperous) prentises v*s*
to Thomas Wolpytt for makyng of the same ij*s* viij*d*

Item payd to Master Clarencius for Alowyng of the Armes of the Crafte & Settyng to his hand xiij*s* iiij*d*

to Robert Porkelyn his servaunte ij*s*
to the Paynter for payntyng of the ij Vnicornes iij*s* iiij*d*

Item payd for the Charterhouse taper from the vth day of October vnto whitsontyd for xv lb quarter of wax redy made & spent with chaunge of iij lb ix*s*

Item payd for the dynner at our hall At the mayers ffeast for Water Sawkyns xxix*s* iiij*d*
for xij of the lyvres dynner to the same Water Sawkyns iiij*s*
more to the same Water Sawkyns for the Surplusage of his stresse vj*s* vj*d ob*
to Robert Bulmer for the dynner of xj of the lyvery at the mayeres ffeast in the secound yere iij*s* viij*d*

Item payd for a newe boke & for the translatyng of the boke of the confirmacion[28] xiij*d*
for x quereis of paper Ryall[29] to Make the boke of our Accomptes ij*s* viij*d*
for making & coveryng of the same boke ij*s* iiij*d*
John lynde for wryttyng of iij Accomptes in to the same Boke & for wryttyng of the Confirmacion xiij*s* iiij*d*
for breade & drynke for hym when he dyd wryhgt in our hall vj*d*
to Mr. Wylford skryvenor wryttyng of our Evidens[30] & drawyng of draughtes for conveyng of the landes of Mistress Spyser in Colmanstret xlvj*s* viij*d*
for the tabyll that stondeth above in the Gallery vj*s* viij*d*
for ij bokys & a quer of paper x*d*

Item payd at Westminster when we went & vppyd ij Swannys & iiij Synyttes at my lorde Barnes place[31]
to the Swaneherd for bote hyre vp and downe & for mete & drynke in the company of Mr Bugh Mr Russell Mr Skampion & Mr Baynard iij*s* iiij*d*
to Thomas Day for his Costes at Swan Vppyng for botehire and meate & drynke v*s* j*d ob*
to William Russell for a Synett & a half iij*s* iiij*d*
for his botehire for iij days & for meate & drynke xviij*d*
to William Ormond for his costes & botehire at Vppyng of the Swannys this yere vj*s* x*d*

Item payd to Wever the mayeres officer for havyng the fforren of Barnet to the Counter xij*d*
to the Counstable in holborne for helpyng vs to parte of his torchis viij*d*
to the wyf of the white lyon at sent Johns where we had more of his torchis iiij*d*
for meate & drynke that nyght & on the morowe yt we toke hym xx*d*
for botehire when we went to present his torchis in to the cheker[32] & for meate & drynke ther xij*d*
to Edmey for havyng of Water Sawkyns to counter for his disobedyence xij*d*
to Middelton of the Chamber for warnyng of Tomson barbour to be afore the Chamberleyn iiij*d*
the same day at Cardynalles hat when Tomson was afore the Chamberleyn in Company of Mr lyne & Mr Skampion xvij*d*
to Edme when he shuld have Thomas Cresse to warde xij*d*
to Edmey sergeaunte for havyng of Water Sawkyns & Alyn Cresswell to warde ij*s*
to Edmey for takyng of a strese at Water Sawkyns & for bryngging hym before my lorde mayer ij*s*
to Wever for havyng of Phillipsons servaunt to Counter xij*d*
Spente the same tyme when we waytyd for hym vj*d*
to Edmey when we toke the Gomyd Wax in temys strete xij*d*
to A porter to bere yt to yeld hall ij*d*

for our Brakefast & Edmeys the same day viij*d*
for havyng of John lambe to Counter for toppyng of a lyght xij*d*
to Edmey when we went to take Stressys xij*d*
to Edmey for havyng of Albryght to Counter & William hull for billytyng[33] of torchis at seynt Alpheis ij*s*
to ij sergeauntes for havyng of Marshall to counter for Sellyng of Thomas Kemps torchis ij*s*
for our dynner when we wayted for that matter in company of Mr Byllyng & Mr Skampion xxij*d*
for havyng of the same torchis to my lord mayere & from thens to the Chamber of London vj*d*
the same day for our Brakefast ix*d*
for havyng of William Ormond to the Counter because he came [to] prosession in nawghty Rayment & for Vngodly wordes xij*d*
to the Quest of Wardmotte in Colmanstret Warde when we were afore them to complayne of the breuhouse for feere of fyer viij*d*
to Edmey sergeaunte for warnyng of the Wardens of seynt dunston[34] to be afore my lorde mayer xij*d*
for enteryng of a playnte ayenst the fforen yt wrought ther ij*d*
to ij yomen for waytyng for the same fforen xij*d*
to Mr Recorder for his counsell iij*s* iiij*d*
for amerssement[35] vj*d*
to Mr Gardyner for his counsell for the matter at seynt dunstons xx*d*
at ffranklyns for our Soper when we had waytyd for Mr Recorder with master Gardener & other ij*s* iiij*d*
at the Roofe taverne when Mr Gardener & we dyd over se the Supplicacion xij*d*
at the Marmayde with Mr Gardener when we sought Mr Recorder xviij*d*
to Mr Gardener for drawyng of our wryttyng iij*s* iiij*d*
to Wryght for writtyng out of our Suplicacion in parchement xvj*d*
to Edmey for warnyng of the Masters of the Rodelyght of seynt dunstons to be at yeld hall[36] afore my lord mayer when we put in our bill of Supplicacion xij*d*
at yeld hall gate vppon Mr Paver Mr common sergeaunt when we putt in our Supplicacion iij*s* j*d*
to Thomas Thrower our Attorney for his ffee xij*d*
to hym for writtyng of a copy of ther Answere xvj*d*
to Mr White for his Counsell iij*s* iiij*d*
at iij Tonnes at yeld hall gate on Mr Paver xvj*d*
to Mr Gardeners servunt for wryttyng of the draught yt his master made xx*d*
at ffrankelyns in the Compayne of Mr Gardener Mr davyll Thomas Darse when we had byn at yeld hall for seynt dunstons matter iiij*s*
to Mr White when he dyd over se our bylles with our confirmacion iij*s* iiij*d*
at yeld hall gate on Mr Pavyer Mr Gardener & Thomas Throer for ther dynner & ours iij*s* iiij*d*
for Mr Pavyars Thomas Throwars and Edmeys Brakefast & ours at yeld hall gate xvj*d*
to Thomas Thrower for wryttyng of all our bylles in to one that our matter myght be red afore my lord mayer & the Aldermen iij*s* iiij*d*
for Thomas Throwers brakefast & ours at yeld hall gate iiij*d*
at yeld hall gate at a court day beyng ther with Vs Thomas Thrower Mr Byllyng & Mr Skampion x*d*
at iij Tonnes at yeld hall gate for our Brakefast iiij*d*
when we went to seke Mr Walsyngham & Mr Mondy ix*d*

to Mr Walsyngham for makyng reporte of our matter before my lord mayer for seynt dunstons ij*s* iiij*d*

to Nicolson that kepith the counsell chamber dore viij*d*

to Nicolson for warnyng of them of seynt dunstons twyse xx*d*

to Nicolson for warning of them of seynt dustons ij*s*

in the company of Mr Wylford Mr lynd Mr Skampion & William Baynard for our Sopper & Mistress Spisers ij*s* vij*d*

for our dynners in the company of Mr Clarencious Mr hall Mr Rogers, Mr lyne Mr Byllyng Mr Skampion Thomas Darse Mr davell William Ormond Mr Russell & William Baynard iiij*s* iij*d*

at the horsehed at a courte day vppon vs & Mistress Burton & her servaunt William Baynard & Kendall his servunte iiij*s*

at seynt Johns hed in the company of Mr hall Mistress Spiser & Garmayn & his wyf when we went to Mr Barnehalys with our wryttyng ij*s*

the xv day of December at the dagar in Chepe when lawles son complayned to the Chamberleyn wher Mr Gardener dyd overse our corporacion[37] xvi*d*

At the Cardynalles hatte when we were before Mr Chanberlyn for settyng Vp of lawles sons Shope with dyvers other of the Company iiij*s* j*d*

to mr hall for his counsell in dyvers thynges concernyng the crafte vj*s* viij*d*

over & above that we had at the buriall of Mr Rogers vppon the company & ther beyng Mr Westm (*sic*) Mr Overton & Coper ij*s* vj*d*

at the Starr in Chepe in the Company of Mr Skampion Mr Davyll Thomas Darse William Ormond William Baynard & other xx*d*

at the Cardynalles hatte in the Company of Mr hall Mr Gardener Mr lynd Mr Skampyon Mr Wilford & other iij*s* x*d*

at ffrankelyns on ffryday in Ester weke ther beyng when William Baynard Mr lane Mr hull & John Shepard spent ther mony for ther Serynges[38] over & above the same in the Company of Mr lyne Mr Byllyng Mr Skampyon Mr davyll Thomas day William Ormond & other iiij*s* vj*d*

at our hall at the buryall of Mistress Shorte over & above that we had iiij*s*

at seynt Johns hed the xxj day of Aprell when we went to Mr Baron halys wt Garman Homan & his wyf Olyver Southworthe Mr Gardener Mr hall & Wylforth iiij*s*

at the Cardynalles hat the xxv day of Aprell when Mr Baron halles was ther Mr hall Mr Gardener Mr Southworth & Mr Wylford at the Selyng of the Reles[39] from Olyver Southworth to the Crafte xiij*s* iiij*d*

the xxvj day of Aprell at our hall when Wylford brought home our wryttynges the whiche was xiiij pesis & he Askyd vj*li* xiij*s* iiij*d* for wryttyng of them & we greed not at that tyme xxiij*d*

the xxviij day of Aprell to Mr hall at the Star in Chepe xx*d*

the same tyme to Mr Gardener xx*d*

the same tyme for over lokyng of our wryttynges that Wylford had made for our mete & drynke ij*s*

when we went to Stratford to serche ther beyng Mr lynd Mr Skampion Thomas Darse with other iij*s* iiij*d*

at a serche day over & above our serche mony ij*s*

at ffrankelyns at a quarter day in the company of Mr lynd Mr Byllyng Mr Skampion Thomas Darse William Perse & others v*s* viij*d*

at ffrankelyns when Mr lyne gave a swan in the company of Mr Byllyng Mr Skampyon Mr Davyll

William Ormond Mr Russell & Baynard vs viij*d*
at ffrankelyns at the settyng vp of Jesus lyght ther beyng Mr Byllyng Mr Skampion Mr Davyll & other ij*s* vj*d*
for Bakyng of venyson that Mr hull gave vs at ffrankelyns ix*d*
at a serche day at the Marmayd in the company of Mr Gardener Mr lynd Mr Byllyng Mr Skampion Mistress Spyser Mr Colte & Perse vj*s*
at Westminster in the company of Mr Sargeaunte of the Chaundry William Perse Mr Overton Mr Byllyng & Mr Skampyon ij*s* j*d*
to yonges wyf for iiij half yeres when she payd her Rent viij*d*
when we went to stratford to Serche xiiij*d*
for bred drynke & ffyer for the space of ij yeres v*s* viij*d*
SUMMA of all the yerely paymentes with other charges for bothe yeres xl*Li* x*s* v*d*

Here after folowith Reparacions for ij yeres

ffyrst payd for makyng clene of the house in Aldergatestret & carying away of the Rubbysshe xij*d*
to Isottson Carpenter for a C & vij fote of borde for ij dorys & for ij purlyns for the stayers in the Seller & for iiij fyllettes to make legis and for bordes to lyne the doris iiij*s*
to ij Carpenters for iij days to make the same dorys & lyne them & to mende the stayres in the Seller & the pale at the dore iiij*s*
to the Goodman Stacy for Reparacions done in Colman strete on Mistress Spisers house & in Aldersgate-stret ix*s* x*d*
to the Smyth for iij boltes with hokys hynges & naylles iij*s* xj*d*
to the Plomer for mendyng of the Gutter xxj*d*
to a kerver for settyng the Armys of the Crafte in ij grete clowde Angelles[40] at powlles next to the Masters of Jesus pewys ij*s* iiij*d*
for mendyng of the lede of the hall & for Soder to the plomer xxij*d*

Reparacions at our hall & yonges house

to Dunnyng for xlj quarters iiij*s* ij*d*
for iiij C di of quarter borde ix*s* x*d*
for di C & xj fote of elmyn borde[41] xvij*d*
for carryage of the same bordes & quarters vj*d*
for xxiij fote & di of elmyn borde for the dore of the galery x*d*
to George Stawker for v ponchons[42] ij*s* v*d*
for xxiij fote of elmyn borde viij*d*
to Burton Carpenter for v days ij*s* iiij*d*
to John Puttell & his man iiij*s*

Item payd to Corrall for iiij days worke ij*s* viij*d*
to John Puttell & his servaunte for iiij days worke v*s* iiij*d*
to Burdon Carpentar for iij days & a half ij*s* iiij*d*
to John higges Smyth for hokys hyngis boltes lachys & Cashis with Remouyng of lokkes & Rynges for dores iiij*s* vj*d*

to Richard fforde for naylles xs xj*d*
for bred & drynke for the Carpenters because they went not home at drynkyng tymes xij*d*
for vij C of hart lathe[43] ij*s* xj*d*
for j C of Sape lathe[44] iiij*d*
for iij days worke of a plaisterer & a laborer iij*s* iij*d*
for a laborer for a days worke v*d*
to Rauf fflemyng for iij days playsteryng ij*s*
to John Dene for iij days playsteryng ij*s*
to ij laborers to serve them ij days xx*d*
for v busshell & a half of here xxij*d*
for iij lode of lome & a lode of Sand xviij*d*
for j C of lyme v*s*
for temperyng of lyme & Sand xj*d*
for bred & drynke for the same laborers xiiij*d*
to Jamys Jefferey Glasier for makyng clene of the glasse Wyndows abought the hall & for xvij quarelles & for mendyng of the Assumpcion of our lady in the parlour x*s*

Summa of the Reparacions for the space of ij yeres Cxv*s* vij*d*

Here after folowith the Dynner the first yere

ffirst payd to the Baker for ix dossen & a half of Brede ix*s* vj*d*
for iij busshelles of Bastard fflouer & ffyne fflower vj*s* iiij*d*
at the Cok & Ster & Ramshed for iij barrelles of Ale xj*s* iij*d*
for a kylderkyn of Bere xij*d*
for wyne at Cardynalles hat in lumbardstret xviij*s* viij*d*

Summa xlvj*s* ix*d*

Item payd for A buk & for fechyng of another xvj*s* ij*d*
to Wryght the Pulter as apperith by his bill xliiij*s* iij*d*
to the Bocher for a Rumpe of Beff xij*d*
for half a lame xij*d*
for vj mary bonys ix*d*
for vij shulders of motton & for suett iiij*s* viij*d*
to the pykemonger for xviij pykys xxj*s*
for ij ffreshe Salmondes & di & a salmond trowte xvj*s* x*d*
for ij Brettes[45] xiij*d*
a lyng & a sydde of Saltfyshe xvj*d*

Summa cviij*s* j*d*

Item payd to the Grosser for Spyse xiij*s* x*d*
for x Gallons of Curdes xx*d*
for peeres xxiij*d*
for Rose Water vj*d*

Summa xvij*s* xj*d*

Item payd to Edme the Meares sergeante for his fee vj*s* viij*d*
to fferrys Butler for his ffee iiij*s*

to the Coke for his ffee vj*s* viij*d*
to the Butteler for white cuppis xx*d*
to the Pewterer for his ffee iij*s* iiij*d*
to the Porter for kepyng of the dore viij*d*
to the Talowechaundeler for salt Sauce trenchers iij*s* j*d*
for Wood & Colles iiij*s* j*d*
to the Water bearer xxj*d*
to ij Tornebrochis[46] viij*d*
to a woman that helpyd them in the kechyn x*d*
for Skowryng of our Vessell xij*d*
to Almondes wyf for wasshyng of our Napery viij*d*

Summa xxxv*s* j*d*

Item payd for butter xx*d*
for Oysters vij*d*
for Erbys ix*d*
to Alman at dyvers tymes when we allowed prentysis viij*d*

Summa iij*s* viij*d*

Summa of the first Dynner x*Li* xj*s* vj*d*

Here after folowith the Second Dynner

ffirst payd to the Baker for x dossen of Brede x*s*
to the same Baker for iij busshelles of meale v*s*
for iij barrelles of Ale at Cok & Sterr & Ramysshed xij*s*
for a kylderkyn of Bere xij*d*
at iij Cranes in the Vyntre for Wyne xviij*s* vj*d*

Summa xlvj*s* vj*d*

Item payd for ffechyng of iij Bukkes that Mr hull gave Vs & in Rewarde to the kepers that seruyd the Warrauntes[47] xix*s* iij*d*
to the Pulter as apperith by his byll lij*s* iiij*d*
more for xiiij Capons vj*s* viij*d*
to the Bocher as apperith by his byll x*s* x*d*
to the Pykemonger for xix pykys xxij*s* ij*d*
for a ffyrkyn[48] of ffreshe sturgeon xxiiij*s* iiij*d*
for iiij ffreshe Samondes xiij*s* viij*d*

Summa vij*li* viij*s* xj*d*

Item payd to the Grosser for Spyce as apperith by his bill xv*s*
to the mylke wyf for Curdes xvj*d*
to Kendalles wyf for Butter ij*s* viij*d*

for peres xiiij*d*
for Erbys & fflowers xvj*d*
for Oysters iiij*d*

Summa xxj*s* x*d*

Item payd to Edme the Mayers sergeaunte for his ffee vj*s* viij*d*
to fferrys Butler for his ffee iiij*s*
to the Coke for his ffee vj*s* viij*d*
to the Pewterer for his ffee iij*s* iiij*d*
to the Talowe chaundeler for Sause trenchers & salte & pottes iiij*s* ix*d*
for di C of ffagottes xx*d*
for vj quarter of Colles ij*s* iij*d*
to the waterberer for water xxij*d*
to a woman that wasshid the dysshes x*d*
to Choppyng for goyng of Arrondes[49] vj*d*
to the Torne brochis viij*d*
to the porter for kepyng of the dore viij*d*

Summa xxxiij*s* x*d*

Summa of the Second Dynner xij *li* xj*s* j*d*

Summa of all the Payments for the Space of ij yeres lxix*li* viij*s* vij*d*

And so the paymentes excedith the Resceyttes by the space of ij yeres xv*d* *quarter*

This Accompte ys Allowed the xvijth Day of January in the xxiiijth yere of the reigne of kyng henry the viij by Vs Edward Byllyng John Skampyon Thomas Darcy & William Baynard Auditours of this Accompte And we the sayd Auditours do fynde that the sayd Accomptauntes shall bryng in for Thomas Stonys gonne[50] xj*s* And for Lawles dett v*s* iiij*d*

Summa of all ys xvj*s* iiij*d*

Arrerages dewe apon this accompte

ffirst Thomas Vawse owith of his Quarterage for this ij yeres ij*s* viij*d*
Item William hilliard owith for the Rest of his nobyll[51] at his commyng in to the lyvere v*s*
Alysaunder Cotyng owith for bothe his dynners iiij*s*
John Blome owith for bothe his dynners iiij*s*
Mr lynde owith for a fyne of xvij torchis v*s* viij*d*
ffyned more for iiij Croppis xvj*d*
ffyned for Midsomer Images iiij*s*
ffyned for iij Torchis xx*d*
ffyned for xij Torchis x*s*

ffyned for Midsomer Images xiij*s* iiij*d*
ffyned for xxij Torchis v*s*
Mr Byllyng owith for a ffyne of xx Torchis x*s*
Mistress Spyser owith for iij quarters Rente vij*s* vi*d*
Thomas Lawles owith for a fyne of xviij torchis iiij*s*
more for a fyne of xij Torchis ij*s*

Summa of the Arrerages iiij*Li* ij*d*

[1]These accounts, for a two-year period starting on 29 September, are transcribed from *MS9481*, fol 7 to 20b.
[2]Rent.
[3]Dwelling house or piece of land.
[4]Money paid by members, either as normal dues, e.g. for the provision of torches or images, or as penalties for misdemeanours.
[5]Half-pound.
[6]Farthing.
[7]St. Paul's.
[8]?
[9]St Olave's.
[10]Underweight (curtailed)?
[11]Wax adulterated with 'pollen', i.e. flour (the botanical meaning had not come in).
[12]Forfeiture of goods (cf distress, distraint).
[13]Of St John and St Peter for midsummer celebrations?
[14]?
[15]Of inferior quality: perhaps mixed with resin, a common adulterant.
[16]Maker's mark.
[17]Torches fixed on staves for carrying in procession.
[18]Rolls of wax.
[19]Rachements were oblique struts used in constructing hearses and perhaps also to support torches in fixed positions.
[20]Too much wick and too little wax.
[21]Services on the last three days of Holy Week, when they were timed to finish at dusk and candles were extinguished in succession.
[22]For use in mortars with a floating wick; or the residue therein?
[23]See page 31.
[24]Office for the dead (from the first word in Latin).
[25]List of names to be prayed for.
[26]Singers or priests hired for the obit.
[27]A coarse woollen cloth.
[28]Of the 1485 grant-of-arms.
[29]A paper size (royal, 24 × 19″).
[30]Title deeds.
[31]The locality is not known.
[32]The exchequer or treasury.

[33]?
[34]There was an action pending against the authorities of St Dunstan's-in-the-West.
[35]Fine or penalty.
[36]Guildhall.
[37]Charter.
[38]Cering of corpses?
[39]Sealing of the release.
[40]See page 31.
[41]'Almaine' (German) timber imported from Riga.
[42]Short beams of standard length for uprights (puncheons).
[43]Heart of oak.
[44]Outer wood of oak, inferior to hart lathe.
[45]Brill or turbot.
[46]Turnspits.
[47]Permits.
[48]Small cask.
[49]Errands.
[50]Gown.
[51]The gold coin or 'noble' usually worth *6s. 8d.* (the standard livery fine).

APPENDIX 7

COST OF A LAW-SUIT, 1544[1]

Here followethe the costes and chardges of owre Sute in lawe.

Paied for searchinge of the Recordes since the whole company sued to the towne Clarcke	ij*s*	
in expences at the Castell in ffisshestreate the xth daye of December and for peruzinge the Evidence[2] of the hawle	x*s*	
for searchinge out of the recognizaunce in the Maiors Courte	iij*s*	vj*d*
the xixth of December at the Castell in ffisshestreate when that wee gaive the Wardens of St John Sackeries there aunswere	ij*s*	vj*d*
the xviijth of January at the Dagger in Cheape when the Mr[3] and the Wardens were arrestedd	ij*s*	
to Mr Cursen his fee	iij*s*	iiij*d*
to Roger Twis, Attorney		xij*d*
item left wth him for fees of the Courte		viij*d*
to Mr Underyll for takenge of suerties in the Maiors Courte		vj*d*
for warninge of the parson and the Wardens of St John Sackeries before my lorde Maior		xij*d*
item spent wt the company when the Mrs[4] cam from my lorde Maiors		viij*d*
to Thorrowyhgood the Maiors officer for fetchinge the Churchewardens of St John Sackeries before my lorde Maior		xij*d*
to the Towne clarcke for makenge of the recognizaunce that wee weare bounde in before my lorde Maior	ij*s*	
the xvth daie of ffebruary at the Starr in Cheape when we had bene wth oure learned Counsell		xx*d*
at the three tonnes at Yealde hawle[5] gate when the men of lawe dydd meete there, Mr Shepperd, Mr Baynard, and Mr Cressey, wth divers other then present	v*s*	
at the Waxchaundlers hawle when the men of lawe did meete there wth the Mrs above written	vij*s*	vj*d*
for bredd and drincke when the Vewers weare at the hawle		viij*d*
at the Myter in Cheape when the Mr and the Wardens wth the Vewers mett ther		xij*d*
to the Vewers for Vewinge of the hawle	v*s*	
at the Bysshoppes hedd in Lumberd streate, the Mr and Wardens beinge there		viij*d*
to the Maiors Officer for fetchinge of the Wardens of St John Sackeries before my lorde Maior		xij*d*
the second daie of Maye to Mr Brooke the man of lawe	iij*s*	iiij*d*
for the entrance of the Attorney		iiij*d*
for the playntys[6]		iiij*d*
for the coppy of the declareacon		viij*d*
for botehiegher to Westminster the fourthe day of Maye		iiij*d*
to Mr Burnell for his fee	iij*s*	iiij*d*
for a Coppy of the vewinge taken out of the Maiors Courte		xij*d*

to the Judge for makenge aunswere for two Courte daies	xij*d*
the xijth daie of Maye when the quest[7] was called and but vj appered, for the Mr and the Wardens dynner the same daye and the offecer	ij*s* viij*d*
the xxvjth of Maye when the Mr and the Wardens wt the Assistaunce dyd appeere at Yelde hall and the same daye for our dynner there	ij*s*
the xth of June when the Mr and the Wardens cam from Yelde hall	vj*d*
the xxvjth daye of June for bredd and drinck when the men of lawe went to seeke the evidence	viij*d*
at the three tonnes at Yelde hall gate when the quest dyd appeere	vij*s* vj*d*
to Mr Brooke	vj*s* viij*d*
to Mr Burnell	vj*s* viij*d*
to two men of lawe	vj*s* viij*d*
to the Attorney	xx*d*
to a Wittness	xij*d*
for bredd meate and drincke when the Officer and I[8] went to seeke the men of lawe	xij*d*
to xij men for a rewarde	iiij*s*
for a dysshe of meate that was geven to Mr Towne Clarck	iiij*s* vj*d*
to the Towne Clarcke for judgement that was geven againest the Wardens of St John Sackeries and the parson	viij*d*
for drawinge out of the Accon[9] againest us	xij*d*
to Thorrowghgood the Maiors officer for the precept againest the Wardens and the parson	xij*d*
for Ingrossinge the pannell[10]	vj*d*
for the bill of Costes	iij*d*
for the precept	iiij*d*
for the coppy of the pannell	viij*d*
on St Johns Eve when the Mr and the Wardens were arested of a Accon of Tresspasse in the Sherifes Courte	xx*d*
the Sargeaunt and the yeomen for gevenge of attendauncs	xvj*d*
to Mr Burnett and to Mr Brooke the two men of lawe for entertayninge of us	vj*s* viij*d*
to Thorrowghegoode the Maiors Officer for removenge the Accon into the Maiors Courte	xij*d*
to the Attorney in the Maiors Courte	xx*d*
for a querelaint[11] removinge out of the Sherifes Court	xvj*d*
to the Attorney for his ffee for three daies	ij*s*
for the coppy of the declareacon	viij*d*
to Mr Blackwell the judge in the Maiors Courte for the Bayle	ij*s*
to Mr Tull for vewinge of the house the xxixth of August	xvj*d*
to Mr Clement for vewinge of the howse	viij*d*
at the Starr in Cheape for our Counsell and the vewers	xij*d*
the xxxth of August at the three tonnes at Yeldehall gate for wyne	iiij*d*
for entertayning of Mr Chamley oure Counselor	ij*s* iiij*d*
to Mr Burnett for makenge out of the pley	ij*s* iiij*d*
to Mr Burnett for vewinge of the house	xx*d*
for plitat[12]	vj*d*
for enteringe of the pley	viij*d*

for engrossinge of the same pley ijs
for the Coppy of the repreevy[13] iijs
Summa totalis of the costes and charges in the lawe [vij*li* xiij*s*]

[1]Transcribed from *MS9481*.
[2]Title deeds.
[3]Master.
[4]Masters.
[5]Guildhall.
[6]Original writ.
[7]Jury.
[8]The writer was the renter warden, Thomas Cressy.
[9]Action (in law).
[10]Names of the jury.
[11]Complaint.
[12]?
[13]Replevin, a writ granting recovery of distrained goods.

APPENDIX 8

THE HALL INVENTORY, 1550[1]

This is the Inventory made by Us walter Sawlk[ins] Mr John Erle and William Wakefelde wardens of the ende of oure Accompt whiche was at Mighelmas in the yere of oure lorde god one thowsand fyve hundred and fyftie and in the fourthe yere of oure soueraigne lorde kinge Edward the vjth of all plate monney Juelles and all other thinges appperteninge to the company of Waxchaundlers of the Cittie of London.

INPRIMIS vj Spoones of syluer waienge a xj ounces and three quarter
Item more iiij spoones of newe syluer waienge vij ounces and di[2] a quarter
Item one Mazer bounde with siluer and gilte with a bosse in the bottom of the same graven with an ymage of our lady cont a pint and di by measure
Item the common Seale of the house in syluer
Item in monney
Item un herst clothe of goulde
Item three garnishes[3] of pewter vessell lackenge two disshes and one Sawcer
Item more to chargars of Pewter
Item a greate brasse pott
Item to greate spittes of Irne
Item two Rackes of Irne
Item iii brazen waightes on half hundered waight one a Quartern of a hundered waight and one ij*li* waighte on j*li* waighte and half a pounde And smale waightes iij quarters di

the Som of all are $\overset{\text{xx}}{\text{iiij}}$ vij*li* (87 lb) iij quart di

Item one dyaper towell cont in lenghte x elles and a quarter
Item another diaper Towell cont in lengthe fyve elles and a quarter
Item two paire of Alman Revettes withe all thinges to them belongenge
Item two swordes and two daggers withe ther gerdles
Item an olde Diaper table clothe broken cont in lengths fyve yardes and a quarter
Item iiij Bowes and iiij Sheaffes of Arrowes
Item two white Cotes reddy made
Item ij stremers and one banner wth iij staves to the same
Item ij Shipp chestes above in the chamber bounde wth Irne where in is contained the Evidences[4] wt the bookes of the accomptes and the corporacion[5] wt other necessary thinges
Item in the same Chamber one paire of oulde tresselles and in the same Chamber the oulde hanginges of the story of Jacob and his sonnes
Item more in the same Chamber on the Sowthe side is a settle of Joyners woorke cont in leangthe vj yardes And in the same Chamber a planck table in lengthe three yardes di

In the Parloure

Item one table cont in leangthe three elles wt two [t]resselles
Item an other table cont in leangthe iij elles wth two tresselles

Item more two fourmes the one cont iiij elles the other three elles
Item more to ioyned fourmes of two elles apeece
Item on Shipp Chest that cam of St blazes brotherhoode and on the same Chest two banners there conesaunce is the Bee hives
Item the same parlour hanged on eche syde wth redd saye and bordered withe Scripture
Item in the same parloure before the windowe over the streate ij Cortens and before the windowe and the gallery doore on the Sowthe side ij Cortens

In the haule

Item the hier table contayninge in lengthe fyve elles wt three tresselles
Item the hier bentche or settle in lengthe of Joyners woorke vj elles and at every ende turninge at the endes on ell and a quarter in lengthe
Item to the same table belonginge ij formes and three ioyned stooles
Item ij tables of three elles a peece with two paire of Tresselles and bothe bentches by the wales wt formes of Joyners woorke And ij formes of ioyners woorke for the oute side of the same
Item the same hawle hanged abowte withe grene saye and bordered aboute wth Pictures of Jhs
Item in an vpper Chamber [one table] of an ell and a half in lengthe withe ij Tresselles

In the Buttery

Item a Byne for bredd and a geist[6] for Ale or beere
Item in the larder house [ ] borded a bowt withe three planckes
Item in the Sellar two planckes reddy leued[7]
Item vj Cressettes of Irne wth there staves

[1]*MS9481.*
[2]Half (L *dimidium*).
[3]A garnish [of pewter] was twelve platters, twelve dishes, and twelve saucers.
[4]Title-deeds.
[5]The foundation charter.
[6]Some sort of vessel?
[7]Levelled, i.e. planed.

APPENDIX 9

A SURVEY OF 1566[1]

A viewe taken the xxvjth daye of Marche Anno Domini 1565[2] in the parishe of St John Zachary, In the warde of Creplegate in London, Bytwene the Parson & churchewardens of the said parishe of St John Zacharye plaintiffs on thone partie & the wardens and felowshippe of the company of Waxchaundlers defendants on thother partie of for and concernynge A certein varyaunce growen and arryssen bytwene the said parties of and for the takynge downe of A brick walle under the partie plaintiffs yoyty[3] & a pece of voye grounde conteynynge in length xvij foote & viij ynches of assice & was in bredthe & widnes vij foote & iij ynches of assise; and furthermore the said defendants hath incroched & made certein ovens uppon the grounde & vawte of A wydraught[4] belongynge to the said plaintiffs from the said kytchen ageynyst the northe stretchynge southeward vj foote & xj ynches.

Which varyaunce we the said iiij sworne viewers have viewed & sene & theruppon we saye yt the said ovens & incrochement ought of Ryght to be withdrawen & taken awaye aswell as the said bricke walle & ought not to stonde there as by A view taken the xv daye of Marche in the xxxv yere of the Reigne of Kynge Henry theight more at large maye appeare.

And ffurther we saye yt by a certein Will & deade which we also did see & Redd yt appereth yt the said partie plaintiffs ought of Ryght to have iiij littell shoppes or howses & A litell howse lyenge on theste syde stretching southe to the partie defendants, as by the said will & deade more playnly also dothe appeere, which the said parties plaintiffs ought of Ryght to have excepte there be any other wrytynges to the contrary etc.

[1]Transcribed from *MS9516*.
[2]1565 was the ecclesiastical, 1566 the historical, year.
[3]Jetty, either the overhanging part of a timber building or a lean-to addition.
[4]Closet, recess.

APPENDIX 10

AN ACT[1] *CONCERNING WAX AND HONEY, 1581*[2]

Whereas by the Goodness of God this land yields great plenty of honey and wax not only for home consumption but also for export, but much wax has lately been found corrupt by reason of deceitful mixture, also makers and sellers of honey have put it in casks of deceitful assize and used deceitful mixtures.

It is therefore enacted by the authority of Parliament that after the Feast of Pentecost next anyone concerned with trade who shall mix wax with resin, tallow, turpentine or other substance for sale, or shall offer it for sale, shall forfeit the said corrupted wax. If any shall have been actually sold, the person responsible shall forfeit 2*s* for each pound sold, whereof half shall go to the Crown, half to the person injured or any who shall sue for it.

To enable offenders to be traced, every melter and maker-up of unwrought wax shall have his own stamp or mark the breadth of six pence, graven with his initials and shall stamp every piece of wax triangle in three places, on the outside of the upper part, on pain of forfeiture of each piece unmarked.

No one shall melt, mix, work or sell any wrought wax, stuff or wares wrought with wax, such as lights, staff torches, red wax or sealing wax, book candles, cering candles, cering of corpses, links, green wax, red wax, etc., except with good wholesome, pure and convenient stuff. Those working or selling wax must have a mark to set on wares, so that offenders may be traced, those working or attempting to sell corrupt and deceitful produce to forfeit same, one half to the Crown, one half to the party deceived or any who shall sue for it.

Every barrel, kilderkin or firkin filled with honey by maker and filler shall be marked with his initials burnt on the head of cask on pain of 6*s* 8*d* for each barrel, etc. not so marked; anyone selling or trying to sell a barrel of less than 32 wine gallons, kilderkin of less than 16 wine gallons, firkin of less than 8 gallons to forfeit 5*s* for each half-gallon lacking; anyone corrupting honey with deceitful mixture to forfeit vessel and honey, half to the Crown, half to any that may sue for it.

The Act concerning the marking of wax is not to apply to those selling wax of their own bees in the open market in small pieces, or to any servant corrupting wax by his master's orders if he confess the same.

No one to counterfeit a mark, or use another's mark without his consent, penalty £5 for each offence, half to the Crown, half to the party injured or any that should sue for it; pillory and imprisonment for refusal to pay fine.

[1]23 Eliz, c.8–An Acte for the true melting making and working of Waxe.
[2]Transcribed from a summary in *MS9488*, fol 29.

APPENDIX 11

OATHS OF OFFICERS AND FREEMEN, 1664[1]

Master and wardens

Ye shall swear that ye shall be true and faithful to our Sovereign Lord the King's Majesty that now is, and to his heirs and successors, and that after the best manner ye can ye shall justly and indifferently execute or cause to be executed your several and respective offices of this your Company, all the lawful secrets, acts, counsels and consultations which touch or concern the good or benefit of this your Company in any of your Courts or Meetings had, done, treated or consulted of, you shall not reveal to any person or persons other than to your Wardens and Assistants not then present, and to the utmost of your power ye shall endeavour to put in due execution all and every the good and lawful Ordinances, made or to be made, touching the said Society, and the said Art or Mystery of a Wax Chandler, without sparing of any person or persons for favour, affection, reward, meed, dread or promise of reward, or assessing or punishing any person or persons, for envy, hatred or malice, and of all and every such goods, plate, jewels, money and other things, that by reason of your said Offices shall come to your hands, custodies or possessions, ye shall make a just, true, plain and perfect accompt in writing to the Master, Wardens and Assistants of the said Art or Mystery of Wax Chandlers for the time being, according to the Ordinances in that case made and provided, so help you God.

Assistant

You shall swear that you shall be true and faithful to our Sovereign Lord the King's Majesty that now is and to his heirs and successors, you shall so long as you continue an Assistant to the Master and Wardens of the Art or Mystery of Wax Chandlers, London, give your diligence and be ready to assist the Master and Wardens, when and as often as you shall be called or warned thereunto, having no lawful let or leave to the contrary, all the lawful secrets, acts and consultations which touch or concern the good or benefit of the said Society, in any of your Courts or meetings had, done, treated or consulted of, you shall not reveal to any person or persons whatsoever other than to your Master, Wardens and Assistants not then present, and shall endeavour yourself as near as you can with all indifferency to give your best and soundest advice, opinion and judgment to the Master and Wardens in all such things as they shall reasonably and lawfully require or desire the same in, touching or concerning the said Society, or the Art or Mystery of a Wax Chandler, or any the Orders or Ordinances made or to be made touching or concerning the said Art, or any person using or exercising the same, you shall not in giving your advice, opinion or judgment spare any person for meed, dread, favour, affection, reward or promise of reward, or assess or punish any person for envy, hatred or malice, but shall uprightly justly and faithfully give your advice according to the truth so near as you can, so help you God.

Clerk

You shall swear that you shall be true and faithful to our Sovereign Lord the King's Majesty that now is and to his heirs and successors, and that you will be obedient to the Master and Wardens of this Company for the time being in all their just and lawful commandments, having no lawful let to the contrary, and will attend upon them at their Assemblies and meetings and make true entries of all things belonging to your

Office and committed to your charge without respect to the person of any for favour, malice, affection, dread, reward or promise of reward; you shall deliver out no copy or copies of any their Ordinances nor shew any books belonging to this Company without the consent of the Master and Wardens thereof for the time being whereby to prejudice the said Company; you shall in all things incident or belonging to your said place and office justly and faithfully demeane yourself to the most of your power and ability, so help you God.

Beadle

You shall swear that you shall be true and faithful to our sovereign Lord the King's Majesty that now is and to his heirs and successors; you shall so long as you continue Beadle or Officer to this Company summon all and every such person and persons as the Master and Wardens or any of them at any time shall command to be summoned according to the Ordinances in that case made and provided without sparing of any person for favour, affection, gain, hatred or malice, you shall endeavour yourself as near as you can at all times to do and execute the lawful Commandments of the said Master and Wardens and Society belonging to your Office; you shall not wittingly or willingly commit or do anything to the prejudice, damage, hurt or rebuke of the said Master, Wardens and Society, but diligently, faithfully and truly you shall execute your said office as a Beadle ought to do so near as you can, so help you God.

Searcher

You shall swear that all wax torches, tapers, prickets, flamboys, links and all other stuff whatsoever belonging to the craft of Wax Chandlers which upon your search you shall view and survey you shall justly and indifferently deem and judge neither for malice or hatred but as indifferently as you can, and make a true and indifferent report thereof to your Master, Wardens and Assistants according to your skill and judgment, so help you God.

Freeman

You shall swear to be true to our Sovereign Lord the King's Majesty that now is and to his heirs and successors; you shall be obedient at all times hereafter to the Master and Wardens of the Art or Mystery of Wax Chandlers, London and to their successors in all matters and things concerning the said Society; you shall not disobey the warning or summons given you by the Beadle or Officer of the same Company without you have a just and reasonable excuse; and for your part you shall observe and keep all and singular the lawful and reasonable orders and ordinances and constitutions made or hereafter to be made for the well ordering and governing of the said Master and Wardens and Society and their successors and shall not do any hurt or prejudice to the said Society but shall let and hinder the same to your utmost power, so help you God.

[1]Since 1839 oaths have been superseded by declarations, but the wording is unchanged except that *Ye shall swear* is replaced by *I do solemnly and sincerely declare*, and *so help you God* by *and I make this solemn Declaration by virtue of the Statutory Declarations Act 1835*. This statute (5 & 6 William IV c.62) was enacted 'to make provision for the abolition of unnecessary oaths', and it authorised corporate and other bodies to use declarations of a prescribed form.

APPENDIX 12

CHARGE TO LIVERY, 1957[1]

You shall be a good and true Brother unto the Master, Wardens and Assistants of the Art or Mystery of the Wax Chandlers of the City of London whereof you are now a full Brother Admitted. You shall keep in your power all the lawful Ordinances and Acts now already made within your said Fraternity, so far as shall concern or belong to your Charge. All these points, as much as in you is, you shall well and truly in your behalf keep and observe to your power as near as God shall send you grace.

[1]The ordinances of 1664 made no provision for any oath or other form of words to be used on admission to the livery. In 1957 it was decided that the master should charge a new liveryman in the terms given above.

APPENDIX 13

MASTERS OF THE COMPANY FROM 1484

1484	Thomas Stone[1]
1486	
1488	
1490	
1492	
1494	
1496	
1498	
1500	John Monk
1502	
1504	
1506	
1508	
1510	
1512	
1514	
1516	John Monk
1518	
1520	
1522	Stephen Warde?
1524	John Tomson
1526	Richard Lynd
1528	William Rogers
1530	Thomas Lane
1532	Edward Byllynge
1534	John Scampion
1536	Thomas Lane
1538	William Hull
1540	Edward Byllynge
1542	John Shepard
1544	John Scampion
1546	
1548	William Sawlkins
1550	Thomas Cressey
1552	Thomas Daye
1554	William Kendall
1556	Thomas Cressey
1558	Walter Meers
1560	Thomas Cressey
1562	Simon Burton
1564	Thomas Cressey
1566	Harry Blower
1568	Harry Blower
1570	Simon Burton
1572	Robert Thrower
1574	John Cressey
1576	Harry Blower
1578	Richard Sharpe
1580	Robert Thrower
1582	John Cressey
1584	Thomas Barlow
1586	Simon Burton
1588	Thomas Barlow
1590	Thomas Shepperd
1592	William Bourne
1594	Thomas Jennett
1596	Harman Jackson
1598	James Skelton
1600	Thomas Jennett
1602	Christopher Dyson
1604	James Skelton
1606	John Coates
1608	Harman Jackson
1610	James Skelton
1612	John Coates
1614	Robert Barlow
1616	Harman Jackson
1618	George Benson
1620	Harman Jackson
1622	William Sharpe
1624	William Hurley
1626	William Sharpe
1628	William Skelton
1630	Twigden Masters
1632	Twigden Masters
1634	John Bewley

[1]Known to be in office on 3 February 1485.

1636 Matthias Westmerland
1638 Bartholomew Hutchins
1640 William Lovell
1642 Thomas Steane I
1644 Matthew Fox
1646 Robert Warner
1648 Bartholomew Hutchins
1650 Grace Hardwin
1652 Hendry Ade
1654 William Graves
1656 Henry Newberry
1658 Robert Warner
1660 John Terry
1662 Josias Ward
1664 William Rutt
1666 Henry Ratcliffe
1668 Thomas Steane II
1670 John Terry
1672 Richard Colborne
1674 Robert Goose
1676 William Phillips
1678 Thomas Hitch I
1680 Francis Thursfield
1682 John Baker
1684 John Gardiner
1686 John Knapp
1687 Francis Thursfield
1688 Thomas Hitch I
1690 John Knapp
1692 Robert Aldersey
1694 Roger Davis
1696 Robert Papworth
1698 John Attwell
1700 James Cooke
1702 James Levett
1704 William Richards
1706 John Gardiner
1708 Robert Aldersey
1710 Thomas Hitch II
1711 Roger Davis
1712 Henry Hues
1714 Richard Casebeard
1715 George Ludlam
1716 William Prince
1718 William Prince
1720 Richard Goggs
1722 George Ellis
1724 Edmund Bick I
1726 Christ Truss
1728 William Jeffrey
1730 Samuel Frearson
1732 James Thomasson
1734 John Mitchell
1735 William Smith
1736 Samuel Willis
1738 Leonard Bolt
1740 William Feast
1742 Daniel Radford
1744 John Lancashire
1746 Round Lampard
1748 Samuel Sandeforth
1750 William Perkins
1752 Stephen Wiggin
1754 Richard Jeffreys
1756 Joseph Gibbon
1758 Thomas Streeke
1760 Thomas Stracey
1762 Isaac Barrett
1764 John Hiorne
1766 Henry Newdick
1768 Nicholas Nixon
1770 William Caldwall
1772 George Turvite
1774 Nathaniel Thomas
1776 George Baughan
1778 Thomas Kippax
1780 Thomas Kippax
1782 Benjamin Batley
1784 Robert Steward
1786 James Dixon
1788 Thomas Rogers
1790 John Ralph
1792 Philip Morgan
1794 Pendock Price
1796 Pendock Price
1798 Joseph Newdick
1800 Thomas Brown
1802 John Scott

1804 Richard Wild
1806 Richard Hill
1808 Hugh Burgess
1810 John Pinhorn
1812 Edmund Bick II
1814 Thomas Fry
1816 Henry Batley
1818 Edward Venn
1820 Thomas Templeman
1822 John Stewart
1824 Henry Hall
1826 Joseph Pulley I
1828 William Pulley
1830 John Field
1832 George Watts
1834 Boughey Burgess
1836 John Cowan
1838 Thomas Brandram
1840 Samuel Clay
1842 William Ryde
1844 Samuel Brandram
1846 James Dummelow
1848 Benjamin Batley
1850 Joseph Pulley II
1852 Charles Pulley
1854 Richard Chambers
1856 William Kippax
1858 Charles Dames
1860 William Clark
1862 Richard Wollaston
1864 Charles Fowler
1866 Samuel Carless
1868 George Watts Quallett
1870 Richard Dames
1872 William Anderson Rose
1874 Charles John Todd I
1876 Thomas Collin
1878 Charles Pulley
1880 Plaxton Samuel Carless
1882 Francis Tullie Wollaston
1884 Thomas Allt
1886 John Ives Vaughan
1888 Charles John Todd II
1890 George Rose Knott
1891 Charles John Todd I
1892 Herbert William Bridgwater
1894 Ernest Henry Gregory
1896 Clement Walpole Burdon
1898 Horace Mark Gregory
1900 Charles Edward Hartley
1902 Thomas Walter Allt
1904 Gerald Maltby Todd
1906 Herbert Cooper Todd
1908 Maxwell Rose
1910 John Roberts Dummelow
1912 Algernon Todd
1914 Charles Samuel Routh
1916 Charles John Todd II
1918 Ernest Henry Gregory
1920 Clement Walpole Burdon
1922 Horace Mark Gregory
1924 Charles Edward Hartley
1926 Thomas Walter Allt
1928 Gerald Maltby Todd
1930 John Roberts Dummelow
1932 Herbert Frederick Robins
1934 Charles John Todd II
1936 Hugh Fraser Collum
1938 Ernest Henry Gregory
1940 Havard Noel Bridgwater
1942 Robert Francis Routh
1944 Herbert Frederick Robins
1945 Robert Francis Routh
1946 Charles George Todd
1948 Claude Barnard Gregory
1950 Edward Christopher Stacey
1952 Albert James Wood
1954 Colin John Wemyss McCallum
1956 Anthony Sancroft-Baker
1958 Alexander Richard Burnet Fuller
1960 John Dummelow
1962 Thomas Hugh Winterborn
1964 Maurice Toller Whinney
1966 Claude Barnard Gregory
1968 Nigel Monckton Miskin
1970 Herbert Twyneham Pike
1972 John Harvey

APPENDIX 14

CLERKS OF THE COMPANY FROM c1651

	John Bennett[1]
1670	Lancelot Monox
1685	William Hitch
1695	*vacant*
1700	Robert Handlapp
1704	John Reeve
1737	Edward Hasted
1741	George Unwin
1765	Barnard Gregory
1798	Mark Gregory
1831	Mark Henry Gregory
1858	Horatio Gregory
1892	Thomas Bridgwater
1930	Albert James Wood
1949	Anthony Sancroft-Baker
1952	Charles George Todd
1970	Thomas James Wood

[1]Known to have been in office in 1651.

APPENDIX 15

CITIZENS AND WAX CHANDLERS, 1972[1]

Master
John Harvey

Upper warden
Richard John Fielden

Renter warden
Anthony John Gregory

Assistants who are past masters

Charles George Todd
Claude Barnard Gregory
Anthony Sancroft-Baker
Colin John Wemyss McCallum
Alexander Richard Burnet Fuller
John Dummelow
Thomas Hugh Winterborn
Maurice Toller Whinney[2]
Nigel Monckton Miskin
Herbert Twyneham Pike

Assistants

Thomas James Wood (*Clerk*)
Hugh Alwyn Lenox
William Burgess Drayson Maile
John Cecil Field

Livery

Thomas Edwin Thornton Shanks
Robert Archibald Hugh Collum
Gordon Cooper Todd
Martin Hugh Routh
Andrew James Lenox
Albert Clements Wood
Arthur Peter Cullerne Allt
Ernest Thomas Floyd Ewin
John Murray Melville
William Maynard Atkins
John Stacey
Tom Hebron
George Mark Archer
Rennie Simpson
John Osborne Lintott
John Henry Gray Burbridge
John Charles Field
William Herbert Tankard
Arthur James Watts
Harold Richard Aldridge
Joseph Robinson
Constantine George Sevastopulo
Harold Albert Harris
Andrew Hugh Olson
Robert Henry Hamblin
Lionel Milner Angus-Butterworth
John Edward Powis Titman
Archibald Gordon Horton

[1]As at 31 December.
[2]An honorary assistant.

Robin Cyril Chaventre
Hugh Robert Collum
Geoffrey Albert Muggleston
John Robert Williams
Bruce Alexander Ross
Michael Hugh Winterborn
John Christopher Robins
Jeremy Hugh Burge
Joseph Mair
Peter John Scott
Michael Harvey
Richard Keith Todd
Christopher Peter Maynard Gomm
John Hanton Clench Davy
Hugh Ian Olson
Michael Pike
Christopher John Francis Watts
Nicholas Bailey
Baldwin Hugh Malet
Peter Bosworth Kirkwood Gracey
William John Sturdy
Henry Alexander Sturdy
Robert Constantine Sevastopulo
Walter Alexander Angus-Butterworth
Reginald Henry Adams
John James George Waller
Roger Noel Price Griffiths
Richard John Percival

Freemen

Arthur Samuel Harvey
Ronald Bousquet Browne
David Ian Bare
Denis Lowther Maitland
John Bousquet Browne
John Anthony Faber
John Wyon Rogers
George Dupin Drayson
David Edward Harman
William Reginald James Pullen
Clarence Edward Mold
Noel Percy Mander
Geoffrey Broadbent Lafone
Stanley Austen Crichton-Baker
Michael Henry Pattison
John St. Clair McCormick
Anthony Hayward Allt
William Trevor Jones
David John Callaghan
Douglas Rodway Millard
Christopher Martin Bakhurst
Howard Jeremy Ricketts
Alec Victor Finch
John Farmer Robertson
James Ashley Boyes
John Harmer Pattisson
Kenneth James Smith
Thomas William Morley
Antony Stewart Bencraft Joly
Raymond Samuel Sancroft-Baker
Charles William Tankard
John Stephen Lintott
Christopher James Drayson Maile
Ronald Anthony Best

APPENDIX 16

INVENTORY OF PLATE

(*a*) *SILVERWARE*

The dates given for British silver are those of London hall-marks except where a provincial assay office is mentioned.

Type	Description	Donor
Standing cup and cover (plate 6 and fig. 4)	Chinoiserie decoration, gilt finial, 20½″ high. Charles II, 1683 (maker: Charles Shelley). See page 89	R. Normansell
Standing cup and cover (plate 9)	Plain, beehive finial, 19″ high. 1897 (Barnard's). See page 101	C. J. Todd I
Standing cup and cover (plate 9)	Lobed bowl, 17″ high. German, imported 1897	C. E. Hartley
Two-handled cup and cover	Oviform, classical band and fluting, acanthus decoration, pineapple finial, 15″ high. 1871	C. J. Todd I
Two-handled cup and cover	Oviform, acanthus and fluted decoration, lion and shield finial, 16″ high	C. G. Todd[1]
Two-handled cup and cover	Plain, applied cut-card decoration, dolphin handles, 11″ high. 1901	The family of C. J. Todd I
Rose-water dish (plate 10)	Gilt. Acanthus and flower lobed border, fluted sides and domed centre decorated with flowers and foliage, inscribed, 18″ dia. George IV, 1827 (Emes & Barnard). See page 103	The family of W. A. Rose
Ewer (plate 10)	Gilt. Oviform, panelled and decorated, rose finial, 13″ high. 1867 (Barnard's). See page 103.	The family of W. A. Rose
Rose-water dish (plate 9)	Oval, shaped border embossed with tulip flowers and ivy leaves, 19½″ long. 1906 (Gilbert Marks)	C. G. Todd[2]
Ewer	Melon pattern, leafage base, dolphin handle, 15″ high. French	T. E. T. Shanks[3]
Tankard (plate 10)	Gilt. Bulbous decoration, domed cover, skirted base. Hamburg, '34–2', c1650. See page 120	C. E. Hartley
Tankards, two (plate 7)	Plain, flat cover, inscribed Samuel Shepheard, 6″ high. Charles II, 1673 (John Ruskin?). See page 89	
Tankard	Plain bellied with decorated cover and foot; caryatid handle, female finial. Dutch	
Tankard	Plain, flat cover, 5½″ high. 1934 (Rossi)	H. N. Bridgwater
Goblets, two (plate 8)	Fluted, square base, four ball feet, 6½″ high George III, 1808 & 1816 (Thomas Jenkinson)	H. F. Collum[3]

13

Type	Description	Donor
Two-handled cup	Plain, 6″ high, 1920	N. M. Miskin[9]
Salver	Shell and scroll border, three feet, 11½″ dia. George II, 1746 (Henry Morris)	Mrs E. B. Todd[3]
Salver	Shell and scroll border, three feet, 9″ dia. George II, 1759 (Ebenezer Coker)	Mrs E. E. Morgan[4]
Salver	Shell, scroll and gadroon border, three feet, 7½″ dia. George III, 1763 (Ebenezer Coker)	
Salver	Shaped classical border, three feet, 10½″ dia. Britannia Standard, 1935	R. F. R. Routh
Salver	Plain threaded, three feet, 6″ dia., inscribed 'Coronation 1937'. 1936 (Barnard's)	
Salver	Carved border, dotted decoration, three feet, 10″ dia. American	
Coasters, two	Shell, leaf and gadroon border, fluted. George III, 1819 (Stephen Adam jnr)	
Wine labels, four	Lisbon, madeira, port, sherry. Irish, c1790 (J—— H——)	
Wine labels, four	Claret, madeira, port, sherry, George IV, 1820 (John Ruskin?)	
Rose bowl	Spiral fluting, 8½″ dia. George III, 1792	G. M. Todd
Rose bowl	Hammered with flower panel decoration, 8″ dia. 1896 (Gilbert Marks)	C. J. Todd II[5]
Rose bowl	Two-handled, fluted with classical border, 14″ dia. 1905	C. J. Todd II[6]
Rose bowl	Two-handled, art nouveau, 8½″ dia. 1908	H. R. Aldridge[7]
Bowl	Engraved border, 5¼″ dia. George III, 1800	
Fruit dish	Circular, gadroon border, 9″ dia. 1961	C. A. S. Pattison[9]
Cups, thirteen	Plain threaded, oviform, on beehive and three dolphin supports. 1898	T. Allt[8]
		T. W. Allt
		H. W. Bridgwater
		C. W. Burdon
		T. Collin
		E. H. Gregory
		H. M. Gregory
		C. E. Hartley
		M. Rose
		G. M. Todd
		H. C. Todd
		F. T. Wollaston
		T. R. Bridgwater
Sauce boats, two	Punched edge, three feet. George III, 1782	Mrs E. E. Morgan
Ladles, two	Fiddle pattern. George III, Edinburgh 1810	Mrs E. E. Morgan

Type	Description	Donor
Sauce boat (plate 8)	Oval, three feet. George III, 1794	H. F. Robins
Trencher salts, six (plate 7)	Plain, octagonal, 7 oz 18 dwt 10 gr. Charles II, 1675 (S—— H——). See page 89	
Salt cellars, four (plate 10)	Gilt. Pierced shaped border, four leaf and scroll feet. 1846 (Barnard's)	L. M. Angus-Butterworth
Salt cellars, four	Cauldron type, three feet. 1883	J. C. Field[9]
Salt spoons, four	To match above	J. C. Field[9]
Salt spoons, four	Fiddle and thread. George IV, 1827 & 1839	C. G. Todd
Mustard pots, four	Domed covers with beehive finials; three lion mask, paw and ball supports. 1903	J. R. Dummelow[9] A. Todd[9]
Mustard pots, four	Domed covers, beehive and three dolphin supports. 1906	G. Winch[9] C. S. Routh[9]
Mustard spoons, four	Old English, beehive crest, as above	
Mustard spoon	Old English	
Pepper casters, four	Plain, vase shape, beehive covers. 1963	
Butter shells, two	Gadroon and scroll border, handles. George III, 1772 (Burrage, Davenport)	Mrs E. E. Morgan
Butter shells, two	George III, 1784	Mrs E. E. Morgan
Sugar caster	Pierced and engraved cover. George II, Edinburgh 1751	Mrs E. E. Morgan
Sugar casters, six	Plain, vase shape, beehive covers. 1908	T. W. Allt
Sugar basin	Swing handle, fluted corners, reeded and bright cut decoration. George III, 1795	Mrs E. E. Morgan
Sugar scoop	Fiddle and thread. 1851	C. G. Todd
Sugar tongs	As above	C. G. Todd
Cream jug	Helmet type. George III, 1784	Mrs E. E. Morgan
Cream pail	Pierced sides and gadroon rim. George III, 1783	H. F. Robins
Cream ewer	Oval, chased	
Coffee pot	Plain, tucked under, 18½ oz. George II, Newcastle 1749 (John Langlands)	Mrs E. E. Morgan
Hot water jug	Plain bellied, wickered handle. George III, 1794 (William Gage)	Mrs E. E. Morgan
Teapot and stand	Pot: oval, barrel-shaped, bright-cut engraving. Stand to match. George III, 1790 (Henry Cowper)	Mrs E. E. Morgan
Tea caddy (plate 8)	Bombé chinoiserie decoration, bird finial. George III, 1763 (T—— G——, I—— G——)	H. F. Robins
Sugar box (plate 8)	To match above	H. F. Robins
Cake basket (plate 9)	Oval, pierced and festooned, swing handles. George III, 1773 (C—— M——)	C. G. Todd[10]
Honey-pot (plate 10)	Gilt. In style of George II, ring finial. 1860 (A. Savory)	L. M. Angus-Butterworth

Type	Description	Donor
Tray (plate 10)	Gilt. Gadroon border, 5″ dia. George III, 1810 (Emes & Barnard)	L. M. Angus-Butterworth
Spoon (plate 7)	Gilt seal-top knop engraved with beehive, 9″ long, stem inscribed. Commonwealth, 1653 or earlier (hall-mark indistinct). See page 89	William Colebourne
Spoons, two (plate 7)	Trifid end, rat-tail, 7¾″ long. Charles II, 1681 (S—— V——). See page 89	
Fruit spoon	Gilt. Fluted bowl, embossed and pierced handles with beehive, date of charter, company's arms and crown. 1897. See page 101	
Table knives, six	Pistol handles. George II, *c*1750. With stainless steel blades	Mrs E. E. Morgan
Cheese knives	As above	Mrs E. E. Morgan
Table knives, twenty-three	One piece with stainless blades	
Cheese knives, forty-two	As above	
Table forks, six	Early English, four-pronged. George II, 1765	Mrs E. E. Morgan
Dessert forks, four	Early English, four-pronged. George III, 1787	Mrs E. E. Morgan
Dessert forks, two	As above, but modern	Mrs E. E. Morgan
Dessert knives and forks, six pairs	Engraved, ivory handles. 1894	
Dessert spoons, six	Old English pattern with bird crest	Mrs E. E. Morgan
Tea spoons, six	Early English. George II? with later chased decoration	Mrs E. E. Morgan
Tea spoons, six	Figure knop, twisted stem. 1916	
Coffee spoons, thirty-six	Old English pattern with beehive crest. 1906	
Tapersticks, four (plate 7)	Round, shaped and shell base, 4½″ high. George II, 1737 (Simon Jouet?)	J. Lancashire J. Thomasson
Snuffers and tray	Snuffers: 1809 (Ernest Barnard). Tray: oval, beaded edge. George III, 1782 (Robert Hennell)	C. G. Todd
Chamber candlestick and extinguisher (plate 8)	Shaped gadroon border, monogram of James, first Earl of Verulam (b. 1775). George IV, 1828 (Richard Sibley)	L. M. Angus-Butterworth
Candelabrum	Seven-light, decorated, vase-shaped stem and triangular base, 32″ high. 1853 (Barnard's)	M. Rose[11]
Candlestick	Three-light. 1928	F. Field
Taper-holder and extinguisher	Taper-holder on wooden handle, 36″ long. Extinguisher in form of beehive. 1971	W. B. D. Maile
Company seal	Die, bearing the company's arms intaglio	
Beadle's staff head (plate 7)	Shaped roped border enclosing company's arms in high relief and surmounting a beehive. 1664 or earlier. See page 89	

Type	Description	Donor
Master's badge (plate 5)	Gilt (with blue ribbon). Pierced, company's arms, shield enamelled; suspended by chain from beehive. Victorian	
Master's gavel and stand	Gavel: ebony and ivory, silver-mounted	C. J. Todd I
	Stand: ebony and silver	H. T. Pike
Upper warden's badge	Gilt. Similar to master's badge but smaller, yellow ribbon. 1965	H. T. Pike[9]
Renter warden's badge	As above, but green ribbon.	J. Harvey[9] & R. J. Fielden[9]
Clerk's badge	As above, but red ribbon	T. J. Wood[9]
Cigar lighter	Elephant-head, with scroll supports and shields, tusk handles. Foreign	G. M. Todd
Cigar lighters, two	Plain threaded, vase-shaped, three feet. Each with two wick holders. 1892 and 1901	C. J. Todd II
Cigar-cutters, four	Engine-turned, gold beehive appliqué. 1970	H. T. Pike
Cigarette box	Oblong, cedar-lined. 1955	M. T. Whinney[9]
Menu holders, twelve	Gilt. With beehive motif. 1972	H. T. Pike

(*b*) *PLATED WARE*

Type	Description	Donor
Rose-water dishes, two (plate 8)	Decorated; fruit, acanthus and wheat borders 18½″ dia.[12] See page 101.	
Salvers, two	Sheffield plate. Shell and scroll border, three feet, 12″ dia	
Wine coolers, two	Basket pattern with vine border	C. G. Todd
Coasters, two	Sheffield plate. Lobed, gadroon border	
Coaster	Sheffield plate. Plain, gadroon border	
Coaster	Pierced vine border, 9″ dia. Continental	
Wine label	Madeira	
Entree dishes, two	Sheffield plate. Flower, leaf and threaded border, two handles. Covers and heaters	C. G. Todd
Sweet dish	Shell pattern, snake handle	C. G. Todd
Sauce tureens, four	Old Sheffield plate. Oval: shell, leaf and gadroon border, two handles, four feet; with covers. *c*1820	
Spoon warmer	Shell type	C. G. Todd
Candelabra, two	Four-light, decorated, flower and leaf	H. F. Robins

Type	Description	Donor
Candelabrum	Five-light, festooned, reeded and beaded column, square base, 28″ high	T. W. Allt[13]
Candelabra, two	Three-light, heavily chased, 22″ high	
Snuffers and tray	Sheffield plate. Snuffers: shell handle. Tray: oblong, gadroon border	C. G. Todd
Dinner service, twenty-four place settings (336 pieces)	King's pattern[14]	
Dessert knives and forks, twelve pairs	Engraved, pearl handles	
Inkstand	Oblong with heavy pierced and scroll border; two ink-bottle holders	
Inkstand	Oblong with domed lid; two ink bottles	C. G. Todd

[1]The cup was won by his father, C. J. Todd II, in 1892 for golf in Singapore.

[2]To commemorate his son's admission to the freedom and the family's 130 years of service (pages 110–11). Originally presented by the Company to C. J. Todd I, the grandfather of the donor, after he had served fifty years on the court; flowers modelled from those on a tulip tree in Todd's garden.

[3]The wife of C. J. Todd II.

[4]Mrs Ellen E. Morgan, who died in 1971, left the company most of her collection of Georgian silver.

[5]Presented to commemorate his election as master for the third time.

[6]Commemorating over fifty years' service on the court. Originally presented to the donor's father (C. J. Todd I) by colleagues in the corporation of London to celebrate his fifty years as common councilman for Queenhithe.

[7]Originally presented by the company to T. Allt, grandfather of the donor's wife.

[8]The donors were the members of the court in 1898; each cup is inscribed with the years of admission to the livery, election as an assistant, and (except for the clerk) election as master.

[9]These items (and probably others) were presented on election to the court.

[10]Presented to commemorate his son's admission to the livery. Originally presented by the company to C. J. Todd II when he was elected master for the third time.

[11]Presented in memory of his father, W. A. Rose.

[12]Said to have been found in the cellar under the street during the 1853 rebuilding of the hall.

[13]Originally a wedding gift from the company.

[14]Purchased in 1971–2.

APPENDIX 17

CALENDAR OF DOCUMENTS (c1200–1959)
available for reference at the Guildhall Library

MS

9481 Renter wardens' account books. (Engrossments) c1529–1597 and 1602–1704
Paper 4to and sm. fo., 3 vol.
Vol. 1. c1529–1597; vol. 2. 1602–1671; vol. 3. 1672–1704.

9481A Renter wardens' account books. 1901–1954.
Paper, la. na. fo., 2 vol.
Vol. 1. 1901–1949; vol. 2. 1950–1954 (mainly blank)

9482 Treasury books, containing renter wardens' accounts, company terriers, inventories and memoranda. 1618–1875.
Paper, sm. fo., 3 vol.
Vol. 1. 1618–1730; vol. 2. 1730–1799; vol. 3. 1800–1875.

9483 Renter wardens' cash books. 1851–1951.
Paper, sm. 4to, 5 vol.
Vol. 1. 1851–1873; vol. 2. 1873–1893; vol. 3. 1893–1910; vol. 4. 1910–1930; vol. 5. 1930–1951.

9484 Renter wardens' ledgers. 1853–1952.
Paper, sm. 4to, 5 vol.
Vol. 1. 1853–1874; vol. 2. 1874–1896; vol. 3. 1896–1911; vol. 4. 1911–1927; vol. 5. 1927–1952.

9485 Court minute books. 1584–1924.[1]
Paper, la. 4to, 5 vol.
Vol. 1. 1584–1689; vol. 2. 1689–1792; vol. 3. 1793–1855; vol. 4. 1855–1889; vol. 5. 1890–1924.

9486 Committee minute books. 1851–1934.
Paper, sm. fo., 4 vol.
Vol. 1. 1851–1875; vol. 2. 1875–1896; vol. 3. 1896–1916; vol. 4. 1917–1934.

9487 Register of freedom admissions. 1633–1804.[1] From 1694 stamp duty book.
Paper 4to.
Indexed.

9488 Register of apprentice bindings. 1666–1749.[1]
Paper, sm. fo. (Damaged).
Indexed.

9489 Register of presentments of apprentices and their admissions to freedom. 1596–1699.
Paper, 4to.

9490 Register of apprentice bindings, with account of orphans duty paid into the Chamber of London. 1694–1857.
Vellum, sm. fo.

9491 Collected quarterage and quarterage arrear books. 1672–1773. Incomplete.
Paper 4to.

9492 Clerk's remembrances, containing:- abstract of the charter of 1663 November 23; list of assistants, livery and yeomanry 1714, continued to 1734; company rental; tables of fees, fines, penalties and forfeitures; notes on charities; formularies and precedents.
S.d. 1st half 18th century.
Paper, sm. 8vo.

9493 Search book, 1574–1649, and 1664.
Paper, sm. fo.

9494 Register of leases. 1584–1810.
Paper, sm. fo., 2 vol.
Vol. 1. 1584–1744; vol. 2. 1749–1810 (latter half blank) with topographical index.

9495 Ordinance, oath and evidence book. Saec. xv-xvii.
Vellum, med. 4to; containing:–
fol. 1r-6v; Kalendar in Latin;
fol. 8r; Order by the company for every member of the craft to give a pound of new wax for sustaining wax taper branches for the rood at the north door of St. Paul's church on the feast of the Cross, 1371 (and every year thereafter); the company's petition to the court of aldermen for establishing certain bye-laws, in French, 1371;
fol. 8v; Bye-laws, in French, *ut supra;*
fol. 9; Oaths;
fol. 10r-13v; Ordinances, 1359, with amendments to 1488;
fol. 14 and 15r; blank;
fol. 15v-20r; Ratification of ordinances, 24 May 1514;
fol. 20v-21r; Supplemental ordinances, 28 February 1597;
fol. 21v; Supplemental ordinances, 22 February 1597;
fol. 22r-25v; Copy will of John Thomason, 4 March 1526;
fol. 26r; Order concerning apprentice binding, 6 April 1599;
fol. 26v; Order concerning search and quarterage, 15 March 1569;
fol. 27r; Memorandum concerning Nicholas Frankwell's gift of £10, 19 April 1621;
fol. 28r-29v; Copy will of Robert Brockett, 22 September 1530;
fol. 29v-31r; blank;
fol. 31v-33v; Inquisition taken at Guildhall concerning the will of William Kendall, 16 June 1567;
fol. 35v-37r; Ordinances, made 17 September 1584;
fol. 38r; Memorandum concerning Thomas Jenner's gift of plate, 9 June 1600;
fol. 39r-40v; Copy will of Richard Powell, 10 October 1603;
fol. 42r-46r; Copy act of parliament for securing and confirming to the several companies of the city of London their several estates, situate within the city, 5 Jas. I 21 July 1607;
fol. 47r; Extract from will of William Parnell, 22 July 1622;

fol. 49v–75v; blank;
fol. 76r–77r; Copy of charter of incorporation by Richard III, 16 February 1483;
fol. 77v–78v; Ordinances agreed upon 10 August 1579 and ratified 14 October 1580;
fol. 79r–80r; blank;
fol. 80v–82v; Tables (index).

9496 Charter and ordinance book, engrossed 1622 (being the gift of William Sharp, master).
Vellum, 8vo. Containing:–
fol. 1r–4r; Application made by the company to the court of aldermen "that they may choose 4 of ye craft to search for bad wares", 13 November 1371;
fol. 5r–6v; Charter of Richard III, 16 February 1483;
fol. 7r–16v; Ordinances ratified 29 May 1514;
fol. 17r; Order by the court of aldermen concerning search and quarterage, 15 March 1569;
fol. 18; Supplemental ordinances, 22 February 1597;
fol. 19; Supplemental ordinances, 6 April 1599;
fol. 20r–22v; Supplemental ordinances, confirmed 27 September 1584;
fol. 23r–25r; Ordinances agreed to 10 August 1579 and confirmed 14 October 1580;
fol. 26; Charter of confirmation by Elizabeth I, 12 April 1561;
fol. 27; Charter of confirmation by James I, 22 May 1603;
fol. 28–36; blank;
fol. 37r–38r; Tables (index).

9497 Contemporary transcripts of the charter granted to the company by James II, 9 January 1685/6, and of documents pertaining to the grant of it and its later use and interpretation, 1685–1696.
Paper, la. fo.

9498 Contemporary transcripts of the charter granted to the company by Charles II, 23 November 1663, and of the ordinances made and agreed upon 13 May 1664 and ratified 28 June 1664, together with copies of documents appertaining to the above instruments.
Vellum, 4to.

9499 Inventory of the fixtures, fittings, furniture, decorative objects, pictures, etc. at the company's hall in Gresham Street, 18 July 1919.
Paper, sm. 4to.

9500 Freemen's declarations. 1840–1891.[1] Incomplete. (Loose).
Paper, 1 file.

9501 Masters', wardens' and assistants' declarations. 1840–1891.[1] Incomplete. (Loose).
Paper, 1 file.

9501A Masters' and wardens' declarations book. 1892–1951.[1]
Paper, 4to.

9502 Quarterage collection lists. 1723–1745. Incomplete.
Paper, 1 file.

9503 Contemporary office copy of the letters patent by James I, 2 October 1619, conveying and confirming to the company the several messuages, lands and premises situate in the Old Change, Queenhithe,

Coleman Street, Aldersgate Street and Maiden Lane.
Paper, br.s., 1 sheaf (ff.73), in file.
Annotated at head (fol. 1.): This is the coppie of our assurance of our lands and rerages of rents made by the King in the yeare 1619 to us and others, the patten itself remayneth in Guild Hall because dyvers companyes are ioyned in the patten.

9504 Original exemplification of the ordinances ratified 24 May 1514.
Vellum, 2 skins, rolled. Illuminated heraldic borders.
Seals missing. Damaged and frayed.

9505 Original exemplification of the ordinances ratified 28 June 1664.
Vellum, 3 skins, rolled. 3 seals in (modern) wooden capsules, on original silk cords. Damaged and frayed.

9506 The Hall deeds:– a collection of deeds and documents relating to property situate in Godron Lane, Inglen Lane[2] and Wood Street, in the parish of St. John Zachary and Cripplegate Within ward, and particularly to the brewhouse known, in and after 1421, as 'The Cock on the hoop' on the site of the later Wax Chandlers' hall. 1298/9–1545. 36 items.
Vellum, 1 box.

9507 Counterpart leases and other documents relating to the company's hall and the site thereof in Gutter Lane in the parish of St. John Zachary. 1477–1730. 27 items.
Vellum and paper, 1 box.

9508 Documents relating to the company's Irish estates. 1587–1705.
Vellum and paper, 1 box.

9509 Deeds relating to company property, being seven houses with garden and appurtenances known as Bungays alley, in the parish of St. Stephen Coleman Street. 1427–1608. 26 items.
Vellum, 1 box.

9510 Title deeds and other documents pertaining thereto, relating to company property, being a tenement with appurtenances, situate in the parish of St. Michael Queenhithe, also a garden plot with chambers erected thereon in Lovelace alley, Queenhithe. 1241–1579. 23 items.
Vellum, 1 box.

9511 Counterpart leases and other documents relating to company property being a parcel of ground with buildings erected thereon situated in Bowling alley near Thames street, Queenhithe, in the parish of St. Michael Queenhithe. 1660–1721. 14 items.
Vellum and paper, 1 box.
Also containing copy decree of the Court of judicature touching burned or demolished property (Fire judges court), about the poor of the parish of St. Michael (upon the company's petition against the churchwardens).

9512 Title deeds relating to company property being tenements and lands situate in Aldersgate street, and 'Britain street' (Little Britain) in the parish of St. Botolph without Aldersgate. *c*1200–1712. 18 items.
Vellum, 1 box.
Charter no. 1 temp. John.

9513 Counterpart leases and other documents relating to company property being freehold premises situate in Aldersgate street in the parish of St. Botolph without Aldersgate. 1584–1854. 18 items.
Vellum (1 paper), 1 box. Some items damaged.

9514 Wills, original, probate and copy, touching upon company properties and charities. 1491–1770. 12 items.
Vellum and paper, 1 file.

9515 Note of the plate belonging to the company, taken 15 September 1664, with list of benefactors for plate.
Vellum, 1 skin (badly damaged and faded).
Transcript attached.

9516 View taken by the four city viewers in a plea between the churchwardens of the parish of St. John Zachary, plaintiffs, and the company, defendants, concerning an alleged encroachment and trespass caused by the erection of a brick wall. 26 March 1565. Contemporary copy, authenticated.
Paper, br.s., 2 sh., in file.

9517 Original charter of incorporation granted to the company by Richard III. Westminster, 16 February 1483/4.
Vellum, 1 membrane, mounted on wooden board. Great seal on original cord. Initial R having royal arms emblazoned. Illuminated borders. Endorsed are notices of enrolments in the Exchequer, Hilary term 1 Ric. III and at Guildhall, also 1 Ric. III, during the mayoralty of Robert Billesdon.

9518 Inspeximus by Elizabeth I of inspeximus by Philip and Mary, 7 June 1558 (exemplification lost), which confirmed the charter by Richard III. Westminster, 12 April 1560.
Vellum, 1 membrane, mounted on board. Fragment of great seal on original cord. Portrait of sovereign enthroned in pen and ink, in initial E.

9519 Inspeximus by James I of previous confirmations of the charter by Richard III. Westminster, 22 May 1604.
Vellum, 1 membrane mounted on board. Initial J having illuminated portrait of sovereign enthroned. Heraldic borders. Great seal on original cord.

9520 Charter granted to the company by James II. Westminster, 9 January 1685/6.
Vellum, 3 membranes, rolled. Initial J having portrait of sovereign, in mezzotint. Great seal (broken) in tin capsule on original cord.

9521 Original grant of arms to the company by Sir Thomas Holme, Clarenceux. 3 February 1484/5. With confirmations by Thomas Benolt, Clarenceux, 11 October 1530, and by Henry St. George, Richmond herald, the latter at the visitation of London, November 1634.
Vellum, 1 membrane, mounted on board. Seal missing.

9522 Original grant of arms by Thomas Hawley, Clarenceux, to take the place of that formerly granted by Sir Thomas Holme, Clarenceux, in 1485, which is described as being obscurely worded and the arms, beasts and crest not rightly set forth. 12 October 1536.
Vellum, 1 membrane, mounted on board. Two seals:– one, office seal of Clarenceux; the other, personal arms of Thomas Hawley.

9523 Summons from Henry St. George, Richmond Herald, to the master and wardens of the company, to appear before him at Guildhall on 8 November 1634, for inspection and registration of their arms, on occasion of the visitation of London. Office of arms, 28 October 1634.
Paper, fo., ld.s., in file.

9524 Papers relating to company property situate in Old Change in the parish of St. Mary Magdalen Old Fish Street, more particularly to lands and tenements referred to in the chantry certificate of 2 Edw. VI (1548), the reference arising from certain provisions in the will of Robert Coldham, citizen and fishmonger (July 1491)* and the eventual vacation of the enrolment in the Exchequer of the above certificate. 1547–1627.
Paper, 1 file.
*Hustings Wills, roll 225, mem. 64; copy will in *MS9514*.

9525 Inventory of all goods found in the house at the sign of the Lamb at Queenhithe, taken 17 June 1611.
Paper, sm. fo., 1 d.s., in file.
Endorsed "A note of implements in Pooles house Queenhine (*sic*)".

9526 Indictment in a suit in the Court of King's Bench, Guildhall, Rex v. William Rutt, Robert Huntley, and William Barrow, upon an allegedly unlawful search and seizure for bad (wax) wares. 15 February 1664/5.
Paper, br. s., 2 sh.
According to the dorse, the verdict was for the defendants.

9527 Legal papers, mainly briefs, relating to the title of that messuage known as The King's head, situate in Old Change in the parish of St. Mary Magdalene Old Fish Street, used in a suit in the court of King's bench, Knight v. Humphreys, arising out of the will of Robert Coldham, citizen and fishmonger (3 July 1491): at Guildhall, Trinity term, 1634.
Paper, 1 file.

10497 Volume containing specification of works to be done in erecting the company's hall at the corner of Gresham street west and Gutter lane, together with plans, elevations and sections. Charles Fowler, architect, of Gordon Square, W.C. 1852–1853.
Vellum and paper, la. 4to.

10498 Volume containing contract with plans (photostat), bills of quantities and pre-contract variations on the latter for the proposed rebuilding after war damage of the company's hall in Gresham Street. Messrs. Seely & Paget, of 41 Cloth Fair, E.C.1, architects; Ashby and Horner Ltd., of 69 Bishopsgate, E.C.2, contractors; and Messrs. Langdon and Every, of 21 Russell square, W.C.1, quantity surveyors. 1955–1956.
Paper, sm. fo., typescript.

10800 Property committee:– minute book. 1934–1949.
Paper, sm. fo.
Latter half blank.

10801 William Kendall's charity (1559):– trustees' minute book. 1878–1946.
Paper, la. fo.

10802 William Kendall's charity (1559):– cash book. 1911–1937.
Paper, sm. 4to.

10803 William Kendall's charity (1559):– ledger. 1877–1918.
Paper, fo.

10804 Inventory and valuation of the tenants' fittings, fixtures, furniture, decorative objects, pictures, plate, plated items, linen, table china, glass, etc., at the company's hall, Gresham street, taken for insurance purposes by Toplis & Harding, surveyors and valuers, of 66 Cannon street, January, 1913.
Paper, 4to. Typescript.

10805 Inventory of the furnishings and other equipment in portions of the company's hall and being the company's property, taken by George Berry & Strouts, auctioneers, estate agents and surveyors, of 140 Sloane street, S.W.1, September 1959.
Paper, fo., 1 sheaf.
Clerk's copy.

10806 Plans, elevations and sections (by Henry Dawson, architect, surveyor to the company) of Albion buildings, 186 (formerly 165) Aldersgate street, in the parish of St. Botolph without Aldersgate, the property of the company, 1885, with further plans 1932–1951, and papers relating to its sale to the Corporation of London, 1942–1956.
Paper, 1 file.

10807 Paper relating to the sale of 23 Coleman street, the property of the company, to the London Investment and Mortgage Company. 1951–1955. Paper, 1 file.

[1]Later volumes are in current use.
[2]An earlier name for Maiden Lane.

APPENDIX 18

LONDON LIVERY COMPANIES[1]

in order of precedence[2]

1 Mercers*
Grocers*
Drapers*
Fishmongers*
Goldsmiths*
{ Skinners*[3]
{ Merchant Taylors*[3]
Haberdashers*
Salters
10 Ironmongers*
Vintners*
Clothworkers*

Dyers*
Brewers*
Leathersellers*
Pewterers*
Barbers*
Cutlers*
Bakers*
20 WAX CHANDLERS*
Tallow-chandlers*
Armourers and Brasiers*
Girdlers*
Butchers*
Saddlers*
Carpenters*
Cordwainers[4]
Painter Stainers*
Curriers[5]
30 Masons
Plumbers
Innholders*
Founders*
Poulters
Cooks
Coopers
Tylers and Bricklayers
Bowyers
Fletchers[6]
40 Blacksmiths
Joiners
Weavers
Woolmen
Scriveners
Fruiterers
Plaisterers*
Stationers and Newspaper Makers*
Broderers
Upholders[7]
50 Musicians
Turners
Basketmakers
Glaziers
Horners
Farriers
Paviors
Loriners[8]
Apothecaries*
Shipwrights
60 Spectaclemakers
Clockmakers
Glovers
Feltmakers
Framework Knitters
Needlemakers
Gardeners
Tinplate Workers
Wheelwrights
Distillers
70 Pattenmakers[9]
Glass-sellers
Coach and Coach Harness Makers
Gunmakers

Gold and Silver Wyre Drawers
Makers of Playing Cards
Fanmakers
Carmen[10]
Master Mariners*[11]
City of London Solicitors
80 Farmers
Air Pilots and Air Navigators
Tobacco Pipe Makers and Tobacco Blenders
Furniture Makers
Scientific Instrument Makers

** These companies now have halls*

[1]There are also two ancient companies, the Watermen and Lightermen's and the Parish Clerks', that have never had a livery, and two newcomers, the Launderers' and the Builders Merchants of the City of London, that have no livery as yet.

[2]The Weavers and the Saddlers claim to have the longest history. The last seven in the list are twentieth-century creations.

[3]The Skinners and the Merchant Taylors take sixth and seventh places in alternate years.

[4]Shoemakers.

[5]Leather-dressers.

[6]Arrow makers.

[7]Upholsterers.

[8]Harness-makers.

[9]Pattens were overshoes with wooden soles.

[10]Carters.

[11]The first grant of livery since Queen Anne was to the Master Mariners in 1932; they have a floating hall in *HQS Wellington*.

APPENDIX 19

THE LONDON APPRENTICE INDENTURE[1]

This indenture *Witnesseth,* That .... doth put himself Apprentice to ...., Citizen and .... of *London,* to learn his Art, and with him, after the Manner of an Apprentice, to serve from the Day of the Date hereof, until the full End and Term of Seven Years, from thence next following, be fully complete and ended. During which Term the said Apprentice his said Master faithfully shall serve, his Secrets keep, his lawful Commands every where gladly do. He shall do no Damage to his said Master, nor see it to be done of others; but that he to the utmost of his Power shall let, or forthwith give Warning to his said Master, of the same. He shall not waste the Goods of his said Master, nor lend them unlawfully to any. He shall not commit Fornication, nor contract Matrimony, within the said Term. He shall not play at Cards, Dice, Tables, or any other unlawful Games, whereby his said Master may have any Loss. With his own Goods or others, during the said Term, without Licence of his said Master, he shall neither buy nor sell. He shall not haunt Taverns nor Playhouses, nor absent himself from his said Master's Service Day nor Night unlawfully. But in all things as a faithful Apprentice he shall behave himself towards his said Master, and all his, during the said Term. And the said Master in consideration of ....
being the Money given with his said Apprentice, his said Apprentice in the Same Art and Mystery which he useth, by the best Means that he can, shall Teach and Instruct, or cause to be taught and instructed; finding to his said Apprentice, Meat, Drink, Apparel, Lodging, and all other Necessaries, according to the Custom of the City of *London,* during the said Term.

And for the true Performance of all and every the said Covenants and Agreements, either of the said Parties bindeth himself to the other by these Presents. *In Witness* whereof, the parties above-named to these Indentures interchangeably have put their Hands and Seals the .... Day of .... in the .... Year of the Reign of our Sovereign .... of the United Kingdom of *Great Britain and Ireland* ...., Defender of the Faith, and in the Year of our Lord One Thousand .... Hundred and ....

Sealed and Delivered (being first duly stamped) in the Presence of ....

[1]This wording remained virtually unchanged from the earliest times until 1889, when an act of common council reduced the minimum term to four years, allowed the clause relating to matrimony to be deleted, and permitted the master to pay wages instead of providing living requirements.

Bibliographical note

At one end of the bibliographic spectrum are the primary sources such as company, city and national records (see page xvi); at the other end are the general providers – encyclopedias, dictionaries and other works of reference. In the middle band comes a wide range of books on English social, economic and ecclesiastical history, on London and the companies (including their individual histories), and on subjects of special concern to the Wax Chandlers; some of those consulted are listed below.

A. H. Dodd, *Life in Elizabethan England*, 1961
Mary R. Price and C. E. L. Mather, *A portrait of Britain under Tudors and Stuarts*, 1954
H. Maynard Smith, *Pre-Reformation England*, 1938
E. N. Williams, *Life in Georgian England*, 1962

Arthur Birnie, *An economic history of the British Isles*, 1935
Sir John Clapham, *A concise economic history of Britain from the earliest times to 1750*, 1957

J. R. H. Moorman, *A history of the church in England*, 1953
J. F. Sullivan, *The externals of the Catholic church*, 1955

B. Ash, *The golden city: London between the fires, 1666–1941*, 1968
Timothy Baker, *Medieval London*, 1970
R. M. Barnes, *The soldiers of London*, 1963
W. G. Bell, *The Great Plague in London in 1665*, 1924
E. Carpenter (ed.), *A house of kings: the history of Westminster Abbey*, 1966
G. H. Cooke, *Old S. Paul's cathedral*, 1955
Sir William Dugdale, *History of St. Paul's Cathedral*, 1658.
Eilert Ekwall, *Street-names of the city of London*, 1954
M. Dorothy George, *London life in the eighteenth century*, 1925
D. V. Glass, *Status and occupations in London* (Studies in London history, ed. Hollaender and Kellaway), 1969
H. A. Harben, *A dictionary of London*, 1918
Martin Holmes, *Elizabethan London*, 1969
William Kent (ed.), *An encyclopedia of London* (rev. Godfrey Thompson), 1970
William McMurray, *A city church chronicle*, 1914
William McMurray, *The records of two city churches*, 1925
W. R. Matthews and W. M. Atkins (eds), *A history of St. Paul's Cathedral*, 1957
C. A. F. Meekings, *The city loans on the hearth tax, 1664–1668* (Studies in London history, *supra*), 1969
Valerie Pearl, *London and the outbreak of the Puritan revolution*, 1961
T. F. Reddaway, *The rebuilding of London after the Great Fire*, 1940
R. R. Sharpe, *London and the kingdom*, 3 vols. 1894

John Stow, *A survey of London . . . , 1603* (ed. C. L. Kingsford), 1908

John Stow, *A survey of the cities of London and Westminster* (rev. J. Strype 1720, with subsequent additions), 1754-5

Elspeth M. Veale, *Craftsmen and the economy of London in the fourteenth century* (Studies in London history, *supra*), 1969

Chronicles of London (ed. C. L. Kingsford), 1905.

The Corporation of London, 1950

John F. Bromley, *The armorial bearings of the guilds of London*, 1961

W. C. Hazlitt, *The livery companies of the city of London*, 1892

William Herbert, *The history of the twelve great livery companies of London*, 1834-7

William F. Kahl, *The development of the London livery companies*, 1960

J. R. Kellett, *The breakdown of gild and corporation control over the handicraft and retail trade in London* (Economic History Review), 1958

Stella Kramer, *The English craft guilds: studies in their progress and decline*, 1927

Sir Ernest Pooley, *The guilds of the city of London*, 1945

Second report of the commissioners on municipal corporations (*London and Southwark*) – Parliamentary report vol. xxv, 1837

Report and appendix. City of London livery companies commission – Parliamentary papers vol. xxxix, 1884

T. W. Cowan, *Wax craft: all about beeswax*, 1908

W. T. O'Dea, *Lighting 1: Early oil lamps, candles*, 1966

W. T. O'Dea, *The social history of lighting*, 1958

Still the candle burns (Price's Patent Candle Co. Ltd.), 1972

General Index

The notes at the end of each chapter are not indexed except where the subject is not directly referred to in the main text. See also indices of persons and places.

Index of Persons

Names printed in italic are those of Wax Chandlers and others connected with the craft or company.
Historical characters are indexed under the names by which they are generally known.
Names occurring only in the appendices are not indexed. Variations in spelling are ignored.

Index of Places

Places outside the London area and those mentioned only in the appendices are not indexed. Names are in modern form. Many places of interest are shown in the end-papers.

The city of London under James I: a south prospect of 1616.—This panorama shows many famous landmarks on the river and for some distance inland (until restricted by the shallow angle of view). The general impression is one of narrow streets and innumerable churches with St. Paul's on its high ground dominating the western scene and, further east, the Guild Hall, Royal Exchange and Leadenhall. Fifty years later, almost every building from Temple to Tower was to perish in the